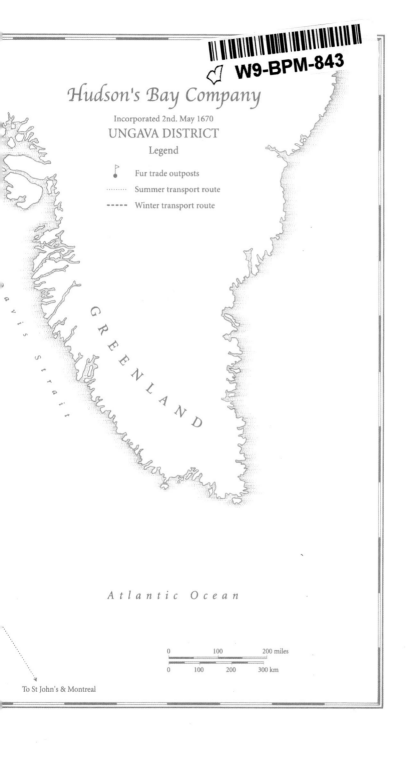

Hudson's Bay Company

Incorporated 2nd. May 1670

UNGAVA DISTRICT

Legend

- ⚑ Fur trade outposts
- .... Summer transport route
- ----- Winter transport route

G R E E N L A N D

D a v i s   S t r a i t

A t l a n t i c   O c e a n

0		100		200 miles
0	100	200		300 km

To St John's & Montreal

The Last Gentleman
Adventurer

Edward Beauclerk Maurice

The Last Gentleman Adventurer

COMING OF AGE IN
THE ARCTIC

Foreword by
Lawrence Millman

HOUGHTON MIFFLIN COMPANY

BOSTON · NEW YORK

2005

First published in Great Britain in 2004 by Fourth Estate,
an imprint of HarperCollins*Publishers*

For information about permission to reproduce selections from
this book, write to Permissions, Houghton Mifflin Company,
215 Park Avenue South, New York, New York 10003.

Visit our Web site: www.houghtonmifflinbooks.com.

Library of Congress Cataloging-in-Publication Data

Maurice, Edward Beauclerk.
The last gentleman adventurer : coming of age in the
Arctic / Edward Beauclerk Maurice.
p. cm.
ISBN-13: 978-0-618-51751-0
ISBN-10: 0-618-51751-0
1. Maurice, Edward Beauclerk. 2. Explorers—Canada,
Northern—Biography. 3. Canada, Northern—Description and
travel. 4. Baffin Island (Nunavut)—Description and travel.
5. Canada, Northern—Discovery and exploration. 6. Frontier
and pioneer life—Canada, Northern. 7. Inuit—Canada,
Northern—Social life and customs—20th century. 8. Canada,
Northern—Social life and customs—20th century. 9. Hudson's
Bay Company—Biography. 10. Canada, Northern—
Biography. I. Title
F1090.5.M38 2006
910'.92—dc22 [B] 2005040449

Printed in the United States of America

QUM 10 9 8 7 6 5 4 3 2 1

*For a much-loved husband and father
whose adventurous start to paid employment has
inspired us all to take up life's challenges.*

*The stories that follow have filled many
happy family times together and we hope this
book will ensure that others also can
share in a young boy's dream.*

Pat, Jane, Sally and Victoria Maurice

Contents

Foreword

EDWARD BEAUCLERK MAURICE almost did not go to the Arctic. His Hudson's Bay Company recruiter, George Binney, thought the seventeen-year-old boy's dark looks suggested "Eastern blood," and in his not necessarily unbiased opinion, recruits with even a smattering of Asian, Semitic, or Indian blood (Binney was at least egalitarian in his prejudices) did not have the right stuff to be fur traders in the Canadian north. If Maurice's headmaster hadn't assured Binney that the boy's brother was "conspicuously fair," Edward probably would have immigrated to New Zealand with the rest of his family, and bookshelves would be deprived of this remarkable memoir.

Yet if it weren't for Binney, Maurice wouldn't have been considered for employment with the Hudson's Bay Company in the first place. For the HBC — to use its popular abbreviation — traditionally looked to the highlands and islands of Scotland for recruits. The company's thinking went something like this: a Scotsman, preferably a poor one, would be thrifty; he would be accustomed to uncomplaining servitude; he would be used to a rotten climate; and, as a Celt, he would be not unlike the primitive people with whom he'd be trading. But Binney felt the company needed educated recruits, what today might be called managerial types, if it was to keep pace with modern times. So he turned his attention to England and to public schools like the one in Sussex that Maurice was attending.

A more unlikely candidate for the northern wilds would be difficult to imagine. Maurice was naïve even for his age, his childhood had been quite sheltered, and his experience of rotten climates seems to have been limited to the drafty corridors of his school. An HBC evaluation refers to him as being "inclined more to indoor rather than outdoor work." But sometimes the least likely person turns out to be the most likely one. After all, Robert Peary was a mama's boy, and his North Pole adversary, Frederick Cook, worked as a milkman.

Maurice started out as an apprentice clerk at the Pangnirtung Post on Baffin Island. Nowadays Pang, as it's called, is a mecca for Arctic tourists, with hotels, souvenir shops, and an interpretive center. But in 1930 it was hardly more than a huddle of clapboard houses surrounded by Eskimo (the then current name for the Inuit) tents. As befits such a high-latitude settlement, there were no trees other than those of the dwarf variety. A lad who'd arrived here from England's green and pleasant land might reasonably feel that he'd fetched up very close to the bleak end of the world. (The actual end of the world was the HBC's Payne Bay post, where it took the trader Charles Duncan two years to receive a telegram notifying him that his father had died.) But not Maurice: he was exhilarated.

According to the oft-repeated joke, the initials "HBC" stand for "here before Christ." But the Hudson's Bay Company didn't actually establish its first post in the Canadian Arctic until 1908 (the first non-Arctic post, Rupert House, dates from 1670). This relatively recent arrival in North America's attic can be attributed to two factors: the overharvesting of fur-bearing animals, especially beavers, down south, and the new global demand for fur from a more northerly animal. The northerly animal in question was the white fox (*Alopex lagopus*).

Before the HBC came, the Baffin Eskimos used the fur of the

white fox primarily to wipe their babies' bottoms. They must have thought White Man's obsession with this fur a little peculiar, at least until they became obsessed with it themselves. For a white fox pelt was virtually the only item they could trade for rifles, bolts of cloth, tools, sugar, and tea. In a decent fox year, an Eskimo trapper would have enough trade goods to fill his tent; in a bad fox year, he would owe his soul to the Company store. Either way, that trapper would be at odds with his own past. In the words of the anthropologist Diamond Jenness, "The commercial world of the White Man caught the Eskimo in its mesh, destroyed their self-sufficiency and independence and made them economically its slaves."

The Company took a paternalistic attitude toward the Eskimos, the better to increase its profits. George Binney (yes, the same George Binney who was worried about Maurice's dark looks) summed up this attitude in *The Eskimo Book of Knowledge,* the official HBC guide for Eskimo trappers, when he wrote: "Our trader has learned to bestow the care of a father upon you and your children." The implication is that father, or the Company, knows best, and the Eskimo knows least.

But Maurice did not regard the Eskimos as an inferior race in immediate need of white parenting. Quite the contrary. In his relations with them, he seemed to be the child and they the parents. In fact, he was so young and inexperienced that they called him "the Boy," but they could have just as easily called him "the Bumbler," since he seemed to have a special talent for getting lost or falling off cliffs. However, he was an excellent learner, and all his HBC evaluations praise his ability to speak Inuktitut, the polysynthetic Eskimo language. Here, too, Maurice distinguished himself from most other traders, who usually didn't bother to learn anything other than a pidgin version of the language. His facility with Inuktitut also earned him high

marks from the Eskimos and probably was one of the reasons
that they ended up giving him a new, unequivocally adult name
— Issumatak ("He Who Thinks").

During his Arctic hitch, one HBC man reputedly browsed
through a catalogue that featured women's underwear and then
wrote away for "the lady on the far right of page 73." Most traders were not reduced to such extreme measures, since they typi-
cally took what's known as a "country wife." Duncan Pryde,
who worked for the HBC in the 1950s and 1960s, sired offspring
from this type of union wherever he was posted, declaring that
"every community should have a little Pryde." Lest you consider
the man a cad, I should note that his Eskimo friends would have
thought there was something wrong with him if he hadn't fa-
thered these offspring.

Maurice seemed disinclined to take a country wife himself, although there was no shortage of applicants. His background, he
wrote, was the reason for this: "My upbringing, both at home
and at school, had run along very strict lines of morality." But as
he acquired what could be called a new background, he also began to acquire a very different sense of morality, one that was
closer to an Eskimo's than to an upper-middle-class English
person's. Meanwhile, he was falling in love, albeit with a culture
rather than a woman, and when he at last decided to take a
wife, you could say that he was consummating his relationship
with that culture.

In the spring of 1934, he was put in charge of the Frobisher
Bay Post at Ward Inlet. This post was considerably more isolated than Pangnirtung and likewise had no doctor or nurse.
Soon he was dealing with an epidemic, which, although never
officially diagnosed (there isn't even a mention of it in the usually thorough HBC records), was probably a virulent form of in-
fluenza. The stress of being forced to treat the sick and the dying

more or less by himself seems to have taken its toll, and by August he was back in Pangnirtung with a condition described by the local medical officer as "an affection of the heart." I suspect the reason Maurice doesn't refer to this ailment in his book is that it was insignificant beside the deaths of those he had come to know and love.

Maurice's narrative ends with his departure from Frobisher Bay, but his life with the Eskimos did not end there. After a year's furlough in England, he returned to the Arctic to manage, respectively, the Sugluk Post in northern Quebec and the Southampton Island Post. At the latter post another epidemic struck. This new epidemic was almost certainly mumps — an indication that white men were giving the Eskimos their diseases as well as their trade goods. At one point Maurice wrote in his journal that "every single man, woman & child in the place is now sick." At least five of them died. But it could have been a lot worse. Thirty-five years earlier, the Sadlermiut, a Southampton Island tribe that had had almost no contact with the outside world, were completely wiped out by an epidemic of dysentery introduced by a single Scottish whaler.

In 1939, Maurice left the Arctic to serve in World War II. When the War was over, he did not go back to the geography that had claimed his heart and that now persisted in sending its ghosts his way. Nor did he ever go back except in the writing of this book. He died in 2003 at the age of ninety, and in his last year he worried that the use of the word "Eskimo" in his soon-to-be-published book might be construed as patronizing. For he had nothing but admiration for the people now commonly referred to as Inuit (the pejorative term for them in the 1930s was "Husky," not "Eskimo"). "They have taught me so much," he remarked in one of his final letters, and this book is a testimony to those teachings.

If Maurice were to visit Pangnirtung today, he might see a cruise ship anchored offshore and its passengers eagerly looking to buy something — a soapstone carving or maybe fox-skin booties — for their mantelpieces. At Ward Inlet he would find a few scattered boards, all that remains of the old HBC post. In Iqaluit, the capital of the new Inuit territory of Nunavut, he might see one or two descendants of his Frobisher Bay friends shivering on the streets, members of the town's burgeoning homeless population. The irony of a formerly nomadic people becoming once again, after a fashion, nomadic would not escape him. Nor would the fact that Iqaluit, despite its relatively small size (population 6,500), suffers from a number of modern urban maladies — drugs, muggings, auto thefts, gang fights. Picking up the local newspaper, the *Nunatsiaq News,* he might read about an eighteen-year-old arrested for dealing heroin and with a start realize that the boy was the grandson of a hunter he knew in another lifetime.

By now our visitor would have seen enough to know that what he had written is in fact an evocation of a lost world.

LAWRENCE MILLMAN
Cambridge, Massachusetts
February 2005

... and when my fiord has no seals and the
   flame of the lamps burns low,
I will visit my friendly Spirit
   in his igloo behind the wind . . .

From the drum song of Padluapik, the Medicine Man

PART ONE

The Boy

I

AT TEN O'CLOCK in the morning of 2 June 1930 about forty young men gathered round a noticeboard set up on Euston station, which bore the message 'BOAT TRAIN, DUCHESS OF BEDFORD LIVERPOOL. HUDSON'S BAY COMPANY PARTY'.

The other travellers hurrying to and fro across the concourse, impelled to haste by the alarming pantings, snufflings and whistlings coming from the impatient engines, hardly spared us a glance, despite the flavour of distant adventure in that simple notice. For in those days, London was still the centre of a great empire and it was commonplace for parties to be seen gathering at railway stations, or at other places of departure, to begin their long journeys to far-away places. Tea planters for India and Ceylon. Rubber planters for Malaya. Mining engineers for South Africa. Administrators for the Indian and other civil services. Policemen for the African colonies. Farm workers to seek their fortunes in Australia, New Zealand or Canada. Traders for the South Seas. Servicemen for all quarters of the globe and wanderers just seeking sunshine or adventure.

We were to be apprenticed to the fur trade 'somewhere in Canada'. In age we were between sixteen and twenty-three. In occupation there were schoolboys, farm labourers, office workers, factory workers, estate workers, forestry people and even two seamen.

We had been told of the wonderful opportunities that awaited us, but what our informants had not known was that the worst depression the world would experience for many years was fast developing. Already the feverish post-war boom was collapsing. The sudden loss of confidence and the general insecurity of the world markets was soon to undermine the fur trade. Before some of us had finally reached our new homes, the whole department responsible for our engagement had been disbanded, with its members released to swell the ever growing ranks of the unemployed. Never again would a party such as ours gather in London.

An oriental philosopher once wrote that no matter how near or far the destination, every journey must somewhere have a starting point. My journey began in the June of the halcyon summer of 1913, to which so many thousands of women were to look back with aching nostalgia for all the rest of their years.

The shadow fell across my mother's life sooner than it did for the others. Six weeks before I was born, in the evening of a long midsummer's day, my father was brought home spread-eagled over a broken gate, dead of a terrible gunshot wound to the head.

Controversy, seemingly inseparable from the human state even in such tragic circumstances, broke out at once. The vicar refused my grandmother's request that her son's body should be brought into the parish church to await burial, on the grounds that he might have committed suicide. The coroner would have to give him earthly clearance from this suspicion before the church could grant him asylum. The clergyman had mistakenly supposed his parishioner, my grandmother, to be a meek and pious woman, an error he was never to repeat. He was astonished by the ferocity with which she defended her son's right to rest in the church, and reluctantly gave way.

So my father, poised as it were on the very threshold of eternity, was brought for the last time into the cool, dim, silent

4

shadow of the ancient building, perhaps there to find the peace he had been seeking. The following day the coroner decided that death had been due to misadventure, thus calming the vicar's disquiet and giving at least some hope of an onward journey to heaven. For those that were left on earth, and in particular for my mother, the problems were just beginning.

Aged twenty-three, with three children already and a fourth expected, her outlook was bleak indeed, for there was no provision at that time for disasters such as this. No help could be expected from the state, since there was no social security or child allowances. Those who fell by the wayside, whether it was their own fault or not, had to pick themselves up or, as a last desperate measure, appeal to the workhouse guardians for relief.

My grandmother then decided she was in need of a house-keeping companion and that her daughter-in-law could fill this position. There would be no pay as such, but food for the young widow and her children would be provided, sparingly as it turned out, and even more sparingly, clothes. Children's garments could be made from oddments, sewn, knitted and handed down. As for my mother, now that she was a widow and would wear black for the rest of her life as Queen Victoria had done, she could inherit the old lady's cast-offs, suitably trimmed to size and shape.

This was how my family came to live in a large, cold Victorian house in a small township on the north Somersetshire coast. My mother brought with her all that she possessed in the world. A few items of bedroom furniture. A dressing table and a little jewellery, a few books and a Colt revolver with six rounds of ammunition. What desperate resolve prompted her to bring these last two items I do not know, nor did I ever inquire.

The year after our arrival, 1914, the Great War broke out. Perhaps the atmosphere of emergency and the heavy emotional demands made upon most of the young women of her generation helped my mother resign herself, at least temporarily, to living the routine of her elderly mother-in-law.

As children we were happy enough, fitting ourselves, as children do, into the circumstances that surrounded us, but mother had to suppress much of her natural jollity, acting as a buffer between her often noisy children at the top of the house and the solemn, easily disturbed downstairs of our grandmother.

Grandmother did not believe in the classless society. Indeed, so convinced was she of her own social superiority that there was not one single person in that Somersetshire township who could justifiably be invited to take tea with her. Ranged behind her in defence of her position were several dukes and other aristocrats, closely followed by admirals, generals and the like, some of whom gazed down at us from the walls of the stairways and downstairs rooms. This meant that there was very little social life to enliven the dull days for mother.

A room at the top of the house was set aside to be used as a school, and armed with a selection of rather aged textbooks, the young widow began the education of her children, my eldest brother being already over four years old. The knowledge contained in these textbooks was rigorously drummed into our heads, for mother was aware of the necessity of obtaining an education of a higher standard than that offered by the free schools, if one was to prosper, and the only way to do this would be by gaining scholarships or similar awards.

One day a visitor called who had heard about a well-known boarding school that had been established with the sole aim of educating suitable children whose parents did not have the available funds. A great number of good people contributed money to the school, and if their contribution was sufficiently large, they were allowed to place an approved child there. I think mother must have written to every single benefactor in order to gain places for her children, and she eventually succeeded in obtaining one for each of us, three boys at the boys' school and our sister at the girls' establishment.

The schooling provided was sound, practical and aimed at producing adaptable adults, able to use such common sense as they possessed. Aware of the undoubted benefits of such an education, I would like to be able to record that this was a happy period of my life. Alas, this was not so. From the very start, the school was like some sort of prison. On my second day I quite unwittingly broke some obscure rule, for which the housemaster, no doubt a brilliant mathematician, but lacking in any noticeably human attributes, accorded me a public beating. A suitably sour start to a relationship which was to lack warmth for the next seven years.

As time went by, my mother began to think increasingly of escape from the situation which had trapped her for so long. The atmosphere in the old lady's house was not a happy one and my mother longed to go to the other side of the world and start afresh. We had no money, but could work hard and New Zealand sounded like a land of opportunity.

My brother blazed the trail by setting off just after the General Strike of 1926, helping to stoke the boilers of an ancient coal burner as it steamed across the Pacific Ocean. He was to work on farms in New Zealand, and two years later my other brother followed him. The three of us who were left at home were to wait until I had finished school, then set off together.

As the time loomed near, however, my prospective life as a farmworker lost its appeal for me. We wrote letters to everybody we could think of to see if they could squeeze me in somewhere else, but the reply was always the same – too young and no qualifications. Christmas 1929 came and went with the problem no nearer solution, but early in the New Year, a chance happening at school provided a possible answer.

A week or two after the start of term, a visitor arrived to take up a long-standing invitation to spend a weekend at the school as a guest of the headmaster. He was the archdeacon in charge of the missionaries working in the Canadian Arctic territories. The news that the clerical visitor was to give a Saturday-night talk was received with some resignation by the boys, but the archdeacon, whose diocese spread from the tree line right away up to the last few humps of ice at the North Pole, had brought reels of film with him and caught our interest and attention immediately when his operator put the first one in backwards. It was the run of a visit by some Hudson's Bay officials to a post above the Arctic Circle. A solitary white building crouched beneath towering black cliffs. A door flew suddenly open and two portly city executive types marched smartly out backwards, skilfully negotiated a short but steep slope then performed an incredibly agile backward leap into a motor boat waiting at the water's edge.

After this entertaining start, the film's chief interest centred on the activities of the Hudson's Bay Company. Incorporated by Charles II in 1670 as the 'Gentlemen Adventurers trading into Hudson's Bay' and led by Prince Rupert, they had been inspired by the thought of getting into Hudson's Bay and establishing trading posts ahead of the French. In this they had been successful, so they later extended their field of operation over the whole of Canada and later still to the islands north of the mainland. The remote Arctic establishments could only be supplied by sea and it was the voyage of the tough little *Nascopie* that the archdeacon had recorded on film. There were hunting scenes, trading scenes, pictures taken under the midnight sun, of polar bears and walrus, of far-away places and people, enough to titillate the imagination of any schoolboy. Moreover, from what our speaker said, it was fairly obvious that this great company employed young people who did not have any special qualifications. I summoned up my courage to confront the authorities and request further details. An interview was arranged with the archdeacon himself. It was to take place in the headmaster's study on the Monday morning.

The missionary was looking out of the window at the boys scuttling about in the quad on that wet and windy February morning when I crept into the holy of holies. I thought that he looked rather surprised when he saw me. He said:

'You wanted to see me I believe?'

'Yes sir,' I replied, not knowing quite how to develop the conversation.

'How can I help you?'

'I wanted to ask about the Hudson's Bay Company and what age the apprentices have to be,' I blurted out. The archdeacon looked at me in silence for what seemed to be a very long time. It was fairly obvious that he did not consider me to be the stuff of which 'Gentlemen Adventurers' are made. Then he said slowly:

'I think they do sometimes take boys of sixteen if they are suitable, mostly they are rather older. Why do you ask? Are you thinking of applying?'

'Yes,' I replied. I knew that I should expand my answers but somehow dried up in the face of what seemed to be disapproval. The missionary sensed my nervousness.

'What makes you think you would like the life up there?' he asked. 'It's not an easy place to live in you know. Many of the posts are just one man among the Eskimos and Indians and no other post near enough even to visit.'

The slight softening of the archdeacon's attitude released my tongue sufficiently for me to explain our dilemma. He listened in silence. When I had finished he actually smiled.

'Well,' he said, 'I can understand your anxiety to help your mother and I can probably help you with the company, but you should understand what it is you are doing. What about your exams? Have you taken School Certificate yet? Even if the company ignores such things, you may need some qualifications later in your life.'

'I should take School Certificate this summer, but that would mean waiting until next year. Things would be very bad at home by then.'

'Do you know anything about northern Canada apart from what you heard in my talk?'

'Only what I have read in books.'

'It's a very lonely life as I have said. The supply ship comes up once a year. At a small post it may only stay for a few hours and that is the only contact with the outside world until the next year. There is just a small house and a store. You will have to forget about cinemas, theatres, dance halls and everything like that. The ship brings up a small amount of fresh food but after that has gone you have to hunt for yourself. There are just six posts on Baffin Island, which is three or four times the size of England, and about fifteen Europeans. The weather is generally cold, except for a week or two in the summer. Sometimes in the winter the temperature goes down to forty below zero. Some posts have a wireless receiving set but they don't work very well because of the distance from the stations.'

The archdeacon made this little speech as though determined to counteract the favourable impression created by his film show.

'What about doctors?' I asked, more from nerves than for any other reason.

'On Baffin Island there is just one doctor. Usually if people become ill they have to do the best they can with their medicine chest.'

I was more careful with my next question.

'What sort of animals do they hunt?'

'Seals,' he replied without enthusiasm. 'Some deer. Ducks. Polar bears. Fish of course, salmon trout mainly and cod further south. Walrus and the larger seals for feeding the dogs.'

It seemed pointless to ask any further questions. After all the months of searching for a way out of our dilemma, the providential arrival of the archdeacon with his news that the Hudson's Bay Company would probably take me on right away decided the issue.

'I would like to go for an interview if it can be arranged.'

'Very well. I will see what I can do. In any case, you will have time in the next week or two to think about it all.'

So ended my first meeting with the Archdeacon of the Arctic.

Within a few days I was summoned to an interview in London. From my point of view it was a great success. They gave me a closely printed contract to take away and study. I never did find out what it actually said for it was written in legal jargon well above my head. Everyone was very friendly, they gave me £1 for expenses and even suggested that I should go to the cinema before returning to school. Perhaps they were thinking of the years that I might have to spend without cinemas.

The second interview was more intimidating. I had to wait half an hour in an ante-room before I was called in to the departmental manager's office. It was a splendid office with a thick red carpet and leather armchairs. The manager gave me a very earnest talk. There wasn't any Mr Hudson's Bay, he said, so that every hard-working apprentice had a thick carpet and leather chaired suite within his sights, or at the very least a chief trader's certificate to hang on the wall, if he could survive forty years in the backwoods.

Eventually the talking was over and they produced the official contract, now with all the details filled in. I was to bind myself for five years to the company, serving wherever they might decide to send me. They would keep me and pay me 10 s. (50p) per week, though should I rise above the apprentice level during the period, some modest increase in salary could be expected.

The terms did not appear unduly harsh. The money did seem to be a little on the short side even for those depressed days, but that was a fairly common complaint at the time, so I signed the document and even light-heartedly agreed to become a competent bookkeeper and typist during the few weeks of waiting before they shipped me off to Canada. Such is the foolish optimism of youth.

One immediate benefit arising from my decision became quickly obvious. I was no longer an inconspicuous monitor of my school. An aura compounded of snow, ice, dogs and polar bears separated me from my fellow boys, even those who had reached the dizzy heights of the First XV. To my astonishment, this also actually clouded the vision of some of the masters. I exploited this situation to the full so that my last few weeks were the happiest of my years at the school.

My housemaster, for some reason or another, was the last to hear of my new status, and when he called me in to go over my end-of-term report he appeared to think that I was still just an ordinary schoolboy. It seemed that my progress in scripture had only been rated as 'fair'. He did not feel it to be satisfactory that the word 'fair' should appear on the report of one of his monitors and he might feel it necessary to demote me.

I quickly set his mind at rest by telling him my news. A curious expression came over his face when he heard that I was off to the wilds, rather as though I had opened some door in his mind that had been closed for a very long time. He wrote to me in the Arctic several times and I later heard that my replies had been read out at prayers, a signal mark of distinction.

At the end of term a special train came to the school station to pick up the boys travelling to London or beyond. The train left just after 6 a.m. in order to avoid the morning rush, so it was very early one spring morning that I discarded my school uniform and, puffed up with sufficient false pride to still any lurking doubts, set off to prepare myself for my life among the Eskimos.

Some years previously, an old great-uncle of ours had died, leaving my siblings and me £52 each. As I was shortly to become an earner in my own right, I dipped into this money to equip myself for my new life and at once purchased a colourful shirt, riding breeches and a horsy jacket. This gave me, on such occasions as I actually appeared in public in my new outfit, a sufficiently bizarre appearance to cause one of the more spiteful of our neighbours to remark: 'He looks quite colonial already, doesn't he?'

My mother, still under forty years old, had hardly dared to even think about the day when she would finally be released to live again, and now suddenly it was within sight. Already she and my sister were filling up the forms necessary to obtain an assisted passage to New Zealand, where they would join my brothers.

Shortly after my arrival home, an important-looking letter came from the Hudson's Bay Company. It reminded me rather sternly that I had undertaken to achieve competence in book-keeping and typing before leaving England, and warned me that I would have to produce certificates to avoid being left behind on the quayside. A visit one afternoon to an established business college in the town indicated that this was not going to be as easy as it sounded. They smiled pityingly and showed us the door. We journeyed round all the other colleges in the town. The answer was always the same. They did not undertake to turn out typists and bookkeepers in a matter of weeks.

Finally, to my horror, mother unearthed a girls' college willing to attempt the impossible task.

My frantic efforts to spare myself this frightful indignity were unavailing. In these days of the easy mixing of young people of both sexes it is hard to credit the conditions that prevailed seventy years ago. At school no females were allowed. Even the maids, unless they were grey-haired, had to operate out of sight of the boys. Consequently, unless there was a good social life at home, boys and young men were awkward in their relationships with girls, even singly. Now I was to be put in with a whole college of them!

Like some rare oddity, I was placed at a desk facing two rows of girls and was so busy watching for slights and suspecting all kinds of indignities that I never got to know any of them. I was to become aware before leaving that these girls had a much better idea of natural behaviour than I did.

The women in charge of the place had pulled a few strings, and a few days before my departure presented me with an official-looking but vague document. This declared me to be indoctrinated, both as to the keeping of books and typewriting, though not accepting any responsibility for the outcome of my activities.

After the presentation, one of the other pupils, a small plain girl whose nose was slightly flattened as though having been pressed against a window pane too long, rushed forward and pushed a small package into my hand. It was from them all, she said, to wish me well in whatever outlandish part of the world it was to which I was going.

This sudden expression of goodwill from my contemporaries, and girls at that, quite overcame me. The unexpected kindness never faded from my mind and the gift, a small silver propelling pencil, remained one of my prize possessions for many years.

The Hudson's Bay Company apparently expected me to

transform myself from a schoolboy into a practical handyman in the few weeks available between leaving school and the departure for Canada. They sent a list of the more important arts which it would be wise for me to cultivate. Apart from the bookkeeping and typing, it was desirable, they wrote, to gain a knowledge of the combustion engine, some idea of first aid and experience of simple cooking.

The far northern districts of Canada, being so isolated, were totally dependent on sea travel by motor boat for summer hunting. There were no mechanics as such, so it was important that as many people as possible should be capable of keeping the engines running. The lack of doctors meant that the post staff would have to deal with accidents and illness and a knowledge of basic first aid was vital. Apparently, few Eskimo women had any idea of cooking, so we would have to do our share of preparing the meals.

As the list of necessary accomplishments grew, doubts began to creep into my mind. Had this apparently ideal solution to our problem blinded me to the reality of the situation in which I was going to find myself? Not even my mother, always prepared to believe the best about me, would have claimed any practical virtues for me. Yet it seemed that it was practical people who were wanted. Of what use would it have been to be top of the German class when the motor boat broke down? How could a sound knowledge of history stop me from being sick when someone came to see me with a bone sticking out of their arm and blood everywhere? Would the promise that the form master had assured me I had shown in English give me any confidence to prepare a meal for the weary traveller?

These fears subsided when the final documents arrived for my mother and sister to sign for their passage to New Zealand. Amid the excitement at the prospect of an early release, my natural optimism reasserted itself. When the last day came, it seemed unlikely that we should ever spend time together in England again, so the three of us took a picnic and hired a boat to laze down a river through the quiet Somerset countryside, where we had passed many happy hours in days gone by.

That night I said goodbye to my grandmother. She seemed much affected. She said that she wished that she had had more money so that we could have stayed in England and not gone so far away, but the family fortunes had dwindled and there was nothing she could do. She gave me a little package wrapped up in tissue paper. It contained two spoons and a fork, silver with her family crest stamped on the handles. This was to remind me of all those people who had stared down on my childhood, and how well some of them had acquitted themselves.

Mother and I set off for London early the next morning, my sister having already gone back to her job in Bristol. We stayed at an old-fashioned hotel, and went to a theatre, and after breakfast the next morning made our way quietly to the ten o'clock rendezvous at Euston station. I remember thinking back to our first parting, on the day that mother had taken me down to start school. The tears had streamed down my face then and she had tried to console me by saying that it would only be a few weeks before the holidays. This time the tears streamed down her face as we began to move, and I did not know what to say.

Five years suddenly seemed a very, very long time.

*

I remember little about the voyage across the Atlantic. Being a summer passage, it was calm and uneventful I suppose, with little to do except eat, sleep and play deck games until we reached the St Lawrence river and had our first glimpse of our future homeland. We had a brief run ashore at Quebec, just enough to say that we had set foot in Canada, then the next day docked at Montreal, where our posts would be assigned.

Our accommodation on the ship had seemed almost luxurious, so our temporary home in the city was something of a let-down. The public rooms were sparsely furnished with trestle tables and wooden chairs and there was little attempt to reach any standard of comfort, but the people who ran the place were good-hearted souls, who kept our spirits up with an ample supply of good plain food.

The Hudson's Bay Company offices in Montreal were in McGill Street, and though half our number had taken the train westward, there seemed to be quite a crowd of us milling about in the comparatively small office space. We met the men in charge of our areas and most of the apprentices were told where they would be going. Another boy, Ian Smith, and I were 'odd men out' for whom a home would be found during the course of the summer travels.

To relieve the congestion, a party of us were sent down to the docks to work on the *Nascopie*, the ship that the archdeacon had told us about at school, now loading up for her annual trip with the year's supply for the distant posts.

After the majestic liner which had carried us so smoothly across the Atlantic, the *Nascopie* seemed very small and insignificant. Her decks only just rose above the level of the wharf, whereas the liner had towered up above the dockside. Her paintwork was dark and workmanlike whereas the *Duchess* had gleamed and dazzled in white. None the less, many of us were, in the years to come, to form an affection for the little ship which no ocean liner could ever have inspired. Sometimes she was naughty. In rough weather there were few tricks that were beyond her, particularly when coming down the Labrador coast with only a few light bales of furs in her holds. She would then creak and groan in the most alarming manner, but survived the worst hammerings the North Atlantic and the Arctic seas could serve up, to return each year, like a faithful friend, to keep us company for a few hours or a day or so in our northern solitude.

More than once the *Nascopie* took on a double duty, when lesser craft than she gave up the unequal struggle against fog and ice. The old ship had been built during or just before the First World War, and was one of the finest steel icebreakers ever constructed. During the war, she was employed smashing the ice in the White Sea, and according to all reports was well ahead of the Russians in this field. Once, in a convoy in heavy ice, the huge Russian icebreaker leading the convoy got stuck. The *Nascopie* bustled up alongside and hailed the Russian.

'Shall I go ahead, sir?' shouted the captain.

'How the devil can you go ahead when I'm stuck?' roared back the Russian.

'Shall I try?'

'Oh, go to hell if you want to,' snapped the Russian.

The *Nascopie* broke through the ice jam to lead the convoy into harbour, and for good measure, on the way home, she sank a submarine. Small wonder that she grew on us almost as though she were human.

On that first Monday morning, however, we were not greatly impressed. In fact by the time we had finished carrying the heavy mail boxes – and it is extraordinary how heavily a year's mail can weigh – we were not sorry to see the last of her for the day.

We soon made friends around our temporary home. One Saturday night, a French Canadian family held a wedding reception in the building. Two or three of us were hanging about so they invited us to join the party. During the evening, we were approached by a rather unsteady-looking man who, after casting a glance at a priest standing near by, said in a deep but penetrating whisper: 'H.B.C. eh? Do you know what that means? ''Here before Christ,'' that's what it means!'

He told us that he had been trading with the company for over thirty years. Ian asked him if he had retired and the man roared with laughter.

'Retired?' he shouted. 'I'm never going to retire. They'll find me one day somewhere along the trail and I hope they'll leave me there.' He waved his arm round the room then went on.

'This sort of thing's not for me. I only came because she happens to be a niece. I'll not be down this way again. Victor's my name. They'll know me up the river. I don't have much in this world but I'm free. I go where I like when I like and I'm off home in the morning.' He waved his arm and marched off towards the table where the food was set out. I was often to think about Victor in the years to come, his boisterous good health, his obvious contentment with the life he had chosen, and his best clothes, which looked as if they had not been worn for many a long day.

We met three sisters at the wedding too who had come from Three Rivers and had made the trip down with their father and mother. They were good fun and Ian Smith and I and another chap took them out for a picnic the next day, as they spent the weekend in the city. It was the first time that I had ever been out with a girl other than my sister, and one of them, Laurette, said she would write to me. I rashly promised to write and send her a fur from wherever I was. She did write too but alas did not receive the promised fur.

By the end of the next week, so far as we could see, the *Nascopie* was just about fully laden. We were not surprised to be told to pack up again in preparation for moving on. Then at the last minute, because of the shortage of accommodation on the ship, Ian, myself and three others were told that we were to take passage on another freighter, which was going up as far north as the Labrador coast and Ungava Bay. Somewhere up there we should join up again with the *Nascopie*. This meant that we should be sailing a few days later.

The evening before we parted we all clubbed together to buy some beer and had a small party – at least we sang songs and were generally very noisy. Now that we knew that we were to be northerners, an air of easy comradeship settled over the gathering and it seemed likely that we should have much to do with each other over the next few years. Such is the remoteness of life in the Arctic that I was only to see three of the dozen or so present after that season.

The five of us that were to be left behind went down to the docks to see the rest of our party depart. Prepared for laughter and banter, we had not expected the sailing of the little ship to be so stirring. The vessel was bedecked in pennants, apart from the Red Ensign at the stern and the Blue Peter at the mainmast. A detachment of the Royal Canadian Mounted Police, in their scarlet uniforms, was drawn up on the deck for inspection by a high-ranking officer. There were priests, government officials, traders, doctors and scientists. In her holds, we knew, were the supplies for a territory ten times the size of England. We shook hands with our friends. Some of the ladies farewelling their nearest and dearest cried, while another group was singing.

Then the siren sounded out in long blasts, the propellor churned the water and she was away. A nearby harbour tug blew her a rousing farewell and more and more sirens sounded their good wishes. Black smoke belched from her funnel and as she moved out into the stream we could see clearly all the things lashed to her decks. Boats. Canoes. Drums of gasoline. All sorts of queer-shaped things covered with tarpaulins.

Ian and I watched her manoeuvre into midstream and then head out of the harbour, the white pennant of the Royal Mail slapping in the wind at the top of her mast. Down river, the

Canadian navy, in the form of two destroyers, dipped flags in salute as she steamed by. Just beside me somebody's friend had forgotten a last message, bawling out 'Happy Christmas' in the forlorn hope of being heard on the ship. We began to understand why they had told us that to think about the Arctic without thinking about the Hudson's Bay Company was like writing a book about sea without mentioning ships.

A few days after the departure of the *Nascopie*, the remaining five of us set off quietly for the docks, taking with us all our worldly possessions. By ten o'clock that morning we were assembled in a rather gloomy shed at the city end of the wharf, where the van had unloaded us. The ship on which we were to take passage, the *Ungava*, was alongside the far end of the wharf, so we had a fair way to go with all our baggage.

One of our party could hardly move, so heavily laden was he with cases and packages, and his crab-like motion attracted the attention of a passing wharfie.

'Why didn't you bring your bed, boy?' the man guffawed. 'Where the devil are you off to with all that load?'

'I'm going north for five years,' came a voice from behind the parcels and cases.

'Well in five years' time you'll either be dead or carrying twice that much on one shoulder,' shouted the man amid his laughter as he went on his way to the dock gates.

There was no glamour attached to the departure of the *Ungava*. She was just a rather rusty old freighter, and an ugly one at that, setting off on a more or less routine passage along the Labrador coast. She was heavily laden. Her well decks were completely filled in with drums of oil, so that care had to be taken when passing across them to avoid falling overboard.

There was no one to see us off, apart from a couple of officials from the office, so without any fuss or palaver, about an hour after we had come aboard, the crew cast off the lines and, belching black smoke, like the *Nascopie* we set off down the river.

The old ship had no licence to carry passengers. We had had to sign on as crew, deckhands, stewards, stokers and the like at a token wage of one dollar per week. I was allocated to a job as 'assistant purser', which did not please some of the others, for they considered it to be a cushy task compared to theirs. As it turned out that I had laboriously to type out page after page of bills of lading while they had little to do after a slight scurry of activity in the mornings, they were quite pleased.

Ian and I went out on deck that first evening, making our way perilously over the oil barrels to a space on the stern, from where we could watch the muddy waters stirred up by the propellor and the coastline dropping behind us. We were somewhere between the two cities of Montreal and Quebec, the former just a distant glow on the horizon, the latter not yet visible. Above the hills, the summer lightning forked and flashed and the thunder rumbled distantly. A few lights twinkled on both shores. A small township, stretched along the bank of the great river, drifted by and dwindled into the distance.

We did not speak much. I think we both realized at last that before long the lights of our accustomed world would have faded behind us. Ahead would stretch the vast empty wilderness of the Arctic to which we had so lightheartedly committed ourselves.

II

THE LABRADOR COAST runs in a north-westerly direction, pointing at the top like an outstretched finger across Hudson Straights toward Resolution Island and Baffin Island. The Torngak Range, mountains of the devil, high and menacing, jut out into the straight above Ungava Bay. Straggling still further beyond the mainland, the islands Killineck and the Buttons jostle each other, desolate and barren as if the Almighty, coming to the end of a coastline with a few black and unproductive rocks left over, flung them in one despairing handful into that grey and uninviting sea.

The other end of the coast is less daunting, but still hostile to anyone used to the gentle countryside of southern England. It begins just above the Gulf of St Lawrence and curves round into the Straits of Belle Isle, the strip of water which separates Labrador from the island of Newfoundland. Here, before we had even really entered the northern seas, the elements served up a warning of what we might expect in the higher latitudes.

During the afternoon of the fourth day out from Montreal, the heavy clouds massed threateningly from the north. Slowly they grouped and crept across the darkening sky toward us, then suddenly, just before nightfall, launched their attack. The wind roared down at us, flinging gouts of rain like pieces of metal into the faces of those foolish enough to stray out on deck to see what was happening.

At the height of each gust, the old ship seemed to waver and stop, shuddering helplessly on the crest of the mounting waves, unable to force a passage through the strength of the storm. Then, as the gust slackened, the vessel slid down into the deep beyond, shaking itself free of the holding wind.

Those of us quartered in the after part of the ship were effectively marooned, since to reach the dining saloon and forward parts we had to cross over the barrels with a near certainty of being flung into the sea. The other apprentices did not seem to mind about this, because the pitching and tossing of the ship had removed their interest in food, but I felt deprived at having to content myself with a bar of chocolate for the evening meal.

Any feeling of superiority was quite dispelled during the night, however, for my bunk, which had not been fastened properly to the wall, gave way with the strain of the ship's movement, flinging me down on to the deck with the mattress and spring on top of me. First aid had to be administered to a gash on my head, necessitating a rather unsightly, bloodstained bandage. My friends thought it much funnier and more undignified that I had fallen out of my bunk (as they soon persuaded themselves) than that they had suffered a bout of seasickness.

Within twenty-four hours the storm calmed almost as quickly as it had risen. We had turned the corner from Belle Isle and were now steaming along the Labrador coast, heading for our first port of call, a settlement called Cartwright.

The harbour was just inside the entrance to a fairly wide bay with an island slanted across the mouth in such a way as to make it almost landlocked. We thought at first that the captain had stopped the ship and dropped anchor to wait until the visibility improved, for all round the vessel there was a low mist stretching to the horizon. Then we noticed straight ahead of us, apparently suspended from the sky, the familiar flag of the

Hudson's Bay Company. Shortly afterwards the fog dispersed sufficiently for us to see that the captain had placed the ship directly in front of the post buildings.

The scenery was not inspiring: a long deep stretch of flat land which looked like marshland or swamp, as if there ought to have been a river delta just ahead of us. We could see no river though, just the flats with some low hills in the distance and, further still, blending almost into the clouds along the horizon but breaking through here and there as a peak or crag, the higher hills of the interior. Just below the buildings, at a jetty pushed out into the bay for about fifty yards or so, a nondescript group of people appeared to be waiting for the *Ungava* to start unloading.

Dotted across the flats were numerous shack-like erections, with larger single-storey buildings here and there, such as a school and a hospital. The whole outlook was as grey and dull as the day itself, but we soon found that we were not there just as tourists. The group we had seen waiting at the end of the jetty was to come aboard and work in the holds, while we were to go ashore to handle the supplies as they came off the lighters.

Our job was to carry the goods down the full length of the jetty and then across to the store, which was situated beyond the dwelling house. It was hard work and a very long way to those not used to carrying heavy weights, which seemed to be most of us. Under my first sack of flour I nearly sank to my knees, but managed to hold up, much to the disappointment, I am sure, of the first mate, who was standing near by with a grin all over his face waiting for one of us to make a fool of himself. Adding considerably to our discomfort was the fact that the place was infested with vicious mosquitoes, which descended upon us in veritable clouds to sample the blood of the newcomers, so that our first day's work on the Labrador coast was misery endured rather than a brave step forward.

25

The apprentice at Cartwright had come out from Scotland two years previously and he warned us not to expect any home comforts. On the evening of his arrival, he had asked the manager where his bedroom was. He had been taken down to the store, shown a mattress squeezed in behind the counter and told that that was his bedroom. He warned us too that a greenhorn in the Arctic was fair game for everyone, especially the old-timers. During his first winter, he had slightly frozen his big toe and had in due course lost the nail. An apparently knowledgeable colleague at the post told him that he must strap the black nail back on to his toe for at least three months, after which time it would have grown back on again. According to our friend he had done this at very great discomfort and not until several weeks later did he discover that his leg had been pulled. I think most of us thought ourselves too clever to be caught out like that, but it was not easy to resist the insistent advice of experienced people, however bizarre it seemed.

The unloading took about twenty-four hours, working quite late into the night and resuming again at daybreak. The mosquitoes attacked relentlessly, but our loads seemed to get less heavy as our muscles became more and more used to the strain, although we were all glad when the last case had been safely deposited in the store. The *Ungava* did not sail at once, so we had an opportunity to look round our first Hudson's Bay Company post.

We visited some of the shacks dotted about on the flats. It was rather like stepping back in time, for these homes could well have belonged to a much earlier era. The first thing that met the eye were the outsize texts hanging near the entrance and at other strategic points inside. 'THE WAGES OF SIN ARE DEATH', 'GOD IS LOVE', 'JUDGE NOT THAT YE BE NOT JUDGED' and other sombre messages set the tone. The occupants sat in their homes, prim and formal, surrounded by their possessions as though they were relics of the Victorian peasantry somehow strayed into the twentieth century. They appeared to be of European descent, with perhaps some intermingling of Indian blood and possibly Innuit as well. They understood some English, but could not be drawn into anything but the most conventional conversation.

During the morning of our departure from Cartwright, the man in charge of our group summoned me to his cabin and told me that I was to become the apprentice at a post called Fort Chimo, a small but long-established settlement situated at the head of Ungava Bay. He advised me to seek the advice of a passenger who had just joined us to travel along the coast and who had spent several years at Chimo. Ian Smith was to go to a nearby post, so he joined me in seeking out this man, Bill Ford by name.

We found Bill asleep in his cabin and at first he did not seem to be too pleased at having his rest interrupted, but he mellowed when he discovered we had brought a couple of bottles of beer with us. He sat drinking the beer and dangling his legs over the bunk.

'Years ago,' he said, 'Chimo was almost a small township. The post staff was much larger than it is nowadays. They had people to make barrels, carpenters, interpreters. There were opposition trading companies, a school, a hospital and government officials.'

'How did the company people get on with the opposition?' asked Ian.

'They didn't have very much to do with each other,' replied Bill, 'they didn't fraternize. If anything went wrong for one of them, the other was always very bucked about it. I remember once that during a gale a boat belonging to the French company Revillon Frères broke away from her moorings. It was a big boat too, about five tons, and the company chaps gathered along the river bank to cheer as she drifted past. The thing went right out to sea and it was several days before they got her back again, with a hole stove in her bow just above the waterline where she had hit a rock.

'There aren't many opposition posts left now though. There hasn't been enough trade for more than one company for the past few years at Chimo and rumour has it that Revillon Frères will be pulling out before long.'

I asked him about the natives in Ungava Bay.

'The Eskimos live around the shores,' Bill replied, 'and the Indians have their camps inland. They're quite friendly and don't really come into contact with each other very much. There's never been any trouble as far as I know. Round the bay, where the Eskimos live, the land is very flat – sometimes I used to wish that the hills were a little higher. The wind comes down from the interior and whistles round the houses during the winter. We had some fair old blizzards. In a real blizzard, you have no idea where you are, the wind can keep changing and you can't see a thing. One of the Chimo mission-aries got caught once coming back from a visit to his flock. He and his Eskimo driver dug themselves into the snow, after struggling as far as they could. They were miserable in what was little better than a hole in the ground for two days. On the third day they were amazed to hear the sound of church bells coming from near by and they struggled out of their holes to find that they had camped almost alongside the missionary's own house. The bells they had heard was his assistant ringing for the morning service.'

We soon found that Bill Ford, who had spent most of the previous winter alone, inland from Cartwright, needed little persuasion to launch off into his stories of the Labrador coast and Ungava Bay. Sometimes it was quite difficult to stop him, but both Ian and I felt that he never did try to make fools of us, a pastime to which many old-time northerners were willing to devote a considerable amount of time.

We made several stops during our voyage along the Labrador coast. At Makkovik, my star did not at first seem to be in the ascendant. Wearing a new beret, purchased under the French influence of the Montreal shops, I felt quite jaunty as I reached the bottom of the gangway and prepared to climb into the first boat ashore. Unfortunately, at that precise moment the fastening, or whatever it was that held the bottom step in place, broke. The step tilted up into a vertical position, allowing me to slide, quite gracefully they told me, into the water. My efforts to grasp something as I went down simply resulted in me pulling the step back down into position over my head. I was able to tell my friends later that although the water looked calm and inviting enough for a swim, it was really too cold to be enjoyable.

Later on during the afternoon, I rejoined the working party on shore and they kept up their ribaldry at my expense for the rest of the day. We finished the work before teatime and a pleasant surprise awaited us, for the post manager told us that his wife wanted us to go and have a meal with them instead of going back to the ship. His wife, a jolly, cheerful person, did not seem to mind how many of us came. She had cooked a huge dishful of cod steaks in batter and on the table was what looked like an old-time washbasin full of crisp chips. She just stood back and let us help ourselves, laughing with delight at our obvious appreciation. When the fish had all gone, the lady produced an outsize apple pie, then cake and bread and jam for any unfilled corner. She seemed much concerned about my plunge into the sea. Had I dried myself properly? What about my clothes? What was the Hudson's Bay Company thinking of, bringing children up into the Arctic? I rejected the suggestion that I was a child at sixteen, but she shook her head and said that it was a hard life and a very lonely one.

After we had cleared up the mess and done the washing up, we gathered round an old piano that had been retrieved from a wreck along the coast. The manager played familiar tunes and we sang and laughed and played silly games until it was time to go back to the ship. When we tried to thank them for everything, they said that they hadn't had such a happy evening for a long time and hoped that one day we might all come back.

Early the next morning we sailed from Makkovik to steam along the central part of the coastline. The scenery improved greatly. There were dozens of islands large and small, where the sea wound in and out in twisting passageways, curious-shaped cliffs and rocks, worn down by time and sea and weather. Birds of all coastal types abounded, from the hungry, cawing gull to the lively little arctic tern.

By the time we reached Hebron, a few days further down the coast, the land was even more impressive, as it rose high and rugged toward the desolate mountains. The weather was fine and sunny and a morning spent on deck was as good as anything an expensive cruise ship could offer.

I found Bill in a cozy spot one morning, behind some boxes, quite sheltered from the slight breeze. He smiled when he saw me.

'So you tracked me down, eh?' he said, but showed no reluctance to talk.

'You wouldn't think that a fine new ship was lying just beneath the water over there, would you? Not that she would be new now of course.' He pointed over to the coast and continued.

'The *Bay Rupert*. I don't suppose you ever heard of her. The company had her built after the war. She was a fine ship, much larger than the *Nascopie* and everything brand spanking new. They put in special accommodation for bringing tourists up here. It was more like travelling on an Atlantic liner than coming up north.'

'Did you ever sail in her?' asked Ian.

'I did indeed,' said Bill. 'I got off just before she went down. It seems that there's a rock along the coast, somewhere hereabouts, which sticks up under the sea but doesn't break water and there was no buoy there to mark the spot. We were coming along the inside passage in beautiful weather, just like today, with a pilot who was responsible for the navigation. The story was that one evening this man made out the course that they were to follow and the captain said that if he did as the pilot wanted, they would run smack into a rock about breakfast time next morning. Some people said that they had a great row about it, but that the course stayed as it was. The next morning, I was just getting out of my bunk when there was a terrific bump and, sure enough, the skipper was right. I'd never been shipwrecked before and it wasn't anything like what I had thought it would be. We just got into the boats and they took us ashore, rather as if we were going for a day out, but the ship sank quite quickly and as the water isn't very deep, it became a kind of treasure trove for all and sundry. Most of the homes along there have to thank the *Bay Rupert* for some item or another.'

'What did they do to the pilot?' I asked.

'I don't think that they actually did anything to anybody. There was a great deal of argument as to what had really happened and nobody seemed to know the whole story.'

'It's a good thing that it doesn't happen very often up here,' Ian said.

'Oh, round about that time there was a jinx on the company,' said Bill. 'Another of the bay boats was lost, the *Bay Chimo*, but she didn't sink, not at first anyway. She was trapped by the ice and it seems that she got frozen in during the winter, after they had abandoned her. Later on, she was sighted drifting about in the pack ice, like a sort of ghost ship, somewhere up in the Beaufort Sea, and for all I know she may still be held together by the ice of the Western Arctic!'

Almost as soon as we left Hebron the weather changed and during the night a thick fog closed about us. The captain groped his way at half speed, with frequent blasts of the fog horn, in case any of the wheat boats on their way to or from Churchill were in the vicinity.

We awoke in the morning to find the fog cleared and heard the rattle of the anchor chain going down, signifying our arrival at a post. When Ian and I went out on deck to see where we were, we did not at first believe that we had arrived anywhere. All we could see of the land was what resembled one humped black rock. Bill Ford put us right.

'Port Burwell,' he said, 'and I hope that I never land here for my sins.'

We could see what he meant. This was one of the islands where the Labrador coast straggled off into the arctic seas. Bleak and inhospitable even on a summer's day, one could well imagine that in the dark grey of the stormy winter the elements would combine to make life as unpleasant as possible.

For once there was little activity, and the dullness of the morning was only enlivened by the arrival of a boatload of Eskimos from the shore. They pulled alongside and one or two of their number came straight aboard the *Ungava*. The crew made them welcome, then the rest came pouring up the gangway, gabbling away to each other and beaming all over their brown faces. A few of the women wore red or green tartan shawls wrapped around their shoulders, but mainly they were clothed in parkas with deep hoods in which to carry their babies. Underneath they had on ordinary summer dresses made of coloured prints of various designs. Many of them looked as though they had got straight out of bed to come to the ship, and a few as though they had worn their clothes all night. The men all wore parkas with coloured braid round the edges; some had bright knitted head coverings, while one or two sported naval caps with gold straps. The chief man of the boat handled his craft very efficiently.

The stewards produced a large kettle of tea and a box of biscuits and another of the crew brought up a carton of mugs. In a moment the Eskimos were squatting all over the deck downing their tea. Some of the women had brought their babies in their parkas, and every now and then one of them would suddenly run to the side of the ship, to hold baby out over the sea to relieve itself.

They were a happy, cheerful lot and looked to me to fit somewhere between the American Indians and Chinese. When the tea was all drunk, they surged back down the gangway to their boat and chugged off, disappearing round a point of land a few moments later.

Ralph Parsons, the district manager for the whole of the Eastern Arctic, who had himself established most of the posts in the district, arrived in his own Peterhead boat about midday and the ship came to life. Ian and I were sent ashore with the first scowload and were surprised to find that the harbour was just on the other side of the point round which the Eskimos had passed. The little cove was only about a hundred yards in depth, but the opening was quite narrow, so there was good shelter from the open sea.

There was not a lot of cargo to handle as the *Nascopie* had already unloaded the main supplies, but the goods had to be carried up a long winding walkway as the store had been built on a rise some way back from the shoreline. By now we were becoming quite experienced stevedores and did not provide the ship's personnel with many laughs. We were also much more speedy, finishing the work in time to go back aboard the ship for a meal.

A surprise awaited us. Ian, myself and another boy were to pack up and go ashore to await further instructions. One of the men who had come up from Chimo with Ralph Parsons gave us the explanation the next day. Ian would not be required as the outpost to which he was to have been sent had sufficient staff, and when the Chimo manager, a Scotsman, heard that I was supposed to join him, he became quite angry and said that he did not want any damned English schoolchildren. Not until much later did I discover that a year or two previously this man had been landed with an English apprentice from a public school who had gone off the rails. At the time, this brusque refusal of my services really upset me for it had never occurred to me that I might not be wanted anywhere.

It was quite obvious that we were not wanted at the Burwell post house either. A small house, built to accommodate two people, it now had to shelter twelve of us, and quite possibly this manager would also have refused us as his 'guests' had not Ralph Parsons come ashore to straighten things out. He directed that Ian and I should sleep on the kitchen floor in sleeping bags. Our thoughts went back to the poor apprentice at Cartwright with whom we had commiserated; at least he had had a mattress to lie on.

Next morning we started on our first shore job, painting the fish house. At that time, a considerable amount of dried fish used to be exported to the Catholic countries for food on Fridays and fast days, particularly to those countries which had a peasant population who could not afford to buy fresh fish. Just outside the harbour, round the southern shores of the island, codfish abounded, the Eskimos often gathering a dinghy full of fish in quite a short time. They sold the cod to the company, who employed women to cut them open, dry them and pack them in barrels for shipment overseas. This processing took place in the shed that Ian and I were about to paint. Neither of us had ever handled a paintbrush before, and it was perhaps unfortunate that the colour of the eaves, where we began, was bright red and not some duller colour which might have blended in better with our overalls.

In the evenings the post manager took me out jigging for cod. This simply meant fixing a double-sided hook to a long length of cord, pushing on a small piece of pork fat for bait, lowering it to the seabed, then pulling it up about a foot or so and jigging the line up and down until you hooked a fish. Sometimes we caught a large fish on each barb of the hook, and even on the poorest evening we collected twenty or thirty fish. All the best cod were thrown into the shed for servicing by the women; the rest we took up to the house or used for dog food.

Eventually most of the visitors left Burwell, until we were the last remaining guests, and actually able to sleep in beds. One day Mr Parsons told us that Ian was to stay at Burwell as the apprentice and I was to join the *Nascopie* when she arrived, to continue my journey northward in search of a home. Ian was sad about this. Burwell was not much of a place, serving more as a summer junction point between Hudson's Bay, Baffin Land and the far northern islands than as a trading post. There was one consolation. He would be among the first to see the *Nascopie* the next year and would no doubt be able to get himself moved somewhere more interesting.

The *Nascopie* arrived one afternoon in late August. The captain intended to waste no time, for there was already a touch of autumn in the air. Once the year's supplies had been landed, I was told not to delay in getting aboard with my belongings.

Ian helped me down to the jetty with my cases. We had become firm friends through the trials and tribulations of our summer's journey and saying goodbye to him was harder than I thought it would be. I cannot imagine how he ever came to apply to the Hudson's Bay Company for a job. He was a timid, gentle sort of person who hated to see suffering either among humans or animals, and it was no surprise to hear a couple of years later that it had not worked out and Ian had gone back to his old Scottish home. I did write to him but he never replied to my letters. Perhaps he just wanted to forget the whole incident.

We steamed away from the island well before dark, heading due north toward Davis Straits and Baffin Bay. At the very top of Baffin Island we were to turn west towards Pond Inlet, at that time the most northerly of the Hudson's Bay Company posts.

Before the light faded altogether, I went to the stern of the *Nascopie* to watch the ship's wake streaming behind us, just as Ian and I had done that first evening out on the St Lawrence River. There were no little townships drifting by, no comforting lights twinkling along the shore or summer lightning forking above rolling hills. Here was only steely grey, incredibly cold-looking sea surging behind us, tipped with long ribbons of hostile foam, while abeam of us the last of the Button Islands passed, black, jagged and with no redeeming feature. I wondered where those other apprentices who had gathered at Euston station that June morning were now and mourned the loss of my friend. Then the captain altered course slightly and a chill damp wind, probably from the northern ice fields, drove me back to my cabin.

The cabin was above a propeller, and as the ship rose and fell to the motion of the sea, so the shuddering vibration swelled and faded in an uneven rhythm. As by far the most junior person on the ship – for there were no other apprentices or post staff of any kind – it was reasonable to expect that the worst cabin should be allotted to me. Somehow, though, the shuddering noise served to increase my growing conviction that nobody really wanted me in this arctic world and the probability that a home would be found for me at the very last post, only because there was nowhere else left, did nothing for my self-esteem.

Our route between Baffin Island and Greenland was one which had been followed by seamen and navigators for more than three centuries, probing restlessly northward then westward among the islands, searching endlessly for the passage which would take them more easily to the riches of India.

Some people believe that the Vikings reached the shores of Baffin Island twelve hundred years ago, but if they did, the expeditions were not recorded and nothing has been discovered to suggest that they ever lived there. It was not until the idea of a short route through to the orient began to exercise men's minds that serious exploration of this inhospitable area began.

As far back as 1497 Henry VII of England commissioned John Cabot to search for a passage, and the explorer is thought to have sailed along the Labrador coast. Forty years or so later, Jacques Cartier attempted to succeed where Cabot had failed but found only impenetrable ice. Sir Humphrey Gilbert, who felt strongly that the journey was possible, inspired others to try by his writings, but was himself drowned while making the attempt in 1583.

Also in the sixteenth century, John Davis made a study of the strait which separates North America from Greenland and joins Baffin Bay to the Atlantic Ocean, though he did not try to push through to the west. The strait now bears his name, and possibly as a result of his findings, Martin Frobisher, a noted navigator of his day, believed that he could find the elusive passage. He became sidetracked when, turning westward too soon, he entered a deep bay in Southern Baffin Land, which took him nearly three hundred miles inland but ended in a range of steep hills. From this bay Frobisher saw some rocks that glittered in the sun. He thought it was gold, and although his find turned out to be iron pyrites, it did not discourage him from arranging two later expeditions to explore the other arms of the bay. He never did find the gold which he had thought to be there, but he did much useful work mapping the bay which was subsequently named after him.

Henry Hudson considered that the navigators of the sixteenth century had all sailed too far to the north, and to prove his theory decided to aim westward between the mainland and the southern coast of Baffin Island. At the western end of the straits, he came out into a wide sea. His crew, superstitious and apprehensive of some unexpected disaster, did not wish to go any further, but Hudson, confident that he was already in the western ocean, insisted that they continue on his course. The men's fury when they discovered that he had led them into a wide bay which had no exit was such that they mutinied, and Hudson, together with his son and seven loyal members of his crew, was cast adrift in a small boat to perish in the icy waters of what became known as Hudson Bay.

We had had clear weather for the first two days and the ship, headed now into familiar northern waters, made good speed. The district manager, who was travelling with us and who hated to see anyone unoccupied, took me on as a temporary, very junior office boy, to sort out the files and account books of the posts which had already been visited. The other people still on board were mainly specialists in one line or another, who seemed quite keen to fill in my remaining spare moments with lectures on a variety of subjects. An anthropologist, an archaeologist, an ornithologist, two scientists, a representative of the Canadian government and two R.C.M. policemen were among those I can remember being on board. From some of them I gathered an amount of useful knowledge, but was never quite sure whether my leg was being pulled or not.

The archdeacon, who six months previously had introduced me to the Arctic, was making the rounds of his widely scattered missionaries and obviously felt under some obligation to take me under his wing. I think he had it in mind to give me a warning as to the possible moral dangers that lay ahead of me, but after two quite lengthy sessions, could get no further than giving me a bar of chocolate and some advice as to how to avoid becoming constipated during the winter months, because of the effort needed to visit the outside lavatory on cold draughty days.

The ice fields were not far away from us. Over towards Greenland, visibility ended in a long line of grey fog, behind which, they told me, the ice blocks were grinding their way steadily southward.

On the morning of the fourth day out, we steamed through a bank of fog and came almost immediately into a large field. The massive blocks crunched against the side of the vessel, but the *Nascopie* pushed them aside. Every now and then we came up against a solid pan which had not broken up into pieces and the captain had to force the ship through by reversing a little way, then rushing back at the ice at top speed. The solid iron bows with the full power of the engines behind them usually sufficed to smash a path through but we made slow speed.

Early in the afternoon, a lookout sighted black objects in the ice ahead of us. Out came the binoculars and the telescopes. 'Walrus,' said the more experienced northerners. Two of the passengers, unable to resist the temptation of trying to kill the inoffensive creatures, went below to fetch their rifles, but were restrained by the older hands, who told them that they would be wasting their time and ammunition, for without proper harpoons with which to secure the walrus the bodies would just sink to the bottom of the sea.

Reluctantly the would-be hunters held their fire. We came

closer and saw that it was quite a large herd. A huge old bull, seemingly the leader, lifted his head to look round every now and then, obviously checking on the safety of the group. He must have seen us, but as our approach was not particularly noisy, he did not raise the alarm until the ship steamed up to the very point upon which the walrus were resting.

We had a wonderful view of the herd and those who had got their cameras out were well rewarded. The old bull who had been so vigilant during our approach took charge. As the *Nascopie* ground into the ice not so very far from them, the leader raised his head again to let out the most enormous bellow, so that they all scrambled and fought to get back into the water. The large bulls, with their great ivory tusks sticking downwards from their jaws and their fierce bewhiskered faces, were a fearsome lot. The cows with their young looked less belligerent, but together they made an awful noise, barging and pushing each other along. For a moment, they appeared to be contemplating an attack on the ship, but suddenly swept round to make off down a lane of open water.

About an hour later, as though we had not had our money's worth for the day, a polar bear, large, grizzled and yellowish against the ice, came out from behind a mound on a small iceberg to stare gravely at us as we passed by. This time our hunters were not to be denied. Three of them rushed down to fetch weapons. By the time they had returned to the deck, the bear had moved off a short distance, wisely having his doubts as to our intentions. The fusillade that followed confirmed his doubts and the animal, now thoroughly alarmed by the noise, raised himself on to his hind legs and dived into the sea, finally disappearing among some nearby ice blocks. He had been wounded though, for we passed a streamer of his blood in a patch of open water. The archdeacon took the marksmen to task for having caused the creature unnecessary suffering.

We then had a spell of fine weather after leaving the Hudson Strait, and although the days were shortening and the breezes cooling as we came north, we had not realized that the summer had really ended until the fall burst unheralded upon us.

The archdeacon was conducting a Sunday-morning service in the *Nascopie* dining room, when the captain turned the ship westward to come out of Baffin Bay toward Pond Inlet. The vessel began to roll as we caught the wind sweeping down the channel through which so many of those early explorers had passed in their search for the passage.

Before the service was over, the storm had really blown up. The congregation swayed all over the place during the final hymn and the archdeacon called a halt to the proceedings when a group on the starboard side collapsed into a most undignified heap. I forced my way out on to the deck, but was nearly blinded by the hard sleet slapping into my face and the stinging spray driven by the violent wind. Sheets of spray streamed across the bows to mingle with the sleet while the ship alternately plunged down into the huge waves, then reared swiftly up toward the clouds, swinging from side to side as the sea took her.

The Sunday lunch was ready to be served and the chief steward was determined not to be beaten by a storm. They put up the sides of the table to keep the dishes from falling on to the floor and they damped the tablecloths to keep things as steady as possible. The chief officer stamped in on a fairly even keel. With great difficulty, one of the stewards managed to get a small amount of soup in a bowl on to the table, but almost at once the bowl leapt into the air, turned upside down and poured the hot soup into the officer's lap.

There was really no time to even think about food as the ship pitched, rolled and corkscrewed. One moment we were clutching on to the table, the next being thrown against it, but we might have managed a little dry food had not our side of the table come apart and those of us to starboard, having lost our support, subsided into an untidy muddle on the deck, closely followed by a shower of plates, knives and cruets. As if to add insult to injury, the wall cupboard above us, which contained the reserve supply of sauces, seasoning and the likes, flew open and a shower of pickles, sauce bottles, salt cellars, sugar bowls, mustard pots and jugs crashed down upon us as we slithered about on the floor. Furniture, passengers, stewards, soup, sugar, salt, tomato sauce and even some milk scrunched and squelched over the deck, swirling about with the motion of the ship.

Some time later, when order had been partially restored, those of us who had recovered their composure and still had any interest in food ate sandwiches in the galley, but few attempted any liquid. Before we had time to finish our meagre repast, a bulkhead door, not properly fastened, was forced open by a huge wave. The sea poured in, sweeping pots and pans off the shelves, extinguishing the oven fire and thumping one of the cooks heavily against the side of the ship. This was the final blow that the storm had to deal us, for after that the wind began to slacken, and though the heavy swell continued for a day or two, we were able to resume our normal routine.

At Pond Inlet, our northernmost call, the scene was dramatic. The tiny buildings almost disappeared into the vastness of the surrounding hills, but there was a bustle of activity as soon as we dropped anchor for there were supplies to be unloaded, not only for the company, but also for the Roman Catholic and Anglican missions, both of which had establishments here.

My assistance did not seem to be required in dealing with the cargo so the ornithologist took me ashore for a walk and told me not only about the birds but also all about the general flora and fauna. His lecture was delivered in such a booming voice, however, that my head was spinning by the time we returned to the ship.

A gentler and most informative chat was had with the anthropologist. He told me much that was to prove useful about the Eskimos I was soon to be living among. I learned that the Innuit (the People), which is their own name for themselves, almost certainly came from central or northern Asia. The physical type, language and culture all tend to confirm this and that they migrated to North America via the Aleutian Islands, starting about 1000 BC. Reversing the usual direction of migration, they travelled steadily from west to east, moving along the northern coastline of the mainland, spreading out into the arctic islands, keeping close to the sea, until finally coming to a halt in Greenland, where the massive ice plateau of the interior blocked further movement.

The development of their culture and of their social life was greatly limited by the severity of the environment, which precluded any attempt at food production. Apart from the blueberries which grew wild on the hills during a short season and a type of edible seaweed, there was no useful vegetation. Hunting of one kind or another was therefore essential at all times, and because they only had the simplest of equipment, cooperation between the hunters was vital.

He also told me about the Eskimo religion, which was based on the belief that everything and everybody had a spirit. A rock, a fish, a polar bear or a human being were all equal in this respect, and it was the activities of these spirits which controlled events and people. They could move about at will. If a person became ill, it might be thought that his spirit had deserted him, or it might be that an ill-disposed one had taken up residence within his body and would have to be conjured out.

This belief provided a continuity of life, softening the reality of death with which they were all too familiar. It was known that although the body became lifeless after death, the essential person remained close at hand, even if invisible. So firm was this conviction that the children, being guarded by the spirit of a dead relative, were allowed to wander into dangerous situations without causing any great anxiety, because their parents felt secure in the knowledge that the spirit would keep them safe.

The shamans, or *angekok* as they were called, supplied a link with the supernatural world by having the ability to transfer themselves, on suitable occasions, into the world of the spirits and by gaining control of one or more of them. Dependent upon the ability of their subject spirits, they would thus hope to have some control over the affairs of everyday life.

The *angekok* did not apparently depend on the miraculous. Generally, it was a shrewd, calculating type of man or woman who was most likely to become a shaman. In a real crisis, matters would have reached a fairly desperate state, from which they could not get much worse, before the *angekok* got to work. So, not infrequently, their incantations were followed by an improvement in the weather, or travelling conditions, or whatever it was that was bedevilling the camp.

As we set off once more, the manager of Pond Inlet, who was due to go out for a holiday, joined me in my cabin, considerably brightening the rest of the journey. When he told me that he had his entire worldly possessions with him, I expected to find the cabin filled with his luggage, instead of which it seemed that his belongings barely filled one small cardboard case, which lay at the bottom of his trunk.

My companion began at once to settle my future.

'You'll be going ashore at Pangnirtung,' he said. 'Geordie Gall will take care of you. He's very strict though you know. Prayers every morning at eight, the youngest apprentice reads the lesson.'

I laughed at this and said that I was sure that he was pulling my leg. He became indignant.

'Indeed I am not,' he said. 'You ask any of the other managers, they'll all tell you the same thing. Geordie is a fine God-fearing man.'

'Well, he must be very different from the other managers up here,' I said.

'And just what do you mean by that?' asked Jimmy threateningly.

'Oh, nothing,' I replied.

'You'll have to be careful about swearing. Geordie doesn't like it and you'll be fined for using bad language.'

I really did not know whether to believe him or not, for he was very convincing, and the next day even produced two witnesses to corroborate his story.

The district manager confirmed his prediction that I would be going ashore at Pangnirtung the next morning. There was nothing very remarkable about this, however, as that post was the last port of call, and short of taking me back to Montreal there was nowhere else for me to go.

Cumberland Gulf, on the east coast of Baffin Island, was visited more than once by explorers hoping to find a sea passage through as far south as possible. They soon had their hopes dashed, but gathered an amount of information about the area. They were later followed by Scottish and American whalers, who for a long period formed the only link the Eskimos had with the outside world. A trading post was not established in the area until the 1920s. The site selected was in a fiord almost at the head of the sound which was reasonably centrally placed for all the camps in the vicinity.

We entered the gulf one morning at half speed, for there was a very dense fog and the captain's wisdom in deciding to travel slowly was soon confirmed. Half-way through the morning, the fog began to lift, drifting away from above the *Nascopie* to reveal a cloudy uncertain sky, a small patch at first, then gradually clearing so that what looked like a darker cloud appeared almost directly ahead of us. Not happy about this odd-looking cloud, the captain altered course about ninety degrees, which was just as well for soon afterwards the fog dissolved altogether and the darker cloud turned out to be a rather solid headland.

Later on the sun came out and seemed to be spotlighting a high and distinctive hill, shaped like a huge man's cap, which they told me marked the entrance to the fiord that was to be my new home. We passed this landmark early in the afternoon and came up the inlet to a point opposite a group of buildings, where we dropped anchor. A quarter of an hour must have elapsed before a boat put out from the shore and a queer party came aboard headed by a man wearing a brightly coloured shirt and a large sombrero hat. His movements were made with such extreme care and his expression was so pleasantly vacuous that it was obvious, even to me, that he was drunk. I thought to myself, so much for the morning prayers and all the rest, for this indeed was Geordie Gall, my new boss.

My grandmother, herself a devotee of the *chaise-longue*, frequently expressed her firm belief that it was better to wear out than to rust away. Comfortably enveloped in rugs and shawls and bounded by hot-water bottles, she rested her own ageing joints while exhorting others to ceaseless activity. At moments during my first three days at Pangnirtung, I had cause to remember this conviction of hers. Once the cargo started to come ashore, the goods came off in an endless chain. While the tide was high enough to unload along the water's edge (there was no jetty), one boatload after another came bustling in from the ship. When the tide had dropped too far back over the rocks and mud for the boats to be able to come in from the shore, the boxes had to be carted up the bank to be piled near the shore. There was a short spell during each tide, at slack water, when it was possible to get some rest, but I was so exhausted that it never seemed more than a few minutes before someone was waking me up again.

The supplies lay scattered about over the flat at the top of the bank, where it was wise to tread carefully. There were cases of all shapes and sizes, bales, cartons, lumber for two small houses to be built for the company's Eskimo employees. Supplies labelled for the Oxford University Arctic Exploration Society. Barrels of oil and gasoline, kegs of molasses. Lengths of steel for sledge runners. A bath loomed up in front of me and I very nearly fell in it. Sacks of coal and flour. Crates of cheese, drums of potatoes, kegs of oatmeal, bags of sugar. Innuit men and women struggled up the bank with vast loads, children with smaller burdens. White men bustled backwards and forwards importantly, missionaries appeared and disappeared, and sometimes even policemen. Always of course the dogs, snuffling round the cases and using them as lampposts.

Suddenly, it was finished, just as it had seemed unending. One of the mates came up the bank shouting that as he had brought the last load, he would accept a drink if anyone were to offer him one, and he went into the house where the last-minute conferences were in progress. The captain decided, however, to get away at once. Although darkness had fallen, the tide was with him, so he blew three blasts on his siren to summon all those who wished to sail. Everybody except Geordie, who had lost interest in the whole thing and was now fast asleep, rushed down to the boats.

We were not allowed to linger on the *Nascopie*. I said goodbye to my friends, including my cabin mate, who was beaming all over his face at having pulled my leg. The ship's engines were turning over and as soon as all the post staff were back in the boat up went the gangway. The little ship swung round toward the gulf and swished past us in a swirl of foam as we aimed for the shore. A group on the deck of the *Nascopie* broke into a spirited rendering of 'Will ye no come back again?' A stern, authoritarian voice from the bridge shouted, 'Not at this time of night.' Last-minute witticisms were bawled backwards and forwards across the water until the captain turned about so that his vessel was stern on to us, blew another blast on his siren and with gathering speed vanished into the darkness.

Alan Scott, the other apprentice at Pangnirtung, had arrived the previous year and had obviously not expected that there would be an addition to the staff. I explained that the district manager had had no option but to leave me here before the ship headed south, but it was too late to go into all the details, so we made the boat secure, climbed the bank to the house and went thankfully to bed.

It was broad daylight when I awoke next morning, but the house was quiet, so I took the opportunity to have a look at my room. It was small and square with a plasterboard ceiling held in place with rough wooden slats. The boards had not been painted but the walls had been done, though some time ago by the look of them, for they were now a dingy sort of white. There was one window looking out over the fiord mouth. Apart from the bed, there was one piece of furniture in the room, some kind of multi-purpose unit. The top did duty as a stand for a washbowl, underneath were two drawers to house my clothes and there was a shelf for anything else at the bottom. The unit appeared to have been home-made, but did not seem to have been constructed to any plan so much as from the random inspiration of the maker, and it was tilted slightly forward, as though the front legs were slightly shorter than the rear ones. There was no other furniture, no chair or wardrobe, and nothing on the walls. The room had a musty, damp odour rather like that of an unused, unheated spare room we had had at home. The whole effect was dreary in the extreme and I could see that it was going to be necessary to do some brightening up before the start of the long winter.

A patch of colour in the doorway suddenly caught my eye. It was Geordie Gall's bright striped shirt. He had drifted up from somewhere and was leaning against the jamb, clutching a bottle in his hand. He gazed at me in silence for a little while with a puzzled expression, as if wondering what to say to me now that he was here. It occurred to me that his shirt, although quite cheerful, did not really suit him. Embarrassed by the silence, I said, 'Good morning.'

Geordie levered himself away from his support and waved his free arm in a broad gesture round the room.

'Not the Grand Hotel, is it?' he said, slurring his words. 'Roof leaks like hell. Doesn't rain in the winter though. Spring's the time when the snow melts on top. You'll have to get some oars then.'

He put the bottle to his lips and took a long swig, gazing sadly up at the offending ceiling as he did so. Belatedly he began to chuckle, perhaps at the thought of me sculling round the bedroom. Then a fly buzzed in near his face and he tried to knock it away with his hand but the effort caused him to lose balance. As he staggered backwards, he jerked the bottle in his other hand, so that some of the liquor slopped on to the floor. He forgot about me, looking angrily down at the pool on the linoleum.

'Damn flies, what the hell are they buzzing about here for?' he muttered to himself as he lurched out of the room.

I did not quite know what to make of the incident at the time, but afterwards realized that Geordie had really just come to introduce himself and welcome me to Pangnirtung. He was a Scotsman who had drifted over to Newfoundland and not having any real trade had moved from one job to another.

Then, when the Hudson's Bay Company opened up the posts in the northern islands, he joined the company and had been managing posts on Baffin Island ever since. He was normally a good-natured man with a liking for order in the post routine and good organizing ability. The Eskimos respected him, but his periodic bouts on the bottle meant that he was never likely to advance further in the Hudson's Bay Company's employment.

Geordie had no hair on the top of his head and the Eskimos, who liked to be able to call everybody by a name which distinguished them personally, christened him 'Shiny Top'.

Shortly after my first visitor had gone, Alan Scott came in to say it was time to get up. He too was a Scotsman, coming from up Peterhead way, where he had been working on farms. He was a few years older than me and being a practical young man had picked up the ropes quickly. This was very fortunate for me as he went to considerable trouble to pass on the lessons he had learned during his first year as a northerner. Alan must have had great patience because I did not at that time readily assimilate knowledge of a practical nature, but he succeeded in teaching me the basic essentials of Arctic life and this stood me in good stead for all my years in the Arctic.

On my way to fetch water from the kitchen I studied the house. It was more or less a square, bungalow type of building with the two apprentices' bedrooms at the far corner being separated by the office between them. From the office, a passageway led down the centre of the house, on one side of which was the manager's bedroom, while on the other was an enclosed space which served as a combined store and bathroom, though to take a bath was a most complicated procedure. The guardroom was situated across the house at the end of the passageway. This name for the sitting room came from the frontier days, when the personnel of the post had to be ready to defend themselves, keeping their weapons at hand in case of attack.

Fortunately there was no danger of attack at Pangnirtung. The ceiling and the walls of the guardroom were painted white with green slats, so the room was not quite so dull as the bedrooms. In one corner there was a large pot-bellied heating stove and from the other wall a door led into the kitchen.

An Eskimo girl by the name of Ooloo had a room at the end of the kitchen. She was supposed to be a sort of housekeeper and did the chores but only had the slightest knowledge of cooking. In fact she was what would nowadays be accepted as Geordie's common-law wife. They had a baby son but were a most unlikely pair. They could not speak each other's language beyond a word or two and perhaps this was just as well, for I found later when she got cross Ooloo could deliver a stream of abuse and insults which would have left Geordie in no doubt as to his shortcomings.

My upbringing, both at home and at school, had run along very strict lines of morality, so that anything that deviated from the straight and narrow was not to be contemplated and certainly not to be mentioned. In my grandmother's house the assumption was that only the lower orders indulged in the sins of drunkenness and immorality, no matter what evidence there was to the contrary. Obviously I now had to emerge rapidly from the Victorian world which had hitherto enclosed me.

In time I was to realize that in fact Geordie and Ooloo's relationship was quite proper among the Innuit, the only anomaly being that he was a foreigner. Marriages were not arranged between families, the young being free to choose as they wished. A girl might pair with several men before marriage, without any obligation on either side; indeed, she might cohabit with several young men at the same time. If the girl had a child, it was likely, but by no means certain, that the association would become permanent.

Hunters might have two wives, and it was quite common for

a man to permit unrelated persons to have relations with his wife, usually, but not invariably, on a reciprocal basis. This was partly a practical arrangement, as the hunters frequently passed through different camps on their hunting expeditions, but it might also be the basis of a very useful friendship.

The Eskimos tended to become interdependent by utilizing each other's skills. If a man was a good carver, he carved; others might have good organizing ability and be called upon to organize expeditions; some would be especially able at making hunting weapons or kayaks, while all who had any flair for hunting went after seals or deer. Each man had to be able in some direction and when there was overduplication it would be normal for a man to leave his group, deserting his wife and children to find another home where he would be more useful.

The effects of this attitude to coupling and marriage were that relationship could be claimed on a fairly wide basis. Apart from the immediate family, if a husband or wife had children not belonging to their present partner, such children would form a link between all the people on both sides of the family. This meant a greatly increased number of potential friends and of camps at which a hunter would have what might be termed residential qualifications, since the camps were organized on a strictly family basis. Family ties were flexible so that a hunter could move from one group to another. Provided that the new group was within the wide family circle, he would at once be accepted as a proper member of the community.

It was sometimes thought that the Eskimos practised some sort of communism, but this was not so, for the foundation of their society was the family grouping in the broadest sense, which resulted in collective responsibility and cooperation with the relatives with whom one was resident at the moment. Thus the whole camp shared the successes and failures, the good times and the bad.

There was a clear division of labour within each home. The men were the hunters and it was they who made the tools and the household goods and built the homes. The women cooked, dressed the skins, tended the oil lamps used for heating and cooking and made all the clothes, using their own tools. Sometimes exceptional women would stray into the men's world, but the men, even though they might be totally incompetent as hunters, did not take on the women's tasks.

The bleakness of my room, as well as the very changed conditions to which I had to adjust myself, had depressed me considerably, but my spirits started to revive as soon as I stepped outside. The house door faced up to the fiord, where the high black cliffs swept round in an arc, rising steadily to a point at which the inlet turned sharply northward. On the far shore, the hills fell slowly away again to a pleasant green valley, just opposite the house. From above this eastern valley, the sunshine spread across the water, picking out the kyaks and boats of the few Inuit who were taking advantage of the calm morning to go seal hunting. The panorama of the high and moody hills, the green valley, the sunshine sparkling on the sea and the kyaks flashing to and fro across the water, lifted my depression completely. Here was a timeless scene from long ago which had somehow managed to remain unchanged in a changing world.

The Pangnirtung fiord settlement of 1930 was one of the largest on Baffin Island. The Hudson's Bay Company post, centrally situated among the buildings, consisted of a line of four houses spaced along the coastal flat just before the land dropped about thirty feet or so to the edge of the reef. There were two storehouses, a main dwelling and a secondary dwelling which had been used as an interpreter's home. The woodwork was, as was usual for the Hudson's Bay Company, painted white with green facings and a red roof. The buildings stood about ten yards apart but were linked together by two straight lines of whitewashed rocks that created the illusion of a purpose-made path. The inevitable flagpole was situated in a neat little square in front of our home and the Hudson's Bay Company flag was flown on any suitable occasion.

About fifty yards beyond us, towards the mouth of the fiord, the Royal Canadian Mounted Police had established their post of two buildings, a dwelling and a kind of storehouse. In front of their house was a little weather station, from the middle of which rose their flagpole, a much more impressive affair than ours, fittingly perhaps, because from it flew the Canadian flag, proclaiming ownership of this large arctic island.

Behind the Hudson's Bay Company post, at the back of the flat, was the archdeacon's mission house, which served both as a home and a church, and the sealskin tents of the Eskimos were spread over the intervening space. Some distance away, we had our 'blubber' sheds which housed the equipment for rendering oil and curing hides. In that year there were three Hudson's Bay Company people, three R.C.M.P.s and one missionary, which represented one of the main concentrations of Baffin Island population.

Ooloo had been busy dishing out tea to the men and women gathered in front of the store waiting to start the morning's work of organizing the year's supplies. The people were dressed in a variety of garbs. Some wore sealskin anoraks, some woollen ones and others ordinary bush shirts. The women, who did not wish to miss the chance of earning a dollar or two, were there, carrying their babies on their backs.

Gradually we sorted the large pile of boxes into the proper places in the store. It was general practice at that time to keep two years' supply of all the more vital commodities on hand, to allow for the possibility of the *Nascopie* not being able to get through the ice. There were large quantities of tea, flour

54

and similar items, each package being marked with the year of delivery indicated by an outfit number.

The first northern trading voyage undertaken by the 'Gentlemen Venturers trading into Hudson's Bay' was in 1668 and the original instructions to one Zachariah Gillam, master of the ketch *Nonsuch* which had been selected for the voyage, are still preserved. The orders were that the master should sail his vessel to such places as were chosen by the traders who had come with him. He was to find safe anchorage and wait there while the trading took place. As soon as a good quantity of furs, skins and the like had been gathered together, the *Nonsuch* was to return home. Two years later, when the first trading post was established, outfit number one was sent north to be put ashore in the bay and the annual voyages had been numbered from that year onwards (1670), so that every item arriving in my first year had the number 260 painted or stencilled on it.

By the end of the day, we had stacked most of the new delivery away in the stores in the appropriate spots, the drums of gasoline had been moved to line up with the old stock, the coal piled behind the post building, the ammunition packed into its own special section and a home found for all that remained. Next morning we were able to turn our attention to the timber, which lay in higgledy-piggledy confusion beside the main store and was destined to provide two shacks for the company's two Innuit employees.

Meanwhile Ooloo had got the stove going in the guardroom and had stretched her culinary abilities to the extent of heating up a delicacy known as 'boiled dinner', which came out of a tin. The guardroom was simply furnished. The square table from which we ate our meal served for all other purposes. There were no easy chairs but several basic wooden ones. A rickety bookcase with a cupboard underneath occupied a corner by the stove. A rather splendid Victrola phonograph filled the opposite corner to the bookcase. It had been retrieved from one of the shipwrecks, so they told me, which perhaps accounted for the haphazard selection of records, six or seven of them, varying from Mendelssohn's incidental music to *A Midsummer Night's Dream* to a bloodthirsty ballad about a certain Turk named 'Abdul Abulbul Amir'.

An elaborate but not very effective radio set stood on the window ledge behind the Victrola. It seldom gave us any continuous session of entertainment without going off into hysterical oscillation. Alan was the only person who had enough patience to attempt to control the thing.

My most urgent need, those first days, was to get fitted out with a pair of sealskin boots. Ordinary shoes were not fitted to the rocky terrain, apart from being very uncomfortable. One of the Eskimos working for the company, Kilabuk by name, said that his wife would make me a pair. She duly appeared, measured my feet with a piece of string in the most casual manner possible and went home, returning the next morning with a pair of sealskin boots which fitted me perfectly. The upper parts, which came to the knee, were of ordinary skin with a few black patches sewn in to make a pattern, while the soles were cut from a larger, tougher skin from a big seal known as an *ujuk*. The boots were secured with drawstrings at the top which fastened below the knee. I paid her one dollar fifty cents, which included the cost of the materials.

Next day, Agiak, for that was her name, sent a message by her husband (who could speak some English) to say that she was going to wash my clothes and would make an arrangement with Ooloo to use the facilities of our kitchen one day a week. I was quite pleased about this for it had not been easy to keep my small stock of clothes clean, and although I had seized every opportunity, my inexpert efforts at laundering had resulted in my garments looking decidedly dingy. What did not please me very much was my discovery, a few weeks later, that the Eskimos had also decided that I was a child and had named me simply 'The Boy'.

By the next afternoon, the ship-time sorting had been concluded and the workers lined up in the store to be paid off. As each one came up to the counter, Alan looked in the book in which the times had been recorded, to find the amount due then spread out the coins to represent the pay. These coins were imitation money, acting as dollars, half dollars and quarters, so that people could see exactly how much money they had to spend. The Eskimo would normally debate with his wife as to what they should buy, generally deciding upon food, tobacco, ammunition and perhaps something small for the children. If the women had any spare money of their own it usually went on print for a dress or some other item of clothing.

The Innuit could not earn very much during the summer season. Trapping did not start until the end of October, but before that time it was necessary to lay in good supplies of dog food, so that the hunters could devote as much time as possible to their traps during the six-month open season for foxes. This meant that they had to be allowed quite large amounts of credit, so they could obtain supplies of petrol, cartridges and other necessities for the summer seal and walrus hunting. Each hunter was assessed according to his past record and allowed to run up a debt of as many foxes as it seemed likely he would be able to catch fairly easily during the winter.

That afternoon, Alan took me down to the blubber house, scene of much of the activity after a whale drive. The place was as unromantic in appearance as in name. Inside one shed was a rendering machine into which the cut-up blubber was stuffed to be processed into oil which was then pumped from the machine to tanks outside. In another shed, the hides were stored at one end and meat which could be used to feed the dogs at the other. The hides had been shipped off on the *Nascopie*, but a pile of decomposing meat remained. This was my first encounter with high meat *en masse* and the smell was too much for me. I had to grasp my nose and retire in haste. I surmised that, as with Geordie's and Ooloo's relationship, this was another aspect of my new life that I would adjust to in time.

III

HOUSEKEEPING ON BAFFIN ISLAND had its complications. We had a plentiful supply of canned goods in the storeroom, but fresh food supplies for the winter then had to be thought about weeks in advance. Hunting was seasonal and whenever possible we took advantage of each season to lay in a stock for the future.

The fall was an especially good time to concentrate on winter food requirements. The plump young ducks gathered on the lakes before their southward flight. The salmon trout, fresh and firm after their summer in the sea, could still be taken on their way back to their home lake, as well as the seals, always with us, though in varying numbers. The deer often came down to feed near the coast before the onset of winter. Apart from this normal plenitude of game, there was another useful advantage at this time of year, which was that with the temperature well down, meat, birds and fish could be stored in good condition right through the winter until the following May.

Geordie had remained absent in spirit from us for a few days after the ship had gone, but Alan set about his rehabilitation with determination and succeeded in bringing him back to our world by the start of the following week, when a party of hunters came in from one of the southerly camps. They reported that they had seen deer feeding near the shoreline of one of the inlets they had passed on their way to the post. Geordie decided that it would be a good opportunity to lay in meat supplies and perhaps a few fish for the winter stock.

Kilabuk and Beevee, the two post servants, were instructed to prepare for the hunt, and then it was suggested at the last moment that I go with them as a reward for all the hard work since ship-time. The suggestion was meant kindly, and no doubt both Geordie and Alan thought I would jump at the chance of a hunting trip, but the idea did not really appeal to me.

My recent journeyings had temporarily satisfied the explorer in me, while I felt that I had put up with enough discomfort for one year, particularly after my long spell on the draughty kitchen floor at Port Burwell. Not that my present quarters could be described as luxurious, but now that my unpacking was completed, so that my own things were scattered about the room and one or two pictures were up on the wall, it had an air of home about it. However, it seemed churlish to refuse what was obviously intended as a sort of holiday, so I took the easy way out, even managing to work up a rather spurious air of excitement about the coming trip. My box was packed with the cooking utensils, such as Primus stove, frying pan, pots and kettles under the mistaken impression that I was acquainted with the use of these things. It looked as though I was going to learn the hard way as usual.

We set off one beautifully calm morning. The hills were mirrored in the waters of the fiord and the seals coming up for air sent the ripples spreading over the sea in ever widening circles. Just down below the post buildings, an inquisitive seal popped up and dallied too long, giving Beevee time to shoot and manoeuvre the boat alongside. Kilabuk jabbed a harpoon into the body, then hauled it aboard with the attached line. Despite this short distraction, we made fairly good progress and stopped to go ashore in a pleasant cove to see if there were any signs of deer. We saw nothing of interest, so decided to boil the kettle.

Kilabuk got the Primus out and showed me in great detail how it worked. Once seen, of course, the operation is simple, but the Eskimo continued the demonstration for an excessively long time, so that a resolution formed in my mind that, come what may, I would get the thing going for the next meal and show them that I was not the complete fool they seemed to think me.

Darkness had fallen by the time we reached the cove where the deer had been reported. We had brought a fairly large tent with us, which the Eskimos now erected on a suitably soft patch of ground. We soon carried up our equipment from the boat, spread our deerskins around at the back of the shelter and formed a little section near the entrance. One of the drawbacks of northern camping is that the cooking space has to be included inside the tent, since conditions outside are seldom satisfactory, there being of course no wood with which to make camp fires.

Before anyone had a chance to forestall me, I lit the Primus, fortunately without mishap. The men cut some meat from a seal carcass and we boiled up a stew in the pot. We ate the meal sedately from plates, not the usual custom, and washed it down with a cup of seal 'soup'. My stomach had protested at the very thought but in fact it was very palatable.

Kilabuk, who had lived most of his life at the whalers' camps where his father had been employed, could speak quite good English, so after our meal we relaxed on the deerskins in reasonable comfort for a chat until the oil lamp which Beevee had got going began to flicker and splutter as the wick burnt low. The men hoped to make a good start next morning so we spread out our sleeping bags to settle for an early night.

I was soon to learn that it is wise, when sleeping among the Eskimos, to get some sleep as quickly as possible, for they are given to extremely loud snoring. As I lay reviewing my first day of camping out in the Arctic, a noise like a slow motion electric saw broke out on the far side of the platform, where Beevee lay, then Kilabuk joined in. I lay dazed by the cacophony of sound and in the end fell asleep only through sheer exhaustion, making up for my disturbed rest by being the last to wake the next morning.

The men had already prepared the breakfast and announced their intention of setting off at once in search of the deer. I decided not to go with them, thinking that they would probably climb the hills at a cracking pace well beyond my capabilities, but after they had gone I planned a little expedition of my own, over the coastal flat towards the banks of a small river and then up towards the hills.

The climb was gradual and just around the first curve in the watercourse a long narrow lake appeared quite suddenly before me. The surface was swarming with birds, most of them, thanks to the lecture my booming friend of the *Nascopie* had given me at Pond Inlet, easy enough to identify. There were old squaw ducks hurrying busily through the water without ever drifting far from the main group, diving every so often with a flurry of feet, then reappearing with seeming nonchalance a few seconds later. Their call, a rather melancholy 'A-ha-ha-lik, A-ha-ha-lik' is a distinctive part of the summer days in the quiet of the arctic islands. Close to a group of rocks in the middle of the lake, a party of eider duck were taking their ease, accompanied by a batch of pugnacious arctic terns. The terns often nest beside the milder, more long-suffering eiders, thus protecting their eggs from the predatory gull, for woe betide any gull attempting to steal eggs while the battling terns are about.

In the old days, when the Eskimos depended entirely upon their own skill and ingenuity for success in hunting, they used to hunt the ducks by 'speed of boat'. During the summer moult, some of the birds had trouble raising themselves from the water to begin a flight. The people took advantage of this fact to pursue them in their large skin boats known as *umiaks* (women's boats, because the women rowed them, leaving the men free to concentrate on the hunting), making the most unearthly din and practically paralysing with fear those birds that had not recovered from the moult, thereby reducing each victim to such a state that all the hunter had to do was snatch the duck out of the water.

Beyond the lake I continued my walk up the slope. The hills rose quite quickly on both sides of the valley, and ahead, in the far distance, a range of snow-covered peaks dominated the scene. Just below me, the river, trapped in a narrow gorge of rock, funnelled into a gushing fall over a short steep cliff drop, the fine white spray drifting far back enough to fleck my face every now and then.

The sun, already dipping down into the west, stretched long rays towards the snow peaks, softening the hilltops with a golden glow as though to form a link between the harsh black cliffs below and the gentle, faded blue of the sky above. The birds, calling from the lake behind me, still sounded faintly above the rush of water down the tumbling waterfall and these sounds served only to emphasize the profound silence of the gulley.

I sat on a convenient rock to eat my biscuits and survey the impressive scene. There was nothing in sight in any direction to suggest the presence of man in this valley. Quite possibly I was the first person ever to climb this slope, for it led nowhere and the deer were known to frequent the other arm of the inlet. My wandering thoughts were suddenly concentrated by a sharp cough coming from close by. To my astonishment a fox had somehow penetrated my solitude and was seated on a boulder at no great distance, calmly observing my every move.

The animal, clearly distinguishable by its ears, looked anything but white in its late summer coat, which was partly brown, partly grey, with only odd patches of dirty white. Perhaps observing my sudden interest, the fox rose to its feet and made off. Very foolishly, I decided to give chase in the hope that it would lead me to its lair.

Once started, the mad pursuit led me higher and higher up the hill, over increasingly difficult terrain. The fox did not appear to be alarmed at being chased, a state of mind which proved well justified before very long. The animal crossed a small cliff face and sat down on the far side to favour me with a contemptuous stare, and my growing conviction that it would be best for me to give up the pursuit and go home faded abruptly.

I rushed out on to the cliff face and was half-way across before realizing the danger of my situation. The sudden realization checked my progress so that, becoming hesitant, I slipped off the narrow ledge which gave me my foothold and slithered out on to the face of the cliff which ended sharply a short distance beyond my feet. There was no further firm ground until the mass of fallen boulders down on the plain, about four hundred feet below. A slim root growing out of a small crack in the rock face held my right foot as I slipped slowly down, enabling me to press my left foot hard enough into the face to stop my slide and come to a halt in a position of extreme discomfort, suspended virtually in mid air, directly above what would surely prove to be the rockiest, bleakest burial place imaginable.

For a moment or two, my thoughts were solely concerned with the estimation of the distance from my position on the cliff to the nearest boulder beneath me and the force with which the rock and I would be likely to meet. When my initial panic subsided, I managed to give out a hoarse cry, but the effort nearly dislodged me completely, so it was several minutes before I dared make the effort again.

After what seemed an eternity, an answer came from somewhere over to my right so I closed my eyes and kept as still as possible, until at last Kilabuk came up from the far side. He took off his anorak, separated it from the waterproof cover, then tied the two together and, bracing himself in a secure position, lowered the 'line' towards me.

Very carefully, holding on firmly to the anorak, I climbed back up the rock face. With my first movement, the root supporting my right foot broke off and, having served its purpose, fell away down to the bottom.

Kilabuk told me that they had only just returned from the hills themselves and that Beevee had gone on down to boil the kettle, which was welcome news in my shaken state.

After a short rest and a meal, I recovered sufficiently to accompany Kilabuk on a seal hunt for what remained of the afternoon. Beevee had brought his kayak on tow behind the boat and set off before us to try his luck.

Versions of the Eskimo kayak are now found in many parts of the world. Originally, the craft consisted of a light whalebone framework, covered entirely with dried, scraped sealskins sewn together, with only the narrow aperture where the hunter is to seat himself left uncovered. The kayak, pointed at both ends, is extremely manoeuvrable and the art of operating it lies mainly in maintaining the balance, for a sudden movement in any direction can overturn the craft. To overcome this loss of balance, the Eskimos developed the knack of swinging themselves right through the water and back upright again, hence the expression 'Eskimo rolle'. Wearing sealskins and moving quickly, they could do this without getting seriously wet.

When Beevee had gone, we puttered off in the motor boat. Kilabuk stopped the engine a little way out, so that I could shoot my first seal, then jabbed accurately with his harpoon to haul the carcass into the boat. All this went a long way to restore my self-respect, badly jolted by the morning incident. Between them the hunters then secured another four seals, so we had a good haul and returned home just as darkness was falling in time for me to boil up a tasty stew from my very first hunting success.

Kilabuk took a great interest in all the details of my morning adventure. As we had settled ourselves among the deerskins and the light from Beevee's oil lamp flickered up and down the tent wall, he told me that the people had a story about this kind of a fox.

'There was an Eskimo man, who lived not far away but a long time ago,' he said. 'He was a bad man, and the people at his camp tried to talk to him and tell him how bad he was, but he would take no notice. He stole from his friends. He told lies, even to his own family and made much trouble. They could not cure him, so at last, the other hunters became very angry indeed and they went off together to see the *angekok*, the man who looked after the people like the missionary does now.

' "Unless you can do something to make this man better," they said, "we shall have to send for the *angekok* from another camp to help us."

'Now their own *angekok* did not like this, as it would not have been good for him to have it said that his powers were less than those of another. He sat for days in his home thinking how he could cure the wrongdoer.

'At last he thought of a plan. Among his spirits – for all the *angekoks* had certain spirits who would obey them – was that of a dead hunter who dwelt in the body of a fox, and the *angekok* went up to the great black rock behind the camp to summon the fox to him. The friendly fox agreed to persuade a polar bear to lure the hunter to his death while he was out hunting, so that when he was dead his evil spirit could enter the body of one of the fox's own recently born cubs, where he could do little harm and where he would remain until someone came to take his place. Thus, a few days later, the man was drowned while going after a bear in his kayak and the people were troubled no more with his evildoing, though they did have more trouble than usual that winter from a marauding fox, who had somehow learned to penetrate even the most secure meat cache to steal food.'

At that time, I knew little about the *angekoks*, who were credited with remarkable powers and were much respected by the people, so it was not until much later that I realized that my Eskimo friend was trying to tell me that it was an evil spirit that had caused me to risk my life and not just my own stupidity.

We turned in early, but my determination to be sound asleep before the night cacophony struck up came to nothing, for despite all the exercise, fresh air and excitement, I did not drop off before the tent was vibrating with the inevitable noise. Long afterwards, it seemed somewhere in the middle of the night, I came awake again when the rain began. The men were silent, but the heavy drops drummed steadily on the tent canvas. Perhaps because I had not done so in the morning, when death might well have been imminent, I began a mental review of my life. Somehow all the more pleasant episodes drifted through my mind. Family Christmases as children. Long summer days in the hills of home. Last days of term. The security of my grandmother's sitting room, with the long heavy curtains, the muttering fire and the clock on the wall which had been ticking and chiming since the days of her own grandfather. These thoughts, combined with the soothing background tapping of the rain, lulled me off to sleep once more.

As their previous day's deer hunt had been unsuccessful, the Eskimos decided to try once more the next morning. They had seen fresh tracks and felt certain that the herd would not be far away. I went with them this time. It did not seem likely that the hunt would be any more arduous than my efforts of the previous day, though certainly less dangerous.

The rain had ceased by the dawn and the day was fresh and pleasant. Beevee led the way. I came next and Kilabuk brought up the rear. They were evidently taking no chances on my falling over any more cliffs.

The sun came out as we set off in fine style to climb the long slope of the river gulley. At the far end of the coastal flat, the land rose quite sharply and the river divided into two courses, one of which was considerably steeper than the other. The men chose the easier route, perhaps doubting my ability to negotiate the more difficult ascent. The Eskimos had of course undertaken a summer deer hunt practically every year of their active lives. Apart from the meat, which could either be dried or cached for the winter months, there were useful by-products. Nearly everybody in the Arctic used the skins for winter clothing. It was common to wear deerskin with the fur inside next to the skin and the short-haired parts of the skin were most useful for this purpose. For an outer covering, the longer-haired parts were used with the fur outward. Short trousers of deerskin reached to the top of the boots and were tied round the waist. Frequently, the winter boots had the uppers made out of deer-skin, with a light and dark pattern worked down the front, as with the sealskin boots.

The thread used for sewing these clothes and boots came from the deer sinew, with the aid of which the women could make the garments mindproof and weatherproof. The sewing was quite intricate, particularly when the skins had been cut up into sections of varying shades and made up into patterns of infinite and sometimes quite original variety. Some men wore trousers of bearskin, but these were considerably heavier and the polar bear was often less easy to locate than the caribou.

When the people went off on one of their summer hunts, the

whole camp went with them, women, children and often the dogs as well. Usually, the dogs were fitted with small packs so that they could help to carry the load when the meat had to be brought home. The speed of the party would naturally not be very great, but as soon as they arrived at an area where there was a chance of good hunting, camp would be made, so that the women and children could establish themselves while the hunters got to work.

We had not walked very far before we came to a waterfall, though it was smaller than the one I had seen the previous day. Beevee got to the top of the fall simply by heaving himself from one rock to the next, Kilabuk going after him. This method looked highly perilous, as it would obviously be an easy matter for me to slip off the rock into the water and bounce down to the bottom. However, the hunters were used to dealing with the women and children of their parties, and so had come prepared.

Kilabuk produced a length of line from somewhere about his person and lowered one end down to me, after which he and Beevee took the strain, thus enabling me to pull myself up from rock to rock and reach the top without harm.

A short distance above the waterfall, the gulley veered away quite sharply to the east. Just as he was about to disappear from view, Beevee stopped quite abruptly and motioned us back. Then he beckoned to Kilabuk and the two men cautiously climbed the bank, presumably to position themselves behind what it was that Beevee had seen.

I stationed myself behind a nearby rock and waited. Suddenly, pandemonium broke out. A fusillade of rifle fire was followed by the pounding hooves of an approaching herd of deer, which swept round into the main gulley. Their sudden appearance took me by surprise, so that I only had time for one shot before they swerved away and charged up the opposite bank. I tried not to appear surprised that my single shot had felled a prime stag, but privately gave thanks to the school corps drill sergeant, who the previous year had given us a course of instruction in the art of sharpshooting.

Between us we had secured five deer, which would give us a reasonable load of meat and skins to take home. The two men started the skinning operations immediately and soon had the first animal ready to be cut up. The hunters worked with a smooth expertise, stopping every now and then to pop little squares of rump fat into their mouths. They chewed the fat with relish and when Beevee noticed me watching him, he handed me a piece which I accepted doubtfully, but then had to admit that it had a most palatable, nutty flavour. This is a much-prized source of fat during the winter months, often taken on the trail to be chewed during the long hours of dog-team travelling.

The Eskimos spent the afternoon in journeying up and down the hill fetching meat and skins. Before long, our camp began to look like a slaughterhouse, with skins, meat, seal carcasses and blubber scattered about beside the tent.

It seemed to me that we had been successful enough without any further hunting, but the Eskimos, their stalking instincts now thoroughly aroused, decided to make another sortie the following morning. They set off straight after breakfast, soon disappearing along the river course in the same direction we had taken the previous day.

I didn't go with them, but pottered around the lower reaches of the river with a gaff to see if there were any fish going upstream to their home in the lakes. I had no success, so took advantage of the Eskimos' absence to make myself a cup of coffee and was enjoying this with a hunk of bannock when there was a sudden noise outside the tent. I called out, thinking it was the men come back sooner than they had intended, but there was no response.

The silence continued for a moment or two, then was broken by a sort of tearing sound interspersed with low growling. Clearly, an animal was helping itself to what it no doubt considered to be our ample meat supplies, and as it did so, an unnerving thought struck me. My rifle was outside, leaning up against the far end of the tent; the only weapon on hand was a small meat knife, not really suitable for a confrontation with a savage creature.

My visitor was obviously wasting no time in getting down to its meal, which it consumed to the accompaniment of an increasingly ferocious munching, growling sound, which did nothing to quiet my rising panic. Once or twice there was a lull, which made me hopeful that the animal had departed, but a few seconds later the meal was resumed, with what seemed to be redoubled energy and noise.

The difficulty of explaining to the Eskimos my apparent inaction while our hard-earned meat supplies came under the fierce attention of a thief at last drove me to take action. As I stood up, silence fell, but my hopes that the creature had been frightened off were soon shattered as the noisy feeding sounds began again. I crept to the door, suddenly flung it open, then slammed it shut again. Except that a piece of the door fell off, this achieved nothing, for the noise continued unabated.

There was nothing for it but bold action, so, feeling anything but courageous, I opened the door again, stepped briskly outside, and forced myself to peer round the corner of the tent.

I had never before seen a wild animal at close quarters, except behind the bars of a zoo, so the sight that met my eyes both horrified and fascinated me. The most enormous creature was sitting on its haunches, tearing blubber from a handy seal carcass and clearly not at all pleased by the interruption. The bear, for there was no doubt as to the identity of the thief, looked hard at me and it took all my resolution to stand my ground in a sort of eyeball to eyeball confrontation.

I had no plan in mind, and do not know how the situation would have been resolved, had not the bear, having completed his inspection of me, slowly shaken its head, dropped quietly on all fours and loped away. I just stood there and watched the great animal wander off, without making any attempt to get my rifle and shoot it. There was something about the casual indifference in the rear view of the bear, moving without haste in its chosen direction, that left me standing and gaping after the thing until it disappeared behind a pile of rocks.

Shortly afterwards the hunters returned. They had not come across any more deer, but when they heard about the bear, they rushed off immediately to try their luck but were too late to catch up with it and lost its tracks somewhere in the rocky ground at the entrance to the gulley. Somehow, although the bear had given me an anxious quarter of an hour, I felt relieved that it had not met its death at our hands.

As we had been reasonably successful with our hunting, we now decided that it would be wise to head for home, before the weather deteriorated, for it was apparently most unusual to experience long spells of fine weather during the fall. We loaded the meat, skins and blubber into the boat before dark, so that our catch would be safe from any more roving beasts, while we would also be saved a delaying job in the morning.

The night was cold and frosty. We rose early while the stars were still bright, determined to get a good run home in daylight if possible, and after we had breakfasted the men did not dally. The tent was packed up and taken down to the boat with all our other possessions. No time was lost, so that as Kilabuk was turning the flywheel to persuade the sometimes reluctant engine into life, the dawn was just streaking the sky along the ridge of high eastern hills.

Despite our good start we did not fare too well, for by daylight the night crispness had gone out of the air and the clouds were jostling angrily along the northern horizon. It was no surprise when the wind burst down on us as we came out into the open to cross the mouth of a nearby fiord. We made very slow progress, for the further we moved out to sea, the worse the conditions became. We could not turn back, since that would have meant contending with a following sea, which might have been dangerous with our heavily loaded stern.

We approached a black, desolate island half-way across the open stretch and eventually came into sheltered water. At the far end of our tiny harbour, a natural path led up between the boulders. We unloaded our tent and the cooking utensils, carrying them up this path for some distance until we came out on to quite a pleasant, short plateau, where the men at once erected our shelter and I attended the Primus stove.

I had by now firmly established myself as chief cook, the main advantage of this position being that, within limits, one could choose the menu. After our cold anxious morning it seemed to me that we deserved a 'special', so I fried some deer steaks in butter. It cooked a little like beef, red and juicy, and though the meat was a trifle tough, at least it was a change from the inevitable seal. My friends made no comment, eating their food in silence. Perhaps they would have preferred a seal stew.

The weather did not abate during the afternoon, as we had hoped it might, so we brought up the sleeping bags and skins and prepared to camp until the storm died down. Shortly after darkness, our lantern began to flicker as the oil ran out. The reserve can of oil and the candles were still down in the boat, somewhere among the skins in the stern where they would not be easy to find in the dark, so we settled in for the night, in the hope that the weather would have moderated sufficiently by morning for us to make another early start. Our hopes were not realized, for when we woke before dawn the booming wind told us that we would not be travelling that day.

During the morning we fetched enough gear from the boat to make ourselves as comfortable as possible, which was just as well for by the afternoon heavier clouds had rolled up and the wind was fairly slapping the rain and sleet into the walls of our tent. Beevee lit his lamp and Kilabuk told me more about his people and how they had made the best they could of the limited resources of this wild country.

Before the Europeans came, and indeed for quite a long time after they had arrived, the Eskimos lived mainly in tents, of either deerskin or sealskin, during the summer months. The fur was generally removed from the skin before drying and scraping took place, and by the time the women had finished and sewn the skins together with deer thread, they had a waterproof tent that allowed a fair amount of light to penetrate to the interior. There was no wood in the country, so whalebone was commonly used to support the tent, which was usually quite low and often sloping gently back in the direction of the prevailing wind, so that when the gales came, the storm swept over the top of the home rather than buffeting into it.

Another of my fellow passengers on the *Nascopie*, an archaeologist, had told me that in the distant past the people had made their houses of stone and whalebone, packing the crevices with earth and mud while covering the top with various kinds of skin. The ruins of these houses were apparently fairly easy to locate, because after a family had left one of them and the roof fell in, the earth gradually covered the remains where they stood, leaving the outline visible for centuries, though less and less clearly as time went by. My friend had been an expert at finding these old homes, sometimes up to a thousand years old, from the smallest clue. A slight variation in the contours of a slope was sufficient to set him digging, and more often than not he was rewarded by the discovery of some old discarded tool or implement, still lying where the owner had thrown it when he shifted camp all those hundreds of years before.

So far as one could tell, the internal arrangements of the house had not altered greatly down the years. At the back of the dwelling, the sleeping space was spread with deerskins, on which the women sat during the day and where the sleeping bags, also of deerskin, were unrolled at night. At each end of this space, in the homes of the better hunters, a woman tended a seal-oil lamp, which provided warmth for the home and for cooking, beside lighting the house.

The oil lamp consisted, as it still does when used, of a slab of soapstone, scooped out to form a shallow dish, which was tilted slightly and filled with small pieces of whale or seal fat. Along the front of the dish, a strip of moss was carefully laid to make a wick, which, when lighted gave off sufficient heat to melt the fat behind, causing it to flow into the bowl, soak into the wick and keep the lamp burning.

It was the woman's task to see that the bowl of the lamp had a good supply of blubber and to keep it poked forward evenly, so that the whole wick would burn smoothly to give maximum light and heat. The cooking pot or kettle hung over the lamp, fixed in position by various methods according to the type of house in use. The condition of the lamp was one of the tests of the ability of an Eskimo housewife that one could apply immediately upon entering a home.

Kilabuk told me that our island refuge had never been used as a campsite because it was very small and the tiny harbour which we had entered was the only shelter from the open sea. There had been quite a large camp, however, on the mainland opposite, at the entrance to the fiord, and the people had used the island as a burial ground.

The rain stopped before darkness fell, so I decided to go out for some exercise and get my bearing. At the far end of the island, a walk of about a mile over rough ground, there was another small flat area, similar to the one on which we had camped. Along one side of the area there were piles of rocks, which had the appearance of having been placed there deliberately.

Among the boulders and stones I came across a rusted mug which had practically disintegrated, and one or two other things so decomposed as to be virtually unrecognizable. This was probably the burial ground, for the Eskimos buried the personal belongings in the grave alongside the body. The hunters had their knives, spearheads and like possessions placed with them, as well as their drinking mugs and other essentials. Women had their sewing materials and trinkets that they must have treasured during their lives in the grave with them, and children had the toys with which they had played.

I wandered about this grim spot for a while, then blundered over a shallow hole filled with bones, and though these might well have been the relics of animals, they gave the place a scent of death and myself an uncomfortable feeling that I was desecrating somewhere better left in peace.

Great care had to be exercised when burying the dead so that the spirit did not become separated from the body. For a spirit angered in this way might bring harm to the camp. The spirit was thought to remain with the body for a short period after death, but a hole had to be left among the burial rocks, so that it could come and go at will to enable it to find another home.

A spirit recalled to guard a child through infancy had to be treated with proper respect. Thus, if a man's father returned to watch over a grandchild, the baby had to be assumed to be a mature person, able to make its own decisions as to how to behave, or what to eat. The parents could not punish the child simply because it did not defer to their wishes, but were restricted to the giving of advice or offering persuasive argument in an attempt to control its behaviour. If the family became angry because of disobedience, the guardian spirit might easily become offended and leave, which might cause the child to suffer a serious misfortune or even to sicken and die. When their offspring reached young adulthood, the parents could begin to take them in hand, for by then it was thought that the spirit with which they had been born would take over guidance, so that it no longer mattered whether the guardian left or stayed on in a secondary role.

The desolation of the little graveyard seemed in keeping with this island of grim black rock, and fitting for the final resting place of the people who had led such a hard and comfortless life.

In this area of Baffin Island, the Eskimos had been in contact with English and American sailors for seventy or eighty years. Cumberland Gulf had attracted the early whalers as a suitable base from which to hunt, and there is no doubt that the impact of these hardy men, with their new equipment for hunting, was very considerable indeed.

Previously, the people had been stuck in a more or less Stone Age period of development, caused not by lack of enterprise but rather by the harsh nature of their existence. The materials for making more efficient weapons were not obtainable in their country, while the climate was unsuitable for food production. The simplest fluctuation of conditions could mean the difference between life and death, for they had no means of controlling the variations of wind and weather.

With such implements as they had, they developed an art in hunting and a patience in enduring, without which they could not have survived. To these men, with such rudimentary possessions, the first whaling ships must have appeared as veritable Aladdin's caves of undreamed of treasure. The knives of steel. The guns that thundered death so fast that the eye could not follow. The little sticks that gave a flame. The pots and pans. The food that was not meat or fat or fish. The cloth and clothing not made of furs or skins. There was no end to the wonders of these ships, for nearly everything they used was new to the Eskimo people.

Very gradually life became a mixture of the Stone Age and the modern. The new equipment cost money, more than most people had from work or trade. First of all, the lance and bow gave way to the rifle, but the whalers had nothing to improve upon the lamps that the Eskimos had always used, nor did the homes of skin or snow give way to wood or canvas for many decades, though only in the most distant and remote places do the people still use the skin tent and snowhouse today.

Without crops of any kind to give them flour or cereals, the Eskimos depended entirely upon being able to kill the wildlife of the country for food. By far the most important single item was seal meat, raw, boiled or frozen, fresh, high or putrid, it mattered not. Every particle of the seal except the bones was utilized. The skins for clothing or tent making, the fat for heating or cooking and the meat for food.

According to the season or place, other food was sometimes available. Fish from the river, sea and lakes. Ducks and geese. Walrus and polar bears, though the dangers of hunting either of these powerful antagonists without a rifle were considerable, and from the stories of the old days, it was certain that few hunters of any account did not have some scar from an encounter with a polar bear.

To the limited food variety, the whalers at once added flour, and though the people could not always afford to buy it in the early days, it came high on their list when they had anything with which to trade. Tobacco also became a much sought-after item of trade for both men and women.

Unhappily, in those days the sailors brought disease as well, in particular tuberculosis. There does not appear to be any record as to when this illness developed among the people of the Arctic. Explorers of the mid nineteenth century speak of them as suffering from the 'bleeding sickness'. The only certain thing is that the first germs were brought in by the men who came from the south.

Nowadays the scourge has been brought under control, but in the days before the Second World War, the Eskimos had no defence against its ravages. Circumstances were such that a family of five or six had to exist closely together in the very restricted space of a tent or snowhouse, without cleanliness or hygiene. They used the same drinking vessels and spat thoughtlessly on the floor of their homes.

Once introduced, the disease spread steadily, even in this land where habitations were so widely separated, for it required only one hunter to travel further afield than usual for the plague to infect a new community, until there was hardly a family on Baffin Island that did not have at least one sufferer.

We did not wake early the next morning, perhaps because we had not really expected the wind to have dropped sufficiently to enable us to cross the remaining stretches of open water, so we had a pleasant surprise when Beevee returned from a morning inspection of the conditions. He told us that the weather was calm enough for us to resume our journey.

We bustled about to get everything ready for departure, though it turned out that we need not have hurried ourselves, for as we came down the short track to the boat we saw that the bow was resting firmly on the shore. The craft was so tightly aground that all our efforts to free it were unavailing. There was nothing for it but to sit and wait until the tide rose high enough to float the boat off again. The Eskimos had developed the virtue of patience to a degree seldom seen among Europeans. No doubt this was forced upon them by necessity, for in a world where survival is difficult enough, even with the help of the rifle, hunting success often came only after long endurance.

The Eskimos came also to possess a shell of resignation, enabling them to suffer, with apparent equanimity, any hardships that might arise. This resignation often became a source of irritation between them and their southern companions when hunting or travelling together, for in such a situation as we now found ourselves, with a shrug of the shoulders the Eskimo would say, 'Ionamut' ('It can't be helped'), and settle down to wait, while his companions become increasingly agitated.

Although the sun had come out the wait seemed interminable, but at last the tide did come up, the boat floated free and we set off on the second part of our journey. As we had lost half of the day, we did not attempt to reach home in one go, aiming instead for an inlet within range of an afternoon's travel where some of Beevee's relations lived.

This was the first real Eskimo encampment that I had encountered. We rounded a headland quite suddenly to reveal twenty-odd tents perched precariously on a narrow strip of flat underneath a very solid-looking cliff – the first consideration in selecting a campsite of course being for the people to place themselves as conveniently as possible for hunting purposes. Just down below the flat was a small, well-sheltered cove, on the shores of which the men had beached their kayaks. The skin tents, the summer homes, were of varying sizes but of the same general design as those in use all over the Arctic at that time, not only along the coastline, but also in the occasional areas where the Innuit were inland dwellers.

As Kilabuk had told me, the skins had been treated to reduce bulk and to allow as much light as possible to penetrate through, though in some cases the seal intestine, of near transparency, had been used as a window let into the skins. At this time the homes were mainly of two kinds. The first, by far the larger, had a long ridge pole down the centre with supports at either end, while the other was obviously suited to poorer hunters, who would not have had either enough skins for a larger dwelling, or enough fat to keep such a home warm. This second lot was of a conical style, rather like an Indian teepee, but not very roomy inside.

We made for the largest home in the middle of the camp, but coming so quickly in from the fresh air, the smell nearly overpowered me, compounded as it was of a strong mixture of decomposing meat and unwashed bodies. Had I not feared to offend my welcoming hosts, I would have asked Kilabuk and Beevee to set up our tent somewhere on the edge of the camp. In fact, as I discovered later, the curious actions of the *kudloonas* seldom offend the Eskimo, who has learned to accept the peculiarities of the strangers' conduct.

I soon accustomed myself to the odours and settled down to examine the native home. The most surprising thing about the 'house' was that it should be the abode of so many people. There were four adults seated on the platform and four children playing on the earth floor near the entrance. Right round the edges of the interior were spread the bags and boxes containing the worldly possessions of the family – clothes, sewing outfits, tool boxes and other oddments. The sleeping space was covered as usual with skins, while along the front edge a row of stones had been laid to form a separating line from the kitchen and work space. That this was the home of a good hunter was clear from the two large, brightly burning oil lamps, for only the more successful men could afford to burn oil on this scale. The family were also well clad, while the bedding skins looked new and clean.

Crouched on one side of the platform was a very ancient woman. Her face had been tattooed with some indistinguishable design and she looked to be about a hundred, though she was probably not more than sixty, which is an advanced age for the Innuit. The old lady was in charge of one of the lamps. Her method of looking after it fascinated me. She had a pot full of fresh seal fat from which she would cut little pieces to pop into her mouth, where she apparently 'milled' the blubber, spitting it out as oil into the dish of the lamp, presumably without mixing it with any of her saliva, for the lamp did not splutter.

This reminded me of one of the first warnings given to me regarding Eskimo hospitality, in the form of a story about a new R.C.M. policeman a year or two previously. It seemed that this man, out on the trail with his Eskimo driver, was welcomed one night into a family home in much the same way as I had been.

Once he had settled in, he was offered a plateful of what appeared to be a rather tempting, creamy mixture which he ate with such relish that his host asked him if he would like some more. The policeman passed over his plate for replenishment, whereupon the hunter spoke to the old woman sitting in the back of the tent, who promptly reached into a container she had by her, pulled out a length of deer fat and cut it into small pieces, popping the bits into her mouth. The traveller watched in horror as the old woman spat the pre-chewed fat on to his plate, his stomach protesting so violently at this revelation of the nature of the delicacy he had so much enjoyed that he had to rush out of the tent.

Kilabuk gave the lady of the house one of our seal carcasses, and considering the limited cooking facilities available, the hunter's wife prepared the meal in a surprisingly short time.

The men dug chunks of meat out of the pot, trimming the size with a knife, and put them straight into their mouths. The ladies used a women's knife called an *oolu*, which consisted of a semi-circular blade with a handle attached that was used, apart from cutting up the food, for all sorts of work on skins. There were no plates and fingers served as forks or spoons. Kilabuk made the tea, producing biscuits from our supply, so everybody had a good blow-out, for the Eskimos seldom pass up the opportunity of having a hearty meal, especially when the *kudloona*'s limitless supplies are at hand, though they are themselves generous with their food, always sharing whatever meat may be available.

Since there were to be six adults and four children crowded together for the night in a comparatively small space, it did not seem likely to be a very peaceful time, but anxiety about the possible noise did not in the end concern me as much as it might have done. Before we retired, the hunter's wife held out her baby over a pot to relieve itself, which it did in no uncertain manner. Not until I had composed myself for sleep did I realize that the pot in which the child had done its business was the same one as had been used to cook the stew. I lay awake considering the implications of this discovery for a long time, but finally fell asleep, taking cold comfort from the thought that it is only possible to die once.

Early in the morning, the boy who was sleeping next to me flung out one of his arms and struck me in the face. I awoke and lay as still as possible for the next hour or two so as not to disturb my neighbour. The oil lamps had gone out, but had left behind a pungent tang of burned fat, strong enough to assert itself above the continuing odours of bodies and meat. A greyish light filtered through the treated skins of the tent. Most of the others were sprawled in sleep. The small child was making soft mouthing noises. Beevee was intoning what sounded like a psalm. The owner of the home lay flat on his back, snorting every now and then. The rest of the people were quiet, but the old woman at the end of the platform was sitting up, staring into the darkness, oblivious to the noise. The hours crept on. It seemed ages before the women stirred themselves, relit the lamps and began the morning chores.

I declined the offer of another helping of stew, freshly cooked in the all-purpose pot, contenting myself with a mug of tea and a couple of biscuits from my dwindling stock.

We had a cold journey home. It began to snow soon after we had left the camp and the damp flakes drifted round our faces all the way back. From time to time the engine coughed sadly and stalled, so that we sloshed about on the water, veering with the wind, while Kilabuk huddled over the thing trying to persuade it to start up again. We seemed forlorn and abandoned, and the scene reminded me painfully of a picture that had been stowed away up in the attic at home, of some doomed vessel wallowing helplessly in a stormy sea. Fortunately this was to the Eskimos all in a day's work and eventually we arrived safely at the foot of the bank below the welcoming lights of home.

Alan brewed a steaming pot of coffee, to the odour of which we added the fragrant smell of a splendid frying-pan hash-up, and I was soon able to recount the stories of my adventures in a light-hearted manner.

IV

I HAD LOST TRACK of the days during our expedition. Some-how it had not seemed to be of any importance what day it was. I was pleased to discover on our return from the hunting trip that it was Saturday night, and though this did not have the same significance up north as in less remote spots, it was special in one way. The Canadian broadcasting authorities used the CKY Winnipeg station, after the usual broadcast pro-gramme had closed down, to relay messages from friends and relations in the outside world to the men and women of the Arctic.

This was the only channel of communication from the south at this time, so practically all northerners spent the early hours of Sunday morning with their heads glued to their radio receivers.

Our set was of uncertain temperament. With the greatest of care and gentle tuning, Alan would bring in the Winnipeg station, often quite clearly, for a period before our programme started, but as soon as the announcer began the messages, the trouble commenced and the old set would go off into shrieking oscillation. Sometimes holding an admonitory finger about an inch in front of the receiver would do the trick, but only so long as there was no movement, for the slightest variation of position would upset everything, bringing on the howling with renewed vigour.

I once got a message through from my mother, who had left for New Zealand during the autumn after my departure, to say that they were safe and well after a severe earthquake. This I heard quite clearly, though I had not known about the disaster. Had it not been for Alan's patient determination with this infuriating piece of equipment, we should have heard nothing at all. As it was, quite often we received at least part of the programme.

On Sunday mornings, Geordie would pad across from his bedroom into the little storeroom and bring out a tin of English sausages. They came in a very special, superior-looking tin and were as different from the ordinary sausages, which flopped like congealed sawdust out of a large can, as a tender beef steak is from a hunk of old bull walrus meat. On the morning after my return, however, we had to pay for our treat. The water supply had run low, and as all the Eskimos would be going to church, Alan and I would have to hoof it back and forth to the river to fill the tank.

Meanwhile, Geordie supervised the preparations of the lunch, consisting of juicy leg of caribou, with roast potatoes and green peas (tinned). Alan came in time to make the gravy since neither Geordie or Ooloo were competent in this department. To round things off, I prepared the peaches and 'cream'.

After our repast, we relapsed into inactivity for a while, then Alan went off to develop some photographs (using the storeroom as a darkroom) and, as Geordie spread himself very inelegantly over two chairs and fell asleep, I had a look at the books in our bookcase. The selection ranged from Adam Smith's *Wealth of Nations* to a lurid thriller entitled *Blood Ran Down the Bishop's Face*. Heaven knew where the books had come from, probably some good-hearted soul had packed all the unwanted volumes from their library into a box and sent them off to us. In the end I settled for a year-old copy of the *New York Times* that carried a report of the great stock market collapse which heralded the terrible 1930s depression.

Early the next week, a whole campload of Eskimos came in by boat to collect their outfit for the coming fur-trapping season. There were about a dozen hunters with their families packed into two boats. This was quite an occasion, so biscuits and tea were made available in our kitchen for the travellers. As they were related to Ooloo, they were of course specially welcomed by her, though all visitors were entitled to the welcoming tea and biscuits.

The leading hunter and his family were the first to come in. The man's name was Evitook. He and his family were well dressed and prosperous looking. They wore new clothes which had obviously been made with great care by an expert seamstress, intricate designs having been worked with the different shades of the skins. The man had about him that air of easy confidence common to people possessing a professional ability of a high order, and some of these hunters were undoubtedly highly able men. Kilabuk stood by to act as his interpreter, so when Evitook had finished his tea they came into the guardroom for him to have his say.

'*Assioyotiddley*,' the hunter greeted Geordie. (This roughly means, 'It's so long since I have seen you that I thought you were lost.')

'Hello Evitook,' Geordie replied. The people had grown so accustomed to this greeting from traders that among themselves they frequently referred to us as the '*halloo-alloos*'. 'Everything all right?' asked Geordie politely.

'We are well,' replied the hunter, 'but there has been much wind during the summer and we have not always been able to go hunting.'

To a trader this sort of opening sounds ominous. When the people have bad news, they lead up to it gradually, beating about the bush until they consider the manager to be in a fit frame of mind to stand whatever it is he has to hear.

'Here the hunting has been good,' fenced Geordie.

'From the north this fiord has some shelter. Across the bay our inlet is open to the north.'

'Did you catch any seals in the nets we lent you?' Geordie was referring to the seal nets that Evitook had borrowed during the spring.

'A few only. One of the nets was badly torn by a shark and we lacked the twine for repairs. The other we lost and have only just found it again.'

'Then I suppose that you are short of dog food for the winter,' said Geordie, bowing as he thought to the inevitable, though there are many possibilities to such a conversation.

'No, we have sufficient meat for the dogs. In the last moon the walrus came up to the point of land just beyond our camp.'

'Good. How many did you kill?'

'We have seven carcasses and this will last us for most of the winter.'

Geordie was becoming suspicious.

'Have you damaged one of the boats?'

Evitook looked shocked at such a suggestion.

'We did not damage the boats,' he replied, 'though with the big winds harm might have easily come to them. One day when we had been out sealing, we were caught by the wind and had to make for home. On our way back, in the entrance to the harbour, we passed a pan of ice on which three walrus were lying asleep.'

By now we were all agog to find out exactly what it was that had happened, for there was no doubt but that Evitook was leading up to a revelation of some kind.

'Yes?' prompted Geordie.

'It seemed an opportunity to add to our cache, although the weather was rather rough.'

'What happened?' asked Alan in English, unable to restrain himself any longer.

Evitook ignored this interruption.

'You will understand that Akpa, my son, was standing in the bow of the boat ready to shoot the walrus as we came close, while I stood ready with my harpoon. My brother was steering the boat.'

'Did you kill any of these walrus?' asked Geordie.

'No,' answered Evitook slowly, 'they sprang into the water on the far side of the ice and swam away.'

'How did that happen?'

'My brother misjudged the distance and steered the boat into the piece of ice, so that the walrus got away.'

'Then the boat was damaged?' asked the puzzled manager.

'No. The boat was not damaged because the bow slipped up on the ice, but my son Akpa, who was standing in the bow, fell forward and dropped his rifle.'

We all looked past the hunter into the kitchen where his son was still standing. There did not seem to be anything the matter with him.

'Well, he's not hurt and probably there isn't very much the matter with the rifle,' said Geordie, with relief.

'I don't know,' replied Evitook.

'What do you mean?'

'My son was standing in the bow of the boat, and as I have said, the rifle fell into the sea and sank.'

Geordie turned away to look out of the window. It was an exhausting business sometimes to get to the heart of the matter with the Eskimos. By this time we had expected a major disaster, so in some ways it was a relief to find that only the rifle had been lost.

Evitook at once pressed his point.

'Akpa now has no rifle and so he will not be able to hunt at the seal holes with us. As he is only a boy, he will not be allowed enough debt to buy one. Therefore it will be necessary for me to have extra debt to buy the rifle for him.'

But debt could not be granted too readily, so Geordie had to carry on with the questioning, to try out every possibility before allowing the extra debt. Eventually the matter was settled and agreement reached as to the amount of the hunter's credit.

Evitook's ability had been established over the years. If the foxes were there, he would be able to trap them. The arctic foxes varied in number according to a rather irregular cycle, which followed a similar variation in numbers of the mice-like lemming, but a year behind. By watching the signs as to the fluctuations of the lemming population, it was often possible to get an indication as to how numerous the foxes were likely to be in the following season, and thus have a rough guide when it came to giving the hunters their allowances.

At the peak of the cycle, a good worker might trap more than a hundred foxes, but a year or two later he might not even get into double figures. The post managers had to take great care not to overestimate the possibilities of the season, for to grant too much debt in a bad season might weigh all the hunters down with debt for years to come. All the signs were that this was going to be a good year, so Evitook was allowed twelve foxes in credit, but before he left for the store, he managed to wheedle another two out of Geordie, on the grounds that since it was now accepted that his son, Akpa, was old enough to hunt with a rifle, he also ought to be allowed a small credit. Alan and I went off with the man and his family, and as we set out from the store, the next hunter came in from drinking his tea, and we heard him say to Geordie, 'I feared you might be lost . . .'

The four visitors, Evitook together with his wife, son and

daughter, followed us happily into the store, obviously with a pretty good idea as to just how the money should be spent. First, there was the matter of the rifle to be settled and the men climbed up into the loft, where the weapons were stored, to look them over.

To the Eskimos of those days, the upstairs of the store was a wonderful place. Kettles, pots, pans and pails hung from the rafters, and lining the shelves were men's coloured shirts, gay mittens, materials for women's summer dresses, socks, white blankets, green blankets, red blankets, duffle cloth, beads of all shapes and sizes for the adornment of the women's clothing, bright braid for the edges. There were long steel knives, pocket knives, underwear, trousers, watches, alarm clocks in all colours, pipes by the score, thin silky grenfell cloth in greens and greys, ropes and twines, threads and cottons, hip rubber boots and, in the corner by the window, the rifles.

The father and son deliberated expertly over the respective merits of the available weapons. Evitook inclined towards an older type, of a make that he knew to be reliable, so this was the eventual choice. Back downstairs, Alan got the coins out of the drawer and spread the money out on the counter.

At that time, each fox was worth $10, so the cash was laid out in ten lines of ten, the money being taken away as the hunter spent it. First on his list was ammunition, some ready made, and some powder and lead with primers for making his own. He needed a new Primus stove and a supply of kerosene, gasoline for the return journey to his camp and for the last of the seal hunting. Tea, flour, sugar and molasses. A knife for cutting up meat. Black twist tobacco for his pipe, a few cigarettes and matches. The money did not last long, the final few dollars being reserved for his wife and daughter. The woman had been promised a length of material for a dress, and though this was not strictly speaking permissible on debt, Alan allowed it as Evitook had spent all the rest of his money on necessities. The very last purchase was a pair of bright mitts for the girl.

The family was fairly easy to outfit; being a good hunter meant that, in normal circumstances, there would be enough cash to buy all the essentials with even perhaps, as in Evitook's case, a little left over. The trouble came when the man was not a good hunter and his debt allowance was insufficient to cover the items the people had come to regard as being vital. This man might perhaps be able to obtain the materials for making cartridges, some tobacco, but no food items such as tea or flour.

In those days, the Canadian government did not accept responsibility for the Eskimo population. Subsistence relief might be allowed to widows or the victims of some gross misfortune, but for the most part the people had to fend for themselves. The Hudson's Bay Company officials were vitally concerned as to the well-being of the hunters and their families. There was only one doctor in the whole of the Eastern Arctic, a territory of hundreds of thousands of square miles, so the Hudson's Bay Company managers had to do the best they could with accidents, sickness or epidemics.

It was undoubtedly fortunate for all concerned that the Hudson's Bay Company had realized, from their long years of dealing with the Canadian peoples, Indian and Eskimo, that their greatest asset lay in the people themselves. The company man registered the births and deaths and tried to solve any problems that arose, economic or domestic. The post managers encouraged any activity that helped the Eskimo towards financial independence. Many of the summer sidelines brought little profit to the posts but did mean a few dollars for the people. This system, though shakily dependent upon world fur prices, for it was only the furs that could justify the annual expensive voyage of the *Nascopie*, did succeed for quite a number of years in keeping the people of the Eastern Arctic in the dignified role of self-supporting hunters, rather than reducing them to the level of purposeless nonentities, which seems to have been the achievement of later tides of 'civilization'.

*

With all the zeal of youth and the help of a few pages of a tatty grammar, compiled with laborious effort by the Moravian missionaries of the Labrador, I had begun a study of the Eskimo. In this respect, I was fortunate that Kilabuk was the Pangnirtung post servant at the time. He was a highly intelligent man, proud of his traditions and very keen to impart information about his people and their customs to any newcomers to the post.

As is typical of the Innuit, Kilabuk was highly sensitive to ridicule and was at first a little tentative in talking to me. He was relieved to find that what he had to say was taken seriously, and this gave him the confidence to tell me his stories without fearing they might cause me to burst out laughing.

During our period of enforced idleness on the Island of the Graves, both of my companions were most helpful in their efforts to increase my Eskimo vocabulary and understanding of their language, and as the long nights came on, Kilabuk was pleased to welcome me into his home to continue the tuition.

Strangely enough, as she knew very little English, his wife Agiak seemed better able to clarify my difficulties than her husband. She made him interpret everything that was said and made many useful suggestions. I thought that with an education she might well have made a very good schoolteacher.

My school, which was noted for sending potential empire builders to the far corners, had somehow imbued in me the feeling that dealing with native peoples was a sort of 'white man's burden'. It was essential to adopt an attitude of lofty paternalism, remembering always that the black, brown or yellow peoples were really little more than children, to be treated with kindly, patronizing patience.

Ironically, in my case the paternalism had become reversed, because the people had satisfied themselves that I was only a child, still capable of absorbing their culture without the obvious scepticism of the older people. I eventually came to the realization that the Innuit were still firmly attached to their old ways and customs, giving them a clearly defined way of life as well as a code of conduct which had served them admirably for centuries gone by.

The others watched my activities with some misgivings, fearing that I was about to become absorbed into an Eskimo world. Geordie, I knew, had my welfare at heart from a funny little talk we had one day.

'Do you learn much about the language from Kilabuk?' he asked.

'Enough,' I replied, 'but his wife is really better than he is.'
Geordie looked alarmed.

'She is there with him,' I explained, 'she ought to have been a schoolteacher.'

The manager shook his head and said, rather vaguely, 'It doesn't do to get too involved with these people.'

I was silent for a moment or two, while reflecting that it was not really possible to get more involved than to actually take one of them as a wife. The same thought must have occurred to Geordie, for he became embarrassed, as though he had only just considered his own position.

'I suppose you think it's funny that I should be the one to tell you not to get involved?'

'No. Not funny at all. You are the manager and you give

me advice because you have had experience of living up here.'

'I am involved I suppose.'

'Not really,' I answered, as a sudden thought came into my head. 'You are involved with one person, not with the Eskimos.'

Geordie looked at me in silence, puzzled as though he didn't know what I was talking about. I seized the opportunity to close the conversation, not wishing to probe any more deeply into the subject. I said, 'Anyway, there's no fear of me getting mixed up with the people. All I want to do is learn the language.'

Geordie, who looked as though he was still thinking about my previous enigmatic remark, which I now heartily regretted, nodded his head and went off into the kitchen.

I continued with my tuition in spite of this seeming disapproval which, combined with the grammatical explanations given in the missionaries' little booklet, helped me in my first year to make great strides towards my goal of being able to talk to the Eskimos in their own tongue.

Kilabuk's father, an old man named Netcheapik, or 'Little Seal', whiled away the hours that fall sawing up the wood dumped from the *Nascopie*'s holds. In his young days he had been one of the chief men of the area. As a hunter for the visiting whalers, he had gone after the mighty Greenland whale in a small boat with a harpoon gun mounted in the bow. Those harpoon guns were notably erratic and sometimes the gunner was flung backwards into the boat by the kick. Many Innuit thought the gun to be possessed of an evil spirit since it behaved so badly, and they would not fire it, but Netcheapik mastered the art of managing the unruly weapon and the Scottish sailors thought highly of him.

One day, Ooloo, who went out each morning to gather the camp gossip, reported that the old man was not well. It was just old age and there was nothing very much anyone could do about it, except to make him as comfortable as possible. I undertook to go up each evening with a bowl of soup or some other titbit to give him some nourishment.

He lived in a dark tent with an old woman. I did not know what relationship they bore to each other for she was not Kilabuk's mother. The sealskin tent was old, cracked and patched in a dozen places. The oil lamp never seemed to be functioning properly, only half the wick being alight and that bit flickering and smoking. So the tent was cold and smoky and smelt of burning oil. The old man's bedding was so placed that he lay with his head close to the lamp, which should have been enough to finish anybody off. The woman sat on the other side, poking ineffectively at the wick with a piece of stick. He often took to shouting when he saw me enter with the soup, which I carried up in a pail. I never discovered why he did this, but as he lifted himself up from his bedding I could see all his ribs sticking out, as though he were already a skeleton. His straggly grey hair was matted round both ears, and the skin of his face was drawn round so tightly over the bone structure that it looked as though it might split at any moment.

He died one evening when I was in the tent. I had never seen anyone die before and it was all rather dramatic and, in a queer way, fitting for the old hunter. He sat bolt upright, waving his arms about as though directing some operation of long ago. Then he suddenly quietened completely, gazed straight past me, gave one huge shuddering gasp and fell over dead.

The woman immediately burst into loud wails, for it was the custom to mourn loudly for a short period. This was sufficient to warn all and sundry that the death had occurred and I crept out before the other mourners arrived. The burial took place the next day. Kilabuk made a coffin for his old father. The procession, led by the missionary, set off for the burial ground down by the river bank. I followed them over the snow and could hear the old man's possessions rattling inside the coffin as they went over the bumps and hillocks. As the missionary read the service, I wondered where they thought old Netcheapik's spirit had gone to await its summons to return.

*

Although the trading post at Pangnirtung had only been set up in the 1920s, the Cumberland Gulf area had long been known to the whalers of Scotland and New England, and there were many tales, some no doubt apocryphal, of strange happenings in this bleak, remote country. Once, it was said, a pirate crew attacked an innocent whaler in our own fiord, robbed them of the furs that they had traded and many of their stores, before departing at high speed for Davis Straits. The people told me too of a ghost ship slipping in and out of a late summer fog, a tolling bell and two graves that appeared mysteriously on a rocky promontory at the entrance to a neighbouring fiord. Later on in my travels, I saw those graves and wondered who it was that had come to such a cold and lonely spot to await eternity.

Less romantic perhaps, but more recent and fully documented, there was the record of the great storm which had roared down from the north one early winter's night not long after the post had been established. Geordie was fond of recounting the graphic events of that night. The wind began to rise during the afternoon and by dark was crashing into the buildings with such force that they shook and creaked alarmingly. The post staff, huddled together in the house, were suddenly appalled to hear a great booming sound followed by an alarming clattering and banging on the roof, as though someone was trying to get in. Then came a resounding crash. No one dared to go outside to investigate so they did not find out until the next day what had happened.

97

The roof of the store, torn loose by the sheer savagery of the wind, had lifted clear of the body of the building, risen into the air and sailed right over the house, discarding some of the kettles and pots hanging from the rafters on to our roof as it passed. On that same night one of the R.C.M. policemen, ill-advisedly opening his back door, said that he saw what seemed to be a small building travelling at some speed in a southerly direction, towards the lower beaches. After the storm had died down it became clear that the Hudson's Bay Company lavatory had disappeared.

The fall sometimes ended with one of these violent gales, which would develop into a blizzard, covering the whole countryside in snow before the weather moderated. And so began my first winter.

The wind had been rising all evening and the icy gusts were hurrying light snowflakes down the fiord, whirling them round and round as they danced past while a long white plume streamed out from the top of the high cliffs.

Back in my own room, I lit my oil lamp, but like a careless Eskimo housewife I had neglected to trim the wick, so it smoked, giving no more than a little circle of light by the top of the bed, while the corners remained in the shadows. It was draughty too, for one corner of the window did not fit properly and every now and then a little puff of snow would drift into the room, causing the light to flutter uneasily. I got into bed quickly and blew out the light, huddling beneath the bedclothes to generate some warmth.

I lay in the darkness thinking about my family in New Zealand. With them the summer would be just beginning. I wondered if perhaps they were stretched out on some beach enjoying the sunshine, or picnicking by a quiet lake. All the while, the wind billowing in from the hills to the north of us slapped the now huge snowflakes into my window and breathed

98

coldly into my room. The house creaked protestingly at the buffeting storm, but I soon warmed up and went off to sleep undisturbed by the noise.

By morning a full-scale blizzard had developed. The wind seemed to be coming from all directions at once, crashing round the building and causing the fire to roar up the stove pipe, so that the bottom of our bulging stove was bright red hot.

After breakfast, I set out on a morning visit to the lav. It was like preparing for a visit to the North Pole. Alan warned me to be careful where I was going, because it was so easy to get lost in these conditions, and I remembered Bill Ford's story of the Chimo missionary who spent two days in a dugout hole in the snow right next to his house. I very nearly did miss the house on my way back, just touching the far wall on my way past.

The storm lasted for three days, but when we looked out on the Wednesday morning the air was again calm. The sky was a very pale, frigid blue and the sun, just hanging above the lower southern hills, stretched cold but dazzlingly reflected rays down the valley, now completely covered with fresh white snow. The morning was cold and crisp. The great wind had swept away the last traces of the fall and the winter had begun.

Now was the time to sort out the winter travelling equipment. First of all, out came the sledges or *komatiks*. They were about fifteen feet long, with solid-wooden runners and crossbars, the latter being lashed on with line made from the *ujuk* seal. This lashing was passed through a hole in the wooden runner, over the top of the crossbar, secured, then on through the next hole and over the next crossbar and so on down the whole length of the sledge. The far side of the crossbar was lashed to the other runner in a similar manner, thus holding the sledge firmly together.

During the early winter and again when the sun had returned

in the spring, the runners were shod with steel to make them slide more easily over the snow. The steel shoeing was about two and a half inches wide and an eighth of an inch thick and, to reduce friction between the runners and the snow to a minimum, was coated with ice. In the cold climate the icing was quite a simple job. The driver would upturn his sledge, take a mouthful of water and squirt it evenly along the steel, smoothing the surface with a skin wiper. This was done at the start of the day and again probably at midday, by which time the first coating would have been knocked off. The traveller would clean the old ice right off before repeating the process. The water froze very quickly, enabling the driver to turn the sledge back upright for loading almost at once.

The load was carefully spaced along the *komatik* to get a reasonably even balance of weight, with the heavier items usually at the rear and provisions for the passengers at the front. Rifles or other items which might be needed quickly during the day were placed in an easily accessible spot out of harm's way. Either deerskin or bearskin was used to cover the load and was lashed tightly on with sealskin line or rope.

In deep winter, the severe frost caused even greater friction between the runners and the surface of the snow, so the steel runners would be removed in favour of a mud shoeing. For this purpose, a black loamy mud gave the best results. The Eskimos had long ago located the marshy areas from which to obtain their supply. The art of making a really good shoe of this kind lay mainly in the preparation given to the mixture. First, the mud had to be heated sufficiently to allow it to be worked up into the consistency of putty, eliminating all rough elements to ensure a smooth surface.

When the mixture was fully prepared, it was packed on to the wood of the runners to a depth of over two inches, roughly smoothed, then left to freeze overnight. When frozen, the surface was planed with an ordinary hand plane, so as to be level from one end of the sledge to the other. For a professional finish, animal's blood, seal or deer, was applied to the top of the mud and this would be iced in the same manner as the steel shoes.

Finally, when the sledge was loaded, lashed and ready, the dogs were rounded up and attached. There was not usually any difficulty about finding and harnessing the team. Having been born and bred as hunters and workers, they were mostly quite frisky in the mornings, keen to get about the day's business. The number of dogs in any team varied according to the ability of the hunter to provide food and was anything from four to a dozen or more.

Each dog had its position in the team and the line attached to its harness varied according to the working place. The harness, made of strips of skin about an inch wide, simply slipped over the head and shoulders, so that the dog could pull with its whole weight. The leader, normally a bitch, naturally had the longest line so that it could work right out in front of the rest of the team. All the other lines were of different lengths, in order that no two dogs would be exactly alongside each other, in which position they would almost certainly take to fighting. The laziest animals were kept closest to the sledge, under the driver's constant observation.

Each team had a boss dog, not usually the leader but the toughest member of the pack, who kept a rough sort of order over the rest of them. As long as the team had a definite boss, there was little fighting. The trouble really started when a boss dog began to get elderly or infirm. The younger ones began to question his authority, fighting with him and squabbling among themselves to decide who was next in line for the 'throne' until a clear-cut victor emerged.

During long journeys, much time had to be devoted to keeping the equipment in good repair, for a stitch in time here almost invariably saved a broken harness. Some dogs developed a taste for chewing their lines and harnesses and even the skin lashings holding on the crossbars. This was a serious problem, the only real remedy being to file down the offender's teeth.

The husky dogs were hard workers, and provided they were kept in good condition would hold a steady pace all day. Just as it was possible to grade the Eskimo housewives by the state of the oil lamps, so a hunter might be judged by his team.

Much practice was needed to achieve an effective use of the dog whip. The whips were very long, since they had to reach at least from the sledge to the lead dog, and they tapered down to a tip, with which it was possible to give any member of the team a painful flick. I found at first that I was more likely to be the recipient of the painful flick than the dogs. The end of the whip was thick line, plaited over a piece of iron, or something solid, to weight it. This end served also as a heavy weapon to separate the combatants in a serious fight or to administer really drastic punishment. Watching an Eskimo flipping the whip casually out to whichever member of the team required encouragement, its use seemed easy, but it took me a long time to handle the thing correctly.

After the storm the temperature dropped at once below the zero mark, the lakes and ponds soon froze over, and it was not many days before the first ice appeared over the fiord. The tidal reef stretched about sixty yards from the shore out to a line of rocks. In this area, between the land and the main sea ice, the water froze when the tide was up, then, when the tide dropped again, broke into pieces on the rocks underneath. This freezing and breaking process resulted in the reef becoming an area of rough ice blocks, which floated freely at high tide, at least during the early winter. Later on, the blocks froze together but altered position with the varying tides, developing into a sort of switch-back between the shore and the fiord ice proper, which we called the 'barricade' ice.

During the period when the blocks floated freely on the high tide, we sometimes took exercise by running from the shore, jumping from block to block out to the sea ice. This was good fun but it was not always possible to avoid a very cold dipping.

My first expedition by sledge was to go with Alan to fetch a load of ice for water from the river. I got left behind when they started off home before we were ready. Alan did not have a very comfortable ride, for the dogs burst off among the rocks and boulders still sticking up out of the snow, as though their lives depended upon getting home with all possible speed. Eventually, the sledge got jammed in behind two big rocks, enabling me to catch up and arrive home seated on the sledge with comparative dignity.

We broke up the load to fill up the tanks, and in view of the good supply I decided to treat myself to a bath in the store cupboard that night. Normally we just used a sort of hip bath for a good wash-down in the warmth of the kitchen. A piece of piping had been taken through the wall of the kitchen into the storeroom, so that it would be possible to use the bath without having to carry all the water round the house. I filled every good-sized kettle that would fit on top of the stove with ice, switching them about from back to front like a general marshalling his troops. Ooloo watched the proceedings with a sardonic smile, finally departing with a shrug of her shoulders, despairing of my inability to deal with life in a straightforward way like the Eskimos.

The storeroom was lit by an electric bulb powered by a battery, which I checked before finalizing my arrangements. I just had time to get in and feel the comforting warmth of the water before someone poured a whole container of ice-cold liquid through the piping, which sprayed out to catch me fair in the back as I sat up to wash myself. This gave me such a shock that I jumped up, catching the battery with my arm, so that it pulled away from the terminal, plunging me into darkness. My head banged into a shelf, dislodging a reserve supply of corned beef which hammered down on to me and into the bath. Dripping water freely on my way, I groped through the darkness to give battle, stamping into the guardroom only to find it empty, for the others, having achieved their fell purpose, had gone off to the police house to play poker.

By early November, the sea ice had become fairly solid, providing a surface suitable for careful travel, so Alan and I were to go off for a few days to set some traps. We spent a day in the kitchen first, preparing the food supplies. We made a lot of meat balls, consisting of deermeat, corned beef and beans hashed up together, then cut up into convenient lumps for freezing, so that we should be able to simply toss them into the pan up at the camp. A big bag of doughnuts was always on Alan's list, for although they froze it was quite easy to thaw them for a morning snack since they contained a large amount of fat. The ship's biscuit, the good old Arctic standby, accompanied us on every trip, as did porridge oats, tea, sugar, chocolate and tinned butter. We cooked up a frying-pan bannock with lots of shortening, sliced up some deermeat and packed away a supply of coffee in the corner of the grub box. Most hunters set up caches of meat along the trap lines (or routes) that they were most likely to be using during the winter months, in order to avoid loading down the *komatiks* with the heavy meat every journey. They simply cut the meat into large chunks, piled it up then covered it over with rocks carefully enough to prevent foxes or wolves from breaking in to help themselves.

Although we had cached a supply of dog food under the rocks near the camp, this still took up a fair amount of the available space on the sledge because a team of a dozen or so dogs consumed a large amount of food, even though normally only fed every second day. Mainly, the dogs throve reasonably well on whatever happened to be the most generally available food in their district, and hence to which they had become most accustomed. Thus the diet might consist of seal, walrus, whale meat or even fish in the Ungava Bay area, though a dog which had been used to a solid meat diet would not thrive if changed over to fish.

Kilabuk was in charge of the loaded sledge with twelve dogs and he was very smartly dressed for the occasion in a new deerskin outfit. We barely had time to say goodbye to Geordie before the dogs, sensing the moment for departure, leapt to their feet and rushed down the bank to burst on to the barrier ice and gallop off. This time, however, I was ready for them and the combined weight of the three of us helped to steady the mad rush over the ice.

The going was good that day, so we bowled along in fine style, taking turns in running beside the sledge, both to keep ourselves warm and to relieve the dogs of the weight. All went well until we reached a spot where, owing to swifter currents, the ice was dotted with holes. There was no danger of the sledge falling through, but I took it into my head to do some running in one of the worst places, jumping off the sledge to land heavily on thin ice, which gave way at once, sending me straight down into the freezing water. The others sitting in front of me did not at first see what had happened, while the suddenness of my descent, combined with the unimaginable coldness of the water, rendered me completely speechless and thus unable to attract their attention. At last Kilabuk, glancing backwards, noticed my vacant place and the sight of him looking round galvanized me into uttering a feeble but desperate cry, sufficient to direct his gaze towards me. He stopped the dogs, ran back to within a safe distance of my hole and tossed me the thick end of the whip, with the aid of which I managed, with some difficulty, to ease my way through the thin ice until it became strong enough for me to climb out on to the surface, safe but perished with cold.

Fortunately, we were very close to a small, permanent camp, consisting of a shack which had been brought up from the post. Alan quickly got the little stove going with supplies of wood that had been brought up by the boat during the fall, and the place was soon hung about with my drying clothes. It was not a very comforting reflection for me that, already in my short life in the Arctic, Kilabuk had twice had to rescue me from a very likely and unpleasant death. This was bound to convince the Eskimos that they had been right in naming me 'The Boy'. I determined that there should not be a third such occasion, but I was less than confident that I would be able to avoid the multifarious dangers which seemed such an integral part of life in the Arctic. I could only hope that Kilabuk would be at hand until I developed an instinct for self-preservation.

We had breakfast in good time the next morning. My skin garments were quite dry but rather hard, so Kilabuk worked them up for a while to soften them. The softening process is normally a woman's job in the Innuit home. Since the Eskimos are not generally given to falling in the sea, the ordinary clothes do not usually require treatment, but the skin boots often become board hard, so the women chew away at them with their teeth to make them soft and pliable, for hard boots mean cold feet.

We made our usual flying start, soon coming to the barricade ice at the end of the fiord, which we crossed to make our way up the river bed leading to the lake above. The river rose fairly sharply through a series of 'falls', which were sometimes quite tricky to negotiate, as Alan had the misfortune to discover.

We had come to one of the biggest 'falls', where the frozen river came down in steps, rather like a large stairway, with a fall, then a stretch of flat, then another fall and so on. Alan had climbed to the top with a length of line which was attached to the sledge at one end, so that he would be able to haul upward, while Kilabuk and I guided the load away from the rocks and pushed from behind. We released the dogs to make their own way up. When the sledge was about half-way up the line broke. Kilabuk and I managed to hold the weight by bracing ourselves against a rock on the far bank, but Alan, who had been standing on a patch of snow at the very top, sat smartly down on his bottom and slithered uncontrollably towards the falls.

We were trapped holding the sledge at an awkward angle, so the best we could do was to watch sympathetically as Alan thudded down towards us at such speed that a broken limb seemed the least we could expect. Fortunately Kilabuk, who was on the outside, managed to grab his deerskins as he went by and guide him off towards a snowdrift, where he came to rest shaken, covered in snow, but unharmed apart from a rather bruised bottom.

That evening it was pretty cold so Kilabuk decided we would put up a snowhouse instead of using the tent we had brought with us for the milder nights. Watching an Eskimo build a home of this kind makes it seem that there is very little to it; in fact it is quite a skilled operation, as many a southerner who has slashed bravely into a virgin bank of snow has discovered. The snow must be carefully selected, firm but not brittle and all, if possible, from a drift formed by a single storm, as a block made up of layers from different drifts fractures easily at the joints.

Having picked out a suitable patch of snow, the next step is to mark out a rough circle. The blocks are cut out from within this circle and placed round the circumference. As a round is completed, the next layer is placed on top, the edges being trimmed with the snowknife so that the two layers fit reasonably well together. This shaping must be done with a view to tilting the second row inward in an even manner, so that as the house grows upward the sides gradually close in, until a single block can be placed on top to seal the shelter. The exact amount of 'tilt' needed varies according to the size of house required, but it is important that all the blocks should sit firmly and evenly all the way round for the snowhouse to be strong enough to resist the violent weather.

When the house is complete, a snowknife must be taken round the outside. All the rough corners are cut off, crumbled and packed into any open joints. Finally, handfuls of loose snow must be applied wherever there might seem to be a weakness of insulation. The floor of a house built in this manner will, of course, be one block below the level of the outside snow since the material was cut from within the circle, so complete 'insulation' is obtained on the ground.

Usually, a ventilating hole is cut in the topmost square. This may be blocked up when necessary with a piece of deerskin. When the Innuit built snowhouses for winter homes, they were often more elaborate than these trail snowhouses. Sometimes they even had two rooms, and invariably a porch, where harnesses, dog food and hunting gear could be kept, the harpoons and spears being stuck in the snow outside the house.

The inside surface of the snow was often lined with sealskin or canvas, which was held in place by thongs passed through the wall and fastened to toggles. This meant that the inside temperature could be kept at a higher level, since the lining tended to hold the heat in the house, while allowing the cool air to circulate from the vent over the surface of the snow. For living purposes, one home would last a whole winter, though by the end of the season it would be getting rather dirty and smelly. If it got too bad, all the Eskimo had to do was to collect everything together and move to a fresh spot.

When our house was complete, we unloaded the sledge, spread the deerskins over the floor and stacked our gear near the door (which consisted simply of a block removed from the wall). We had brought two Primuses and I lit them both, one for the purpose of melting down a block of snow into a kettleful of water, the other to begin the heating up of the meatballs for our meal. I was glad to have had my previous camping experience, for the Primus now held no mysteries for me, and the cooking routine came to me quite easily. The cook's job suited me well. The last hour or two of travel had not been too pleasant. There was a slight but chill wind and running over the rough terrain in the pitch dark was difficult, particularly with my feet becoming steadily paralysed by the cold. But with the Primuses going our little home soon warmed up.

In fact the temperature rose rather rapidly as the cooking got under way. Without any lining, walls soon started to drip, but our companion showed us that by smoothing over a handful of loose snow the water could be conducted down far enough for the drops to fall harmlessly round the edges of the house. We had a fine supper of meatballs, ship's biscuits and hot coffee and were not sorry to slide into our sleeping bags without delay.

Next morning we continued our journey up the river and soon came out on to a smooth lake, over which we rattled at top speed towards a sheltered spot at the far end, just right for a camp. Here we decided to set up our main trapping home, another snowhouse, but a trifle more elaborate this time since we should be probably using it fairly often.

Alan had done some trapping the previous year and was going to show me the ropes during an afternoon tramp. We must have looked bloodthirsty characters as we set off carrying a hatchet and a .22 rifle with traps draped over one shoulder and dangerous-looking knives thrust through scarves tied round our middles. We set the traps as far as possible in little hollows dug in the snow, with a very thin slice of snow to cover the top. The bait was fastened between two rocks, with another over the top to prevent the bait from being taken from the other side.

Half-way through the afternoon we came round a corner on to a large group of ptarmigan wandering about pecking through the snow. We shot several of the plump little birds, which were excellent for the pot. They did not at first appear to be alarmed, seeming not to have taken in the fact that several of their number had been removed, which enabled us to gather quite a haul before they finally flew away across the lake. During the winter, the ptarmigan are white all over except for one or two black patches round the eyes. From about the end of June, their plumage changes to a mottled brown, so that at nesting time they fade into the background, although the male bird also stands on guard to sound the alarm in case of trouble.

We took our catch home and boiled up a very good stew with the addition of a packet of dried vegetables. While we had been away, Kilabuk had put the finishing touches to the camp. He had brought up a seal-oil lamp with him, which he had lit before our return, so that when we came in the snowhouse was warm and brightly lit. Our driver intended to return to the post the next day, leaving us to our own devices until the end of the week, when he was to come and fetch us.

Once the traps had been set the next morning, Alan and I split up, going off in different directions so that we could cover the line more frequently. I did not take easily to being an arbiter of life or death, even to the heartless fox, and one of my first victims, somehow caught by the tail, defended himself so vigorously that I just opened the trap and released him, though I never dared to confess this to anyone. The arctic trappers actually helped the environment by controlling, to a small extent, the number of foxes roaming their district, for there was some evidence that in the years when they were most numerous they became subject to a distemper-like disease which could spread to other animals.

Our days were spent on foot, tramping round the shores of the lake land up the northern arm of the river to where we had set our traps. The going was mostly rough and hilly, and though we continued to take our lunch with us, by the time we got home in the evening we were famished and always ready to do full justice to our supper, sometimes the meatballs, sometimes ptarmigan stew, and once Alan brought home an arctic hare which had somehow wandered into one of his traps.

Alan usually got home before me, then hung a lantern from the top of a tent pole stuck in the snow to guide me home. Coming into view of the flickering light, then picking up the odours of Alan's cooking activities, was one of the best ways I have ever known of ending a day's hard work.

Coming back one night from the far end of the lake, I had my first experience of the famous northern lights. It was a calm, cold night. My route lay across the last stretch of plain at the top of the lake. Half-way over the bark of a fox made me raise my head just in time to see a sudden beam of light sweep into the sky, so rapidly that it had gone almost instantaneously, yet bright enough to dazzle me with a clear green flash. Then came a whole series of golden lights, changing smoothly to rainbow colours as they spread far across the sky. When the first bursts died down, new beams rose into the empty spaces, twisting and twining together like slithering snakes. The lights seemed to move towards me, illuminating the whole scene with their brilliance, picking out the high, bleak hills to the north as though with a beam from a soft, golden searchlight, while the lonely valley dipped and rose in the rainbow colours as the display swung across the sky. Travellers sometimes claim to have 'heard' the northern lights, but although I listened carefully on this and other occasions, I cannot say that I ever heard any sounds other than those normal to an arctic winter's night.

We were most fortunate that during this spell at the camp the weather remained fine, but on the day that Kilabuk returned with the team, we noticed a line of small, sinister-looking clouds ranged along a wide stretch of the horizon, a warning of approaching bad weather that even I recognized. Fortunately, the threatened storm did not materialize at once, for there was little more than a briskish wind as we came down on to the flat by our camp that evening and the howling of the dogs told us that our friend had returned.

Kilabuk had not wasted his time, having relighted the seal-oil lamp, so that the snowhouse was comfortably warm and cosy after the cold walk home. Our companion was in good form that evening. When we had finished our supper, he filled up the spaces in the bowl of the lamp, poked up the flame and we settled down for a traditional winter's evening of storytelling.

Nearly all the Eskimo stories have been handed down from generation to generation with astonishing accuracy, for the same tale, from two far-distant sources, is often almost identical. Mostly, the stories are of a folklore type, but they sometimes have a background of historical record. One or two of the historical narratives connect vaguely with the activities of European explorers. In the Frobisher Bay area, there were references to the doings of white sailors, which might well have originated with the journeyings of Frobisher himself. Kilabuk finished up with a fable telling how the fogs began.

'A long, long time ago,' said the Eskimo, 'far away up in the hills above a great lake a hill spirit lived with his family. Now they lived by themselves, for food was scarce in those parts and everyone else had gone down to the coast, where the seal were plentiful. This spirit did not choose to leave his home, so he fed himself and his family by stealing the bodies of the coastland people from their graves and dragging the corpses back to his home in the hills. One day, the son of a very good hunter died and was buried under a pile of rocks just behind the camp. The day after the burial, the father went back to make the grave secure against the animals, only to find that the body had gone, which made him very angry indeed. He determined to discover who it was that was stealing their dead, so told his friends that they were to bury him alive in the hope that the thief would then reveal himself. The hunter dressed himself in his furs, pushing a stone under his deerskin in case the thief should try and stab him before dragging him away. Very soon, the hill spirit appeared, removed the rocks over the new grave and started to pull the body off towards the hills. This was not easy for him because the hunter made himself as heavy as he could, catching hold of any protruding rocks as he passed by to make the spirit's job more difficult. At last they arrived at the thief's home, by which time the spirit was so exhausted that he flung his burden towards the back of the house before lying down to rest. His wife tended the lamp in preparation for the forthcoming meal, but the hunter, curious to see where he had been brought, opened his eyes to look around. The children of the house screamed in fear for they had never seen such a thing happen before.

' "The man is opening his eyes," they shrieked, "he will see us and do us harm."

' "Nonsense," replied the father, "his head has been hanging down as I brought him up here and the eyes have opened."

'At that the hunter sprang up from his place at the back of the house, killed the spirit and the children, then ran from the place, passing the spirit's wife in the porch where she had gone to cut up more seal fat for the lamp. In the darkness, the woman, thinking it was her husband brushing past her, asked him where he was going, but the hunter ran off without answering. The woman set off after him as fast as she could go. The ground was flat outside the spirit's home and the wife, being fast, might easily have caught up. However, the hunter was something of an *angekok*, having spirits who did his bidding, so he called out, "Come from the ground, O boulders, in front of this woman," and great rocks came out of the ground to block the path of his pursuer. This delayed the woman sufficiently to give the man time to reach a small stream, over which he jumped.

'As soon as he was across the stream, he shouted loudly, "Come down from the hills, O water, and pour into this stream, so that the woman will not be able to cross."

'Down came the water so that no one could have crossed. They looked at each other from either side of the now fast-moving stream.

' "How did you cross this brook?" called the woman.

' "I lay on the bank and sucked the water out so that I could walk over," replied the other.

' "What thou canst do, so also can I," shouted the spirit's wife, kneeling down to gulp up the water.

'After she had drunk a large quantity, the hunter laughed and called out, "See, thou hast drunk so much water that the fish wait on the ground behind thee."

'The woman got up to see the fish, but when she turned round to bend down and look, she was so full of water that she burst and, in bursting, gave off clouds of steam, which rose up from her to drift among the hills and become the fog which is still with us.'

The next morning was a little cloudy, but there seemed no reason for us to delay our departure. We set off in good time, but the day did not go well. Going down one slope, the sledge shot away from us, knocking down three of the dogs and overtaking the rest. The toggle fastening the bridle slipped open, so that the dogs were free to gallop in all directions. Kilabuk just managed to bring them back before they dashed off home. Descending one of the 'falls', a sledge runner pushed hard into a narrow crevice and jammed there. We then discovered that the bung of the coffee Thermos had come loose, so that the liquid, though not actually frozen, was stone cold. Finally, darkness fell while we were still a long way from home and we decided to camp on the lake at the head of the fiord.

The weather was still mild, so we put up the tent almost in the middle of the lake, although Kilabuk was not altogether happy about our exposed position. We made up our minds to aim for an early start next morning, so retired to our sleeping bags in good time. Falling asleep almost right away, I had a few hours of peaceful slumber, but being in the middle, I woke up when both Alan and Kilabuk converged on me at the same time. I pushed them away, but could not go to sleep again.

The walls of the tent had become rather slack, with a tendency to flap in and out, but it did not at first appear to be a noisy night. The canvas on the far side had been stained at some time and this stain made a sort of pattern which changed as the material billowed with the breeze. In the grey, shadowy light, I thought I could pick out a shape resembling that of a Victorian house, rather like the one we had lived in as children. As it bulged inward, a window of the top storey on the side nearest to me looked remarkably like the one from which my brother had once nearly fallen to the ground.

This reverie might easily have drifted me off to sleep again, had not the whole house burst suddenly apart as a gust of wind swept down the lake, pushing the canvas in as far as it would go. A noisy booming followed from somewhere high up in the gulley to the north, which undoubtedly heralded the approach of a storm of some violence. While I was debating with myself whether to waken my companions or not, the wind came thundering down the gulley, roaring round our doubtful shelter, gleeful at finding victims so completely unprepared for resistance.

Kilabuk shot up out of his sleeping bag to brace the ridge pole. Alan grabbed the support nearest the entrance, already bending with the pressure. I made for the far end but the top of the pole broke off before I could reach it, striking me a formidable blow on the head as the tent started to collapse. We struggled to hold everything together but were clearly fighting a losing battle. We held steady for a few minutes, then, blasted by a sudden acceleration of shrieking wind, the end support gave way. Alan went over head first, disappearing from sight as our shelter tore away from its moorings to wrap itself round him and Kilabuk, flinging them both to the ground. Somehow, the tent had gone over my head leaving me standing freezing cold in my underpants with a useless piece of pole in my hand. The storm soon tore the flapping canvas away from my friends, leaving them totally exposed on the snow. Our boxes, overturned by the tent as it pulled away to depart, spilled their contents on to the slippery snow and ice. The tins of our reserve food supply shot away at considerable speed over the lake, heading towards the river, closely followed by three rolls of deerskins. Even the saucepans slithered off as though intending to journey home under their own steam. Kilabuk jumped to his feet and was blown off into the darkness, but somehow managed to track down our shelter and returned shortly with it draped around him. Fortunately, I had managed to see that our sleeping bags did not blow away. We retrieved most of the tins and pans that were conveniently at hand, but the rest of our equipment was now dispersed over the lake.

There was no question of re-erecting the tent. The wind was far too rough and two of the poles were broken. We were not a happy group as we huddled together to prepare to spend the rest of the night in what comfort was possible under the very trying circumstances. The dogs howled in protest at the violent disturbance of their rest as we made what use we could of the remaining supports. Eventually, the three of us lay in our sleeping bags with the tent more or less wrapped round us, while the storm raged on derisively.

We did not need any persuading to give up the pretence of sleep at the earliest possible moment. We started our breakfast preparations before five o'clock, by which time the gale had calmed sufficiently for us to make the shelter firm enough to permit the use of the Primus stove. It was my turn to make the porridge and the climax of our unfortunate twenty-four hours came when I split the boiling mixture over my knees and into my sleeping bag. Kindly, my colleagues said nothing. My Scottish friend took over the cooking and succeeded in producing a hot breakfast.

The dogs were as keen as we were to get away from the unhappy spot and, with the following wind urging them on, they set off into the darkness determined to show us that they could handle their task efficiently, even if the same could not be said about us.

The mild, windy day produced conditions excellent for fast travel, so that even after several stops to pick up our truant belongings, we made the descent to sea level in quick time. We pulled into the wooden shack to have our coffee in comfort, and our spirits were quite revived by the time we trundled over the barricade on to the main ice again for the last leg of the journey.

So began my life of hunting and trapping. I already knew that I was not one of those people who thirst to put an end to the lives of wild animals simply because they come within their range of vision. Nor would I ever derive much pleasure from exhibiting the trophies of the chase. But hunting for food was no different from slaughtering unsuspecting lambs, calves, chickens, ducks and turkeys for the table, and no one ever thought of killing more than they could handle or use. Nevertheless, it took me a long time to develop a completely professional attitude to hunting and not feel a shiver of guilt as I pressed the trigger.

V

ON SATURDAY NIGHTS at the trading post we played poker while waiting for the messages to come on the air from CKY Winnepeg. One evening, the subject of Christmas celebrations came up and it became obvious that the reserve of liquor in the settlement had fallen to an abnormally low level. We lacked the wherewithal to make spirituous beverages, so there did not appear to be any way by which we could right this sorry state of affairs. Then one of the policemen remembered about Father William and his wine.

The good father, it seemed, having been faced with a shortage of wine, took to making his own with no little success and afterwards, being a good-hearted man, he communicated the recipe freely to anyone with any interest. One of our colleagues had written it all down and brought the instructions over the next day for an immediate start to be made. The brewing was to take place in our kitchen, since it was probably illegal and thus not fitting for the Royal Canadian Mounted Police to be the actual instigators.

The father's method consisted of a bagful of raisins being suspended in a cask of water with a few pounds of sugar thrown in to produce the fermentation. We hung the bag just beside the guardroom door, where it naturally attracted the attention of every passer-by, some of whom, being doubtful as to the efficacy of the mixture, poured in concoctions of their own to ensure a satisfactory final product.

The whole thing looked revolting; a thick yellowish scum covered the surface of the liquid, but those in the know declared all to be well, and at last bottling day arrived.

In our foolish haste we had made no provision for drawing off the liquid through a spigot or tap of any kind, so the brew had to be sucked out with a length of rubber tubing. Wisely it was thought necessary to limit each person's spell of sucking duty to not more than four bottles at a time. As a finale, it was decided to squeeze the bag containing the raisins, so that no liquid should be lost. Fuelled as we were by at least two spells of sucking duty each, there was much discussion as to how this should be achieved, but it was finally decided to carry the precious mess carefully down to our reserve store, to be put in an old fur press. In our inebriated state, we put far too much pressure on the press and it flew apart under the strain. Alan was flung out through the door into the night, while one of the policemen received a substantial blow on the head, which considerably reduced his interest in the proceedings. We pushed the mess out on to the snow with a broom and, led by Geordie with the lantern, filed out into the darkness to rescue our comrade.

Quite a large number of bottles and containers were stored in various frost-free parts of the buildings. Although not allowed to mature for the full six months recommended by Father William, the wine did provide us with a very pleasant refreshment for the Christmas season.

Early in December, the people started to arrive with the first of the winter's catch. That it was going to be a very good fur year was soon obvious. Our kitchen was full, morning and evening, with the deerskin-clad forms of the hunters. They would come to the guardroom door, after finishing their tea and biscuits, smiling as they shook hands with Geordie.

'*Assioyotiddley?*' they would say gravely, producing a sack of furs.

As it was such a good year, they had no difficulty in clearing off their debt and even fixed their sights on expensive replacements, such as rifles, engines, boats and the like. Gone were the rough and ready days, when the hunter had to pile up the furs so that they reached the top of a weapon before he could claim it for his own. The good hunters knew as well as the managers that the peak fur year was the time to replace expensive equipment. The very costly items, such as engines or boats, were often bought by several people clubbing together, or possibly by contributions from a whole camp.

The sacks of furs were shaken out on to the floor to be valued and the man's name and the amount due was entered into our log book. Alan and I would then light the gas lanterns to set off for the store, where we spread the money out before the hunter so that we could begin the trading. Most of the men knew what they wanted, rattling quickly through the list of such items as cartridges, powder, tobacco, tea, flour, molasses and other essentials. Many of them had made notes of any special purchases in the syllabic writing that was introduced to them by the missionaries. The women differed little from any other women when it came to shopping. They wanted this, but not in that colour, or that, but a little thicker. The needles were not broad enough, or were too short, and so it would go on.

The place soon filled up like a meeting house, the atmosphere heavy with the thick, blue acrid smoke of the black twist they all used, while every now and then there would be a burst of laughter as they exchanged a coarse joke. An especially good joke would merit one of their number coming up to the counter to tell us about it, if they could, interrupting the trading while the whole store rocked with laughter. It was a jovial gathering, particularly on these rare occasions when the people had money to spare for little extras that they could not normally afford, such as sweets for the children, new pipes and fancy knives.

From the time that the trappers started to bring their wares in until Christmas there was hardly a break in the furs flowing inward and the trade goods outward. The skins were rough-sorted to be hung upstairs in the reserve store, from which they would be taken in the spring to be cleaned and hung out in the air. The days became shorter and shorter. At Pangnirtung we were just below the line of the Arctic Circle, but being practically surrounded by high land, there was quite a long sunless period and by Christmas time there was hardly any daylight at all. The gas lanterns glared all day down in the store, but there was no heating, so after a day's trading none of us were sorry to get back to the warmth of the house and a hot meal.

The largest group of arrivals of the whole season came in on Christmas Eve, which meant we were hard at it in the store from quite early in the morning until about ten o'clock at night. Later, our erratic receiver put on its best behaviour and we heard practically the entire programme of messages in a special Christmas edition. Well on in the morning it all came to an end, so we banked up the stove, wished each other a 'merry Christmas' and trooped off to bed.

In the rush of trading, I had forgotten to fill my oil lamp, so it was to bed by candlelight for me. I stuck the candle on an upturned case, which served me as a bedside table and got into bed. As I lay studying my room by the flickering light, I remembered how dismal it had seemed to me that first day of waking under the dun-coloured ceiling when Geordie came in and slopped his liquor on the floor, making me wonder whether I should ever become accustomed to my strange new life. Just as I was sinking into sleep our dog team all gathered outside my window and began to howl, soon to be joined by dozens of their visiting friends. The whole settlement echoed to the mournful wailing until the sound died away quite suddenly. The silence was broken only by the cracking and grinding of the shore ice, easing into new positions with the high tides of the full moon, a familiar sound which no longer disturbed me.

Our good friends at the police barracks had invited us for Christmas dinner, so, after a morning's trading with the late arrivals, we drank a toast with Geordie to ourselves, then set out, dressed in our town clothes for the first time since the ship left, to walk across the snow to the police buildings. I thought of the jovial Victor of the wedding party in Montreal and how awkward he had looked in his party clothes. I felt at that moment how easy it would be to slip into his attitude to the world.

The fellows had put on a really splendid spread: soup made with caribou stock and flavourings, eider duck garnished and prepared with stuffings and sauces of a standard high enough to make a gourmand's mouth water, Christmas pudding of course, Stonewall Jackson cigars, and coffee. Father Williams's wine circulated freely round the table as we settled down to digest the excellent meal. The wine was pleasantly palatable and of sufficient strength to loosen tongues, so that many strange tales were related, most of which we had heard before, but in our close-knit little community this was perhaps unavoidable.

The story-telling ended when the Eskimos started to come into the kitchen, for the sergeant had promised them that they should have a dance in the barracks. On these occasions, the people danced a mixture of formation and reel, obviously imported by successive groups of whalers in years gone by. The dances varied from place to place according to local adaptations, but there was always a fiddler calling the turns, usually in English. The movable furniture was taken away and the available space was quickly packed with intending dancers. All the adults joined in, with the exception of the very old.

The dancing was a serious matter. The Eskimos lined up in a row to bounce up and down for some time before moving into a turn of some kind. Some of the older ladies remained jigging on the same spot indefinitely, their bosoms rising and falling with the rhythm, their faces devoid of expression other than that caused by the exertion of energy. Undoubtedly they were enjoying themselves immensely.

When the dancing had got under way, we returned to the wine and, as was normal at such times, the conversation lapsed into the wishful descriptions of what everybody was going to do once they had succeeded in tearing themselves away from the Arctic. Geordie was going to buy a chicken farm somewhere in Ontario. Two of the policemen were planning a descent upon the hula girls of the South Seas. Alan was going to remain to save money, as he hoped to get married before too long. The police sergeant had been a prisoner in one of the coldest parts of Germany during the First World War. Little had he thought then that he would afterwards be living in the Arctic of his own free will.

Gales of laughter from the kitchen drew us out to see what was going on. We found that Geordie, having got his piece about the chicken farm off his chest, had slipped out and was now jigging, like one of the old women, with a deadpan expression, up and down in the middle of the room, so we all joined in, each with our own interpretation of the dance, to the delight of the Eskimos, and in a few minutes even the elderly ladies were laughing.

I had not been used to the consumption of strong drink, even of the limited alcoholic content of the wine, and what with the heat of the room, together with all the jigging and noise, I felt the need to slip outside and lean on a big rock in the fresh air, in order to preserve my dinner. Afterwards, I went back into the room furthest away from the noise, to sit quietly, and Beevee came to join me, telling me about the real Eskimo drum dances or songs. I was deriving an unexpected bonus from the interest

I had shown in the Innuit language and affairs. People were keen to tell me about their customs.

I did not understand all that Beevee said that night, but years later I saw both the dances and the songs performed. The drum song in particular was a traditional entertainment of the Eskimo people, varying from district to district but with a basic similarity common to all. Many hunters frequently made up a series of songs which would then belong to them alone. These consisted mostly of a recitative against a rhythmic background, but the key to the type of song lay in the rhythm and chorus.

A hunter sometimes sang a song commemorating some great deed of his own bravery. At one song session that I attended, the people all used the same drum, made in this case from deerskin parchment, pulled across a circular frame of whalebone. The singing was held in a large sealskin tent, the oldest inhabitant being the first to strike up.

He was really past it, mumbling into his beard as though he had indigestion. I hadn't the faintest idea what he was supposed to be telling us. The rest of them knew, since these songs, like our own stories, were repeated fairly often, and they egged him on with frequent promptings whenever he faltered. They were really just showing their respect and affection for an old hunter who had led a long and useful community life. Not for the first time, I felt that here were people without my initial advantages, showing a generosity of spirit which I lacked.

Later on, the chief hunter of the camp got up to give his song. It went something like this:

> It cannot be helped
> That the seals do not come to me,
> Though I stand many hours waiting,
> My rifle is too crooked,
> While my spears have no point . . .

This sort of self-depreciation is quite common. Another version of this type of song might tell how a hunter has had to beg food for himself and his family, whereas of course he is the one who is likely to feed the others. This is quite understood by the listeners, and the further he can distort the truth the more the song is appreciated. Occasionally, he will sing a 'straight' song describing a long, difficult journey from the past.

The people were not above poking hearty fun at the strangers from the south, who often adopted a patronizing tone towards them, little realizing that their oddities of appearance and behaviour were quickly noted, and might be recorded for posterity in a drum song:

> She opens her mouth like
> A fish out of water
> To show off her tooth
> Like a walrus tusk . . .

Sex, of course, has never been a neglected subject in this type of entertainment, though this applies more to the dances rather than to the songs. When they really got going little was left to the imagination. The singer steps out into the ring of people, in fact eagerly, but protesting his own inadequacy in the manner expected:

> I am the poorest drummer in the camp.
> I have no song that the people wish to hear.
> My memory is so bad that I can think of nothing.

He taps his drum once or twice, the people shout and suddenly he has begun. He starts slowly, beating the drum steadily. The women's chorus sways backward and forward, chanting whenever the man stops at the end of a verse.

> Aiyah . . . Aiyah . . . Ayiah . . . Ayiah . . .

The man quickens his tempo. The women chant more loudly in the flickering light of the oil lamps, their voices rising to a crescendo as the drum beats become more intense and wild and the man, oblivious to his surroundings, flings himself from side to side in a sort of trance, abandoning himself to the raw rhythm. Then he gradually comes back to reality, slowing down his song, quieting the chanting and finishing with a few soft taps on the drum. If he has excited his friends, before he has time to sit down they will start to sing another of his 'songs' and he has to go through the whole process again. Another will then follow him and the drums beat and the women chant throughout the night with unabated passion.

*

So slowly did the snow melt during the weeks of spring, that it sometimes seemed that the fresh falls might start before the old drifts had gone. The levels must have been sinking all the time, but somehow, after quite a hot day, there was little obvious change, while at night there would be a hard frost, consolidating where the sun had softened the snow. Then, quite suddenly, we would hear water running under the drift. A trickle began to appear on the river ice, soon broadening into a stream, which gushed quickly through a narrow, restricted course, carving out strange shapes along the banks and in the bends and crooks of the river. The flow then increased to a torrent fed from the melting snows above, throbbing and pounding with life after the deadness of winter.

Sometimes, later in the spring, a southerly gale would blow up from the mainland, streaming from the barren hills of the remote Canadian northland above Ungava Bay down to the deserted bays and inlets along the coastline. Funnelling through the valleys and gullies, it would gather strength to burst across the still frozen straits before scattering at random among our arctic islands. With such a wind, the faint scents of the southern summer came to us. A whiff of spruce and pine. A slight, tantalizing tang of smoke from the fires of the faraway timberlands.

The mildness of the air started new, twisting streamlets down towards the fiord, crumbling still further the already rotting ice, until it looked as though the winter covering was held together only by narrow bands and strips criss-crossing the surface like some huge pattern of lace, and the whole fiord became a dirty mess after the stiff white drift of the winter.

By this time of year, all the fresh food stored for the winter had gone, so we had to rely upon our stock of tinned foods to see us through until we could take to the water once more. Before the ice had cleared from the fiord, we welcomed the first birds' eggs.

Around the shoreline of Cumberland Gulf, apart from the many inlets, bays and fiords, there were hundreds of islands of all shapes and sizes. Gulls, terns and ducks laid eggs in their thousands on these islands, so we were able not only to vary our immediate diet, but also to put down a barrelful to keep us supplied until the *Nascopie* returned.

Soon after a supply of eggs had been collected, the fish started to move down from the lakes to the sea and on to our menu. The salmon-like arctic char were not at their best until they had been in the salt water for a while, revitalizing themselves following a rather stagnant winter on the bottom of the lakes. Later on, we fitted up a small shed to smoke suitable fish, using the aromatic moss which grew on the hills. A primitive arrangement, it consisted of racks from which the cleaned, split fish could be hung. Holes were drilled at the top of the shed to let out the smoke. Underneath the racks we started a small fire, covering it with the gathered moss to smoulder and flavour the fish. The result, cooked slowly in dissolved milk powder and eaten under a midnight sun, made the trials of winter seem well worth while.

The river increased its spate, tearing at the sides where the ice still held, bursting down to pour over the sea ice now retreating from the mouth. On the land, the under-surface streams sucked away at the snow. Little patches of earth appeared, gradually widening until at last only the drifts on the shaded slopes were left. The sea ice held on tenaciously, usually until a strong north-east wind broke the pans away from the shore, and carried the crumbling blocks off towards the gulf. We often saw large seals taking advantage of the moving ice to travel away from the fiord, no doubt aware that, at least for the time being, they were beyond the reach of any hunter.

One quiet afternoon in late July, our peaceful skies reverberated to the unaccustomed, frightening sound of an approaching aircraft, the first ever to come to our fiord. A boy came rushing into our house, so overcome that he could hardly speak, waving his arms up in the direction of the sky. We rushed out on to a large flat rock, which gave us the best viewpoint. People soon gathered around to see what was afoot.

We had had supplies landed the previous year for the Oxford Arctic Air Route Exploration Society, an outfit who had also written to say that they might be coming over from their headquarters in Greenland and would we hold their equipment until they arrived. We naturally assumed that this would be their machine and we mentally adjusted, as far as possible, so as not to appear totally backward.

The Eskimos gazed up into the sky with amazement. Beevee appeared quite dumbfounded, which surprised me, until he later told me that he had been unable to understand how anything could fly through the air without flapping its wings. As the thing came nearer, the noise became very loud. One or two of the women did not like it at all, put their hands to their ears and would probably have run off, had we not all stood our ground.

The aircraft descended to just above the fiord. We could see that it was short and squat, with large pontoons for landing on the water, giving it the appearance of an outsize bird. The fliers brought their machine roaring over our heads, almost sweeping us off the rock, before turning back to come down smoothly in the centre of the fiord and taxi quietly to an anchorage just below us.

There was a general scramble down the slope to obtain a satisfactory vantage point from which to study the arrivals. Geordie was making a visible effort to brace himself for the meeting with the university men, when the lanky pilot swung himself out of the cockpit to shout, 'Howdy folks!' in a broad American accent.

He told us that he and his companion had come up from Chicago. They were attempting to fly this machine to Europe, at their own risk, to make the first flight by way of the arctic islands, using whatever fuel they could pick up *en route*. The depression had robbed them of their jobs as engineers, so they had set off on this desperate venture. They were as carefree a couple of fellows as ever could literally have dropped out of the sky on to a far-away trading post. They gave us one of our most entertaining evenings of the whole year, regaling us with wild stories of Prohibition Chicago in the gangster-ridden years of the late 1920s.

The two men had nothing. They were down to their last half gallon of petrol, they were without food and their only hunting equipment was a .22 rifle. Had the weather been unfavourable, they could certainly never have reached us, and if they had had to come down on a lake in the middle of Baffin Island, they would never have been heard of again. Astonishingly, they appeared to have no foreknowledge as to the type of country over which they had planned to make their flight.

Their main consideration was whether we could give them enough fuel to get them over to Greenland. By collecting together all the available supplies of kerosene from the various establishments, we had just enough to fill their tanks.

The evening went too quickly. I tore myself away at about ten o'clock to write some letters for the Americans to take with them the next morning. What a surprise it would be for my family in New Zealand to get a letter out of the blue like this, when they were not expecting to hear from me for another two or three months. I was up all night, for having once started on my saga it was not easy to stop. Outside my window, the people were strolling about as though it were daytime, because only the clock said it was night. Except for a brief interlude, the sun shone right through until I laid my pen down at seven o'clock.

All hands turned out to assemble the fuel for the aviators. We rolled the nearly empty drums down the slope to pump the contents out into handier containers. There was a tank in either wing I believe, and I remember one of the Americans, a very tall fellow, standing with legs outstretched, taking the cans as they were pushed up towards him, as though they were glasses of water, then handing them on to his friend, who poured the contents carefully into the tanks. Everybody pressed round, trying to be helpful, though most of us probably just got in the way.

When the refuelling was completed, the two men came ashore to say goodbye. I handed over my letters, together with some old currency which I hoped would buy the stamps needed wherever they landed. They had told us that they had no money but thought that, once they arrived in Europe, the people who owned the aircraft would stake them.

The airmen climbed back into their machine. There was a

roar and a blast, water sprayed up on to the beach where we were standing. The craft turned slowly round to face out towards the straits before taxiing away from us. A hand appeared from somewhere to wave a final farewell, then the engine revved up, our visitors began their run down the fiord and very soon they were in the air, disappearing rapidly in the direction of Davis Straits and Greenland.

Two years later, one of the letters that I wrote that summer's evening came back to me, sent from God knew where, with a note to say that it had been picked up with some others in an oilskin wallet by some Danish fishermen. They had been working somewhere in Denmark Strait, between Iceland and Greenland, when the package appeared unexpectedly in one of their nets.

No trace of the aircraft was ever found and this little wallet of letters was the only clue as to whereabouts the disaster, which must have threatened all the way up from the Great Lakes, finally engulfed the travellers.

*

After the departure of the airmen, we settled back once more into the routine of daily life. There were several projects in hand. The buildings all had to be painted at regular intervals, which meant work on a couple of them each year. The pathways connecting the store buildings and the house were picked out with lines of stones which were whitewashed annually. This year we had become rather more ambitious, extending the path right down to the blubber sheds, which meant quite a lot more work. Inside the dwelling house, too, there were decorations to be brightened up and essential repairs to be carried out.

The seal nets were put out at the head of the fiord, and Alan and I went net fishing one evening just below the post. We took a fine net mesh over the reef and operated just below the rocks.

During the time it took for the tide to go out and come back in again about half-way, we caught about three hundred fish. Some of these we distributed round the camp, some we salted, some we smoked and the rest we ate ourselves or used for dog food.

Gradually, our thoughts and conversation turned almost exclusively to the forthcoming arrival of the supply ship. There were endless combinations of possibilities, for the ship did not always follow the same itinerary. The faintest chance did exist that they might decide to come north first before going into the bay. This never did happen while I was in the country, but it had to be considered, as indeed did the awful thought that the vessel might not one year be able to force a passage through the ice, as had been known to happen.

The days grew shorter as all the summer tasks were completed. The caches were filled once more with the winter dog food. We put up a good stock of smoked and salted fish. There was fat and to spare for the people's lamps to burn through the winter. The ptarmigan were plump and tasty now and there were reports of deer grazing in the area where Kilabuk and Beevee had taken me for my first arctic expedition.

One weekend we had a big storm, warning us that the fall was almost upon us. We began to be anxious that the ship might not be coming at all.

Then, on a fine September afternoon, I went up by myself to the top of the hill behind the post, hunting ptarmigan. It was a fair climb, but there was a good stretch of plateau on top where the walking was quite easy. I saw no birds, but strolled about for a while, enjoying the view over the gulf and towards the fiords and inlets. Then, far out to sea straight ahead of me, a plume of smoke suddenly rose up into the sky, seemingly from nowhere. The obvious truth did not dawn on me until a black dot appeared, pinpointing the distant merging of the blue sky with the grey sea, while another puff of black smoke belched upward. I shouted, although it didn't seem likely that anyone would hear me from the top of this hill, '*Umiakjuak* ... The Ship ... *Umiakjuak* ...' and a few seconds later the cry was taken up by many voices below. '*Umiakjuak* ... *Umiakjuak* ... *Umiakju aaaa ak.*'

I slithered and fell rather than climbed down the hill slope to prepare for my first ship-time.

Out came the suits and sports coats. I pulled my case up from under the bed to get out the attire which had caused our spiteful neighbour to sneer at my 'colonial' appearance. Somehow, after their long stay in the box, the clothes did not hang very well. The collar of my shirt did not fit properly and the tie kept trying to work its way round under my ears. Geordie, though perfectly sober, made little concession to civilization, simply adding his ridiculous hat to his normal get-up. As we set off happily down the bank to our motor boat, intent on greeting the little ship, the anchor chain was already rattling down into the waters of our fiord.

Time was never wasted by the crew of the *Nascopie*. Once the anchor had taken hold, down went the gangway so that, within minutes, we were aboard. Geordie went straight off with George Watson, the new district manager, to tell him about the year's trading, while Alan and I wandered off to a favourite spot on the old ship, a long settee built into the bulkhead at the top of the main companion-way, where we found no lack of willing talkers to bring us up to date with all the latest northern gossip.

Strangely enough, world affairs, though certainly historic enough over the previous year, took only a secondary place. Perhaps we had been so long detached from the world at large that we felt the year's events did not concern us, in which view we were gravely mistaken. The Hudson's Bay Company were aware of the tendency of the northern traders to withdraw from the outside world and did their best to counteract it. One long, rather coffin-like box which came ashore contained one whole year's editions of the *New York Herald Tribune*, which I first dismissed as being of no interest. Picking up a copy to idly scan the advertisements, however, I soon found myself getting down to reading the whole paper from front to back, finally even sorting the issues into chronological order to make for continuity of reading.

Naturally, my interest centred chiefly on the box marked 'mail', which some thoughtful person soon looked out for us. But before we went ashore again, we had a meal served on a starched linen tablecloth by a white-coated steward. There was chicken and bread sauce, fresh potatoes and not quite so fresh peas. There was real cream with the sweet, too. We were sharply jolted back to reality by the arrival of a messenger, before digestion had been properly completed, to say that unloading had commenced: the first scowload was ready to depart shoreward and if we wished to check our goods ashore, we best delay no longer.

Once unloading began, there was the usual hectic rush of goods coming pell-mell off the scow, but the pressure was not quite so fierce as it had been the previous year. There had been no last-minute additions to the captain's itinerary, nor did any large quantity of building materials have to be brought ashore. In fact there was a lull during low tide after lunch the next day. The people of Pangnirtung were welcomed aboard the ship as usual. There were the usual shouting matches indulged in when the European attempts to converse with those who do not understand his language. The Eskimos beamed at the visitors, unable to comprehend what they were saying, but smiling happily, thereby confirming the ship people in the erroneous belief that the arctic inhabitants were simple and childlike. Tea and biscuits were served, while children scrambled for the sweets graciously tossed down to them by the captain. Afterwards came the film show, cartoons and the promise of free smokes. Every available boat in the place, filled with men, women and children, headed for the ship for the people to climb aboard and take part in the fun. No matter how worn and scratched the films were, they were all greeted with roars of laughter and approval.

Meanwhile, Alan and I slipped ashore to read our mail in the now quiet post house. My mother had written her letter in an exercise book, filling in little details as events occurred, rather than waiting for the mailing date before writing a long letter. I read of their encounter with the notorious Bay of Biscay, of the storms of the Atlantic, of the day-long tropical sunshine of the Pacific Ocean as they steamed south of Panama, of the flying fish and the palm trees and the orange groves of the South Sea islands. Now and then there was a hint of her sadness that I had not gone with them in search of a new life. I looked at the dingy walls of my room, then at the home-made washstand, and a tear or two trickled down my face as I felt the remoteness of it all from my family and the events about which I was reading.

They had not found life easy. The depression had hit New Zealand, as it had hit other agricultural countries, with great severity. Many of the farms were kept going only under the strict control of the banks, who would sanction only the purchase of absolute necessities. There was no money to provide work for people coming from overseas. Anyone who did get hired had to give very long hours for very little money. So it was with the jobs that my mother and sister had taken in Wellington. It was not until the end of the diary that a note of acceptance of the life they had found began to creep into the letter. The latest of mother's news was already several months old, and a sense of real isolation came over me with the thought that there would now be complete silence for another whole year.

Before I had come to the end of the letter, the scows were creeping in with the new tide, so my mail had to be put aside to be read later. Now that he had given everyone a break, the captain was going to waste no more time. No doubt he had the thought of the Labrador coast and the fall gales in mind.

The clouds were rolling up to mingle with the black smoke pouring from the funnel of the *Nascopie* as the scows were taken back on board ready for departure. It was a dark and starless night and a brisk wind was blowing as we came down the gangway for the last time to the sound of the sea slapping against the ship's steel plates.

Almost before we had cast off, the propeller was churning the sea astern of the vessel and the skipper manoeuvring to head out of the fiord. As Kilabuk started up the engine, there was a blast from the siren, a shout from the deck above us and by the time we had crossed the reef, the *Nascopie* had disappeared into the darkness. Only the wind, blowing the smoke from her funnel back into our faces, could tell us whither she had gone.

VI

THE DAILY PROBLEMS of our arctic home were those of wind and weather, sickness or misfortune among the people, and the settlement of an occasional dispute. There was an ease about the routine that could never have been part of life in the world outside. One did not have to rush for transport to reach an office by a deadline, nor check the observance of convention in one's attire. Each season had a fascination of its own, only the winter lasting long enough to drag into a tedium which made the spring seem extra welcome.

During my first year, I often wondered whether my sudden decision to come up into this wilderness had not been a mistake. Perhaps, after all, I should have joined the others and gone to chase sheep around the wide green acres of New Zealand, where there would have been fewer opportunities for me to make the near fatal blunders which rather overshadowed my early days of apprenticeship. And yet it was possibly these foolish mistakes that concentrated my mind on a determined course towards becoming a competent hunter, traveller and trader. In time, the difficulties began to drop behind me, so that by my third year I could talk quite fluently with the Eskimos and no longer fell through holes in the ice or slipped out on to cliff faces. The dog whip no longer held any mysteries, and by looking round the horizon I could make a reasonably accurate forecast of the weather conditions for the day.

We developed a kind of resistance against the imagined city life and a vague resentment at the intrusion of the office managers, so that while we welcomed the ship's arrival, we were not sorry to see it depart again. To some people it was astonishing that anyone could contemplate life in such a place. Taking passage on the *Nascopie* on the occasion of my third ship-time was a naval commander availing himself of one of the arctic tours offered by the Hudson's Bay Company. He was a typical grizzled navy type, who paced round the deck, even while the ship was at anchor, with his body braced as though the vessel were listing in a heavy sea. He buttonholed me one morning just as I had come up the gangway leading to the dining saloon.

'How long have you been here?' he asked me.

'Three years,' I replied.

'Are you staying much longer?' he inquired.

'Well, my contract is for five years,' I said.

'Not worth the paper it's written on,' he snapped.

'Oh, the company would take me out if I wanted to go.'

'Wasting your time, young man. Just wasting your time. All right for a couple of years. Something to tell your friends about. You'll never get anywhere in a god-forsaken country like this.'

'Well, I mightn't get anywhere sitting at a desk all my life. That's what seems to happen to most people and I don't suppose that they really like that very much.'

'Maybe they don't all make the grade,' he barked at me, 'but they are alive, they've got other people to talk to and places to go. They know what's going on. This is a hideaway, that's all. A hideaway!' and the commander, in true naval fashion, did a smart about-turn, assumed a list of thirty degrees to port and marched off.

This was the first time that anyone had really queried my career prospects as a trader. My own doubts had been more concerned with my ability to survive than about the prospects of a trader's life. I had not yet begun to consider whether a training in hunting, boating, sledging, two-finger typewriting, elementary bookkeeping, and a knowledge of a remote language and people, would ever have anything more than an interest value. At the time, I dismissed the conversation as soon as I had left the ship, but it was to return to my mind in days to come, bringing me to a state of doubt and indecision. To this day, if I close my eyes, I can see the solid figure of the commander standing before me, barking out his advice before pacing off for his morning exercise.

Our naval visitor was right about the isolation of our home. During the early 1930s, for nine months of the year, the winter closed like a curtain around Baffin Island. A shelf of ice, reaching several miles out to sea, barred the approaches, so that from early October to late June all communication ceased completely.

There were no radio transmitters on the island, nor any aircraft or helicopters to link us with the south. The motor boats we used for summer hunting were not suitable for travel on the open sea in the conditions to be expected up there, and were used for local hunting or coastal travel. Winter movement required much thought and preparation, if any great distance was to be covered. Once the snow had fallen and the ice formed, we became dependent upon the dog teams for any expedition of more than a few miles. A well-cared-for team could pull a sledge thirty or forty miles under normal conditions, but allowance had to be made for days of unsatisfactory progress or slow going. Indifferent weather might halve the distance covered or, if things got really bad, halt progress altogether.

Our most distant camps were a good journey of several days from the post. These hunters did not normally bring in their furs until the longer days of early spring, when the main trapping season was over, and we did not usually expect to see them before that time. One year a message somehow reached us to say that the hunters' dogs had died from a sickness of some kind and the snow had been too soft for them to hunt properly for many weeks. Men, women and children were starving, the report said. They could not survive much longer without help.

Preparations were put in hand immediately. It was decided that I should go with Beevee to give what assistance we could. Kilabuk went off with a good load of dog food to establish a cache as far away as possible, so that more space could be devoted to the carrying of the relief supplies when we set off. We heard that the missionary was also planning to help the stricken camp, so, thinking we might coordinate our efforts, I went up to see him. Much to my surprise I found that he was already prepared for departure, travelling light to make greater speed and disdaining any cooperation. Presumably the Lord would provide.

We loaded our sledge carefully with seal fat, paraffin in two containers, biscuits, soup concentrates, milk powder, some medicines and as much ordinary food as we could carry.

With some misgivings as to the adequacy of our outfit, should conditions be as bad as the report had indicated, we set off, heading up the fiord in the direction of our trapping camp. By working hard ourselves, running, pushing and helping the dogs in every possible way, we made good time. We fed the team from the cache established for the trapping season, which was not yet empty, then followed in Kilabuk's trail as far as we could before camping for the night.

Kilabuk passed us on his return trip on our third day out. He told us that he had dropped his load off right up on the height of the land. Now he was hoping to rattle home at top speed. We all had a mug of tea and discussed the situation for a few minutes before going our separate ways.

Beevee was concerned about the probability of soft snow

down the river gulley which we would normally have used. He knew this area quite well because he had lived not far away in his youth. Conditions would almost certainly deteriorate once we started to go down the river, for, in his experience, if the going was bad down on the coastal flat, as we had been told, the snow would also be deep and soft a long way up the river course.

There was an alternative route. By swinging north now, a day's travel would bring us to another gulley, where we might find things more in our favour. The prevailing wind of winter blew down this way and the snow was seldom really soft, which gave us much more hope of bringing our supplies within a short distance of the camp. It would mean adding a day to our travelling time, but if we were less likely to get stuck while still a long way from our destination, there was no doubt that it was the route we should take.

We swung out of the gulley into a defile which headed us north towards the other river. Somebody's good spirit must have been watching over us, for after an hour or so we noticed that the dogs showed a great inclination to head up the bank on our left. We stopped the team and climbed cautiously up on to the plateau. Not far from us, scrabbling in the snow for moss and grass, was a herd of caribou. Such wind as there was came straight from them to us, so there was no danger of them becoming alarmed by scenting our presence.

We retired beneath the bank quietly to discuss our tactics. There was little point in trying to use the dogs for the hunt. We should do better to move up the defile ourselves, until we were abreast of the herd, then crawl over the bank to come as close as we could without alarming the deer and secure as many as possible.

The luck which had so seldom come my way in the past was really on our side this time. When we pushed our heads over the bank, to our amazement the herd had moved quite significantly in our direction and were well within range. We shot seven of them. We could have had more, but felt this was as many as we could handle. The dogs came up as fast as they could when they heard the rifle fire. Although it meant slowing us down for the rest of the day, we fed the dogs immediately with the warm entrails. A hot meal was exactly what they needed to keep them in shape, and from what we had heard, quite a few people depended upon this team being in good condition.

We travelled on a short distance before building our snow-house. We had a really heavy load now, for we had brought three deer with us. I felt that since things seemed to be going our way, we could afford to take a few chances which might make all the difference to the unfortunate camp.

The next morning we came out of the defile into the gulley which we were to follow downward. At every turn, we half expected the soft snow we were dreading. A long way down, we followed the river course through a sharp westward bend and shortly afterwards we ran into deeper snow, which worsened after a mile or two until we could hardly move the sledge at all and we came reluctantly to the conclusion that we should have to dump part of our load.

We climbed to the top of a hillock to see what lay in front of us. The long coastal flat stretched up to the river on the far side, the one down which we had decided not to travel. In the middle of the flat, but nearer to the sea than to the hills, was a mound of earth, somewhat resembling the hump of a camel, with a very large black rock poised perilously on the top. Apart from this rock, the whole plain was one huge, lifeless expanse of whiteness. In the distance, on a shelf of land slightly above the level of the flat, a patch of messy snow with the slightly blurry outline of several winter homes indicated the location of the camp we were seeking.

The silence was profound. Even the ice blocks seemed to have reached a final settlement on the floor of the reef, for there was no sound of the restless creaking normal to the quietest shores. A feeling of alarm began to creep over me. There was a deadness here which I had never encountered before. Was it possible that our relief expedition was already too late?

Beevee had been viewing the outlook from a different angle. He said that although it would be best for us to cache some of our meat up here, he thought that the snow would be less heavy when we came out of the river trough. We should have to work hard for a little while longer, then things would ease, so that there was no reason why we should not take most of the supplies right up to the people's homes.

We came up to the settlement quietly. There were a few dogs about, mostly at the far end of the camp. They did not howl to greet our arrival. Perhaps the general lifelessness of the place had affected them, or perhaps, if they were the missionary's dogs, they were too exhausted to show any interest. Now that we had arrived, Beevee revealed that he too was apprehensive as to what we might find in these homes. He stood aside so that I should be the first to enter.

With some trepidation, I went into what seemed to be the largest home, pausing in the porch for my eyes to become accustomed to the darkness after the whiteness outside. There were two long bundles wrapped and sewn in old sealskins down one side of the porch. They were each about the size of a person and there was little doubt as to what they were. Steeling myself to cope with whatever dreadful sight was about to confront me, I went on into the interior. There was a candle flickering at the far end of the sleeping platform, giving enough light for me to make out the features of our missionary, who was lying back against a box with his legs stretched out in front of him. He looked a very different person from the one who had so readily refused our cooperation a few days previously. He said, waving a hand dejectedly towards his feet, 'I hurt my ankle on the way in. I can't walk yet. These people are in a bad way. There are two bodies in the porch.'

There were four other people on the platform. Two, a man and a woman, covered with deerskins except for their heads, showed no sign of animation. Next to them on the far side a girl was kneeling. I caught a glimpse of her face in the flicker of the candle. Her hair had been cut short, but unevenly so that it was all at different lengths. Her face was thin and starved looking, but her eyes were clear, seeming too large for her emaciated face. She looked hard at me, as though wondering whether I should be able to understand her if she spoke.

She must have decided favourably and said, 'I am the only one able to move about here. My brother and my aunt are both dead. We have not been able to bury them yet. The dogs are dead, they died of an illness before the snow came. The men walked out to the seal holes for a while, but when the snow came without the wind, they were no longer able to do this. We had no food until the other white man came, but he did not bring much. My name is Keeta, who are you?'

'I am from the trading post. We have brought food and oil because we had heard of the bad things that had been happening to you.'

Beevee came in just then and the girl asked him if I was the one the people called 'the boy' and whether we had brought enough food for everybody, but before he had time to answer a voice came from a corner at the back of the platform. It said, 'Akpak has told me that the seals do not come to the holes any more and that the deer have gone many miles up into the hills . . .' The voice petered out into a long, mournful groan, then continued, 'Why does it not come out now that I have cut the way open?'

The agonizing groans continued. I looked at the girl.

'That is my grandfather,' she said. 'His leg became very swollen and painful. He cut himself with his knife, so that whatever was inside could come out. This was several days ago, but the pain has become worse and he talks much about things that are in the past.'

I began to feel totally inadequate. This was only the first home and already there were two dead bodies, two quite inanimate people, one probable case of severe blood poisoning and a damaged ankle. Thinking about the ankle reminded me that I had not so far spoken to the missionary.

'Sorry to hear about your injury. I hope it is not too painful. We have some cloth we can tear up to make a bandage.'

I could not think of anything else to say. His ankle seemed unimportant.

After the initial despondency, my mind began to function again. The dead we could not help, but those that were still living stood a good chance now that we were here with a stock of fresh meat. Fortune had favoured us so far. We must not lose heart. I decided we should first give everybody still able to eat a small hot meal. Then we might have a chance of convincing them that they were not going to die after all. By now their natural fatalism would have brought them to such a state of resignation that death would seem the only outcome.

I was thankful that the girl, Keeta, appeared to be in a reasonable state. She was evidently a survivor and I decided to use her as an assistant. As a person who was well acquainted with all the people of the camps, she would be invaluable in our dealings with the various families.

Beevee and I went round all the homes we could see. The situation was pretty serious. We were going to need a largish snowhouse to use as a centre – for us to live in, but also for communal cooking and to provide warmth for those that were able to move, at least until we could get some heat into their own homes. With our fresh dogs it was vital that we should as soon as possible organize a seal hunt with the two or three hunters still on their feet. Obviously we should also have to go back for the rest of our load.

Two of the men helped Beevee to put up a good-sized snow-house while I cut up some material to make a tight bandage for the minister's ankle. He refused our offer of immediate food, saying that he would not eat until the people had been fed, so the preparation of a meal became our top priority.

Our snowhouse was basic, for we did not bother about making platforms or any fancy touches. We threw deerskins over the floor, gave Keeta our oil lamp with enough seal fat to get things going, and fixed a line above, so that we could hang a cooking pot in the flame. Meanwhile I lit our Primuses and before long our preparations were well under way. I sent the girl round the camp to tell everyone who was able to move to come to our place bringing utensils with them. They would have their meal, but should bring with them a container of some kind to take away meals for those not able to come. They must look after their own people. They should let me know about anyone who was ill as we did not want anyone else to die unnecessarily.

Keeta went off while Beevee and I assessed the situation. We had enough food for the time being, but our stock of seal fat would not stretch very far, as it was going to be essential to get sick people warmed up as soon as we could.

Those hunters that were still up and about were pretty shaky, but we could not delay the seal hunt. Weather permitting, Beevee would have to go out with them the next morning, preferably to the floe edge where there was more chance of a reasonable hunt.

Six or seven men and women came up to our snowhouse.

We had cooked a big potful of deer stew over the oil lamp, with additional small stews in pans heated over the Primuses. We fed all the people in the house first, giving each of them a cupful of hot deer broth and one biscuit each. The people then went off to feed the sick, while Keeta took what remained in the big pot for her relatives and for the missionary, who would now probably consent to partake. After we had eaten our own food, Beevee came round the houses with me to dole out shares of our seal fat, so that each home would have at least one lamp going for long enough to cheer things up a bit.

We got into our sleeping bags satisfied that we had done everything possible as a first step towards the revival of the camp.

Next morning, we cooked a larger stew, having borrowed another big pot from one of the homes. We gave out rather larger portions than the night before, as no one had complained of pains after their last meal. The biscuits were still limited to one each as our supply was not inexhaustible. Three of the hunters elected to go out with Beevee to the floe edge while our dogs were still fit and frisky, and it was time for me to do something about the sick people.

So far, I had not brought out my first-aid kit, which was quite comprehensive, including a range of medicines as well as bandages, a thermometer, iodine and the like. The moment had now come to admit that starvation was not the only malady from which the people were suffering. The people who were ill appeared to have developed a chronic tubercular condition, brought about by the lack of nutrition and the cold. I was under no illusion as to the medical effectiveness of my ministrations. It would have taken a miracle actually to cure them, but there was no doubt that they had some faith in me. The thing that would help them more than anything else would be for me to appear confident of my own ability.

One man was going downhill. Keeta's grandfather was now

in constant pain, his thigh and groin were terribly inflamed and the perspiration was pouring off his forehead. He could eat nothing. I told his relations, who were now beginning to show the first signs of animation, that what the old man had done by cutting himself like that was to let a lot of devils in rather than letting the old ones out, and that he was not beyond my help, though indeed he was.

The missionary's ankle had improved overnight. He thought he might be able to hobble about very soon. We agreed that the burial of the dead should be left until he was mobile. He seemed a different man from the previous day and it was largely his efforts that galvanized the previously lifeless pair still lying on the platform into some slight awareness.

Keeta followed me back to our large snowhouse, when I went over to replenish my supply of food. She seemed ill at ease. She was a vital part of my present arrangements, so it was necessary to find out what was wrong.

'What's the matter, Keeta?' I said. 'I can't help it about your grandfather, he shouldn't have cut himself like that with a dirty old knife.'

'I know,' she said quickly, 'I understand about that. He's an old man and would not live much longer.' She became silent, as though not knowing what to say next.

'What is it then, have you given someone too much food?'

'No. There is something which I should have told you about yesterday, but the *angekok* told me not to speak about it. I do not wish you to become angry with me.'

'The *angekok*?' I was puzzled as to what it was the missionary did not want her to tell me.

'The *angekok* of the people, not the white man.'

This startled me. I knew that the shamans still operated on a limited basis, but had certainly not expected to find one dictating what I should or should not be told.

'Well, you'd better tell me what it is that the *angekok* does not want me to know.'

'There is another home that I did not take you to yesterday.'

'Where is it then? I went into all the houses.'

'No. There is another, under the cliff behind a rock, so that it cannot be seen from down here.'

'Did they not have any food yesterday, then?'

'I took them food, but I do not think that it will have been eaten.'

Expecting to find some trivial matter which would be easily overcome, I said, 'Come then, we will go over there now.'

Keeta led the way across the flat at the back of the homes until we came to a sealskin tent tucked away at the foot of the cliff. When we arrived at the entrance, the girl stood aside without speaking. I went in. The brightness of the day penetrated the scraped sealskins to a certain extent, so that there was a kind of yellowish light, but the place felt as though there had been no heating for many days. There was a slightly sickly smell about the home. Keeta followed me in and stood by the door.

A woman sat in the middle of the platform staring straight ahead, apparently quite oblivious to her surroundings or to our presence. The cup of soup which Keeta had brought over the previous day was on the ground in front of the platform untouched. I wondered vaguely why there was only one cup of soup, when there appeared to be three in the tent. For I could just see the hair and outline of two children lying one on each side of the woman. Something was wrong, but I could not make out what it was.

I had brought some of the broth over in a Thermos flask and now poured out a fresh mugful, handing it to the woman for her to drink. She ignored the mug. I said, 'We have come a long way to help you. It has not been easy. Will you not eat the food we have brought?'

There was no reply. I said to Keeta, 'She has not eaten the food you brought yesterday. She will not speak to me.'

Keeta said, 'Have you looked at the children?'

I looked hard at the platform again. I put out my hand to touch the head of the nearest child. The woman switched her gaze towards me. 'He will not harm you.'

'No,' I said. 'He won't harm me. He's dead, isn't he? Is the other one also dead?'

'Yes.'

The woman became silent again. A band of stronger light, penetrating a well-scraped piece of skin, fell across her face. She was quite young but had the same starved look as the others.

Keeta said, 'He has brought you some food. You must eat.'

'I do not wish to eat.'

'How did this happen?' I asked.

The woman's lips began to move, but no sound came out at first, then suddenly she started to talk loudly: 'The people said that it was because of my husband, who had no relatives here, that the dogs caught the sickness and died. It was said that an evil spirit came through my husband and caused the sickness.'

I looked at Keeta, who said, 'She and her husband were strangers here. They came in a small boat from a camp up the coast, but the *angekok* said that they were to leave again because they would only bring us harm. They could not go because of the weather. Then, when the dogs died, Padlu said that we were to have nothing to do with these people and they were not to be helped. In this way the sickness would end.'

'Where is the husband now?'

'He went away. Walked off one morning. This woman could not go with him because one of the children was not well. The *angekok* said that even though the woman was now alone, we were still not to help her, but I have brought her food and oil when I could, from my father's home.'

Realizing that at some stage I was going to have to confront the shaman, I said, 'The words spoken by the *angekok* were untrue. The sickness of the dogs is not caused by evil spirits, but comes from the foxes, who become ill when there are too many without enough food. From the foxes it spreads to the dogs. This we know because we had such an illness at our post last year.'

Keeta said, 'When the heavy snow came after nearly all the dogs had died, my father was not able to hunt. I could not bring food and the children died.'

'How long have they been dead?'

'A few days only.'

'Does the white *angekok* know about this?'

'Only that the children are dead. He has not been here because of his foot.'

I turned back to the woman and said, 'It has been very hard for you but you are young still, you will have more children. If you do not want to die, you must eat this food.'

Keeta said, 'My father will let you come and live in our home now that you are alone. In the spring perhaps you will be able to return to your family. Drink this soup now, Aiyah.'

The woman, Aiyah, took the mug of broth and began to sip hesitantly. I put a biscuit down beside her and Keeta brought out some seal fat from the sack she had with her, which she put beside the empty lamp.

She said, 'We will bring you some more meat later on. If you light your lamp, you will get warm and be able to cook your food. We must go now because we have others who need help.'

As we went round the homes, I realized that these people did have faith in my ability to work some sort of miracle on their behalf. The mere fact that we had appeared out of the blue like this to dole out seal fat and deer meat, when they did not even know that we had heard of the disaster that had befallen them, convinced the camp that their ills were about to be cured. After we had completed the morning round, I felt strong enough to tackle Padlu the *angekok*.

Walking across the snow to the house where the *angekok* lived, I reflected upon Geordie's dictum about not becoming involved with the Eskimos. Perhaps learning the language had been a mistake. If you could not talk to them, theirs would be a world you could not enter or expect to influence in any way other than the economic.

Yet, what might happen to this woman if someone did not speak up for her? The *angekok* was thin and emaciated like the others, but his wife was far worse than he was. She had been very low when we arrived and perhaps had not been able to tolerate the food we had given her. The poor woman was unable to keep even the broth down. Now she was very weak after vomiting during the night. Something had to be done or she would die. We were going to have one death, without any doubt. Keeta's grandfather was not going to pull through, but if we were to keep the revival of the camp going we must keep this woman alive.

I temporarily shelved my plan to give the *angekok* a sound dressing down and went back to our house to fetch a bottle of a kind of beef extract, part of our medicine-chest outfit, and a Primus stove to melt some ice and boil up the water.

The patient sipped the hot drink, very slowly but without any noticeably adverse effects. I told her husband that if he came with me, he could have some fat for his lamp and also some milk powder which I would show him how to mix up as a drink for his wife. As we walked across, I thought up a suitable line of attack. Inside our house, I said, 'I have heard that you told the people here that the man from Kevitou caused the illness from which the dogs died and that, because of this, none of them were to go into that house or help the family.'

Padlu looked taken aback, but not silenced. 'The ways of the people are not the ways of the white men. In this camp we believe as our fathers did before us. This may not be understood by those who come to our country for a short time only.' The *angekok* gave me a stern look, but perhaps remembering that he still needed our help, said no more.

I replied, 'Some of us may only be here for a short time as you say, but we have brought with us our own taboos, which must be obeyed by everyone no matter what their own ways are. It is not permitted to say things about others which are not true and which might cause harm. The things you said to stop your people from helping that family may have caused the children's deaths. The police would not like to hear this and they might come to take you away if they thought you were causing trouble.'

The man wilted visibly at the mention of the police. He said, 'The children died because the father went away.'

'He went away because of what you had said. Now listen carefully, Padlu, you are to tell the people of this camp that the woman, Aiyah, did not cause the dogs to die, nor is it her fault that the snow came and lay so deep. She is to be free to live where she chooses and anyone may help her. If she comes to harm, I shall have to tell the police about you and they will not be pleased.'

I dismissed him with a wave of the hand and he was out of the house almost before I had finished speaking.

Keeta came in to say that the old man was very much worse and was frightening the family with his wild talk. We went over to see him. He was in a dreadful state of agony and delirium. The only thing left in the medicine chest which had not been tried were the two bottles of painkiller. We got him to drink one of them and for a while he quietened. I tried to talk to him. By all accounts he had been a fine hunter in his day, but it was too late to communicate with him now. Although less restless, he had already withdrawn from reality. Keeta gave me a pageful of syllabic writing which he had written before he became so ill, but if this was meant to be a last message, I could not make any sense out of it nor could his family. We could only watch him drifting away from us. He died during the night.

As though to make up for the dreadful gloom of that day, Beevee and his companions returned late in the afternoon with four seals. They had fed our dogs and the missionary's team out on the ice, now they cut the meat and fat up to share it equally among the homes, with a fair portion for Aiyah.

The tide had really turned now. The fresh seal meat worked wonders for the morale of the camp. Hunters started coming into our house who had given themselves up for dead at the time of our arrival, thin and decidedly shaky but snatched back from the grave.

The missionary was now able to hobble short distances, so we were to collect the dead and bury them together. Keeta said that she would come with me to Aiyah's home and fetch the children, but though it would have made things easier to have had her with me, it did not seem fair to involve her in business which might result in her incurring the displeasures not only of the already ill-disposed *angekok*, but of others in the camp as well.

Bracing myself for this awful experience, I went alone into the silent tent. Aiyah sat motionless, staring intently at the tent door as though there was something that only she could see. She had put the skins ready but had not wrapped the bodies of her children. When I went over to make them ready for burial the tears began to trickle down her face, slowly at first, then more quickly, splashing down on to her hands as they lay on her lap. As I tended to the little girl, the boy's body rolled over as if he were stirring in his sleep and one arm fell across his sister's chest, perhaps in a last protective gesture against the danger of the spirit world. I wanted to say something reassuring to the desolate mother, but I couldn't speak, so busied myself wrapping the children into their skins together with the few possessions which Aiyah had put ready for them.

Outside, the faithful Keeta was waiting with a hand sledge and as I brought the bodies out she took charge of them, then helped me to drag our sad load over to the burial place, a large empty meat cache which we were to use as a communal grave.

The missionary joined us at the graveside to conduct a burial service in a proper Christian manner, but I afterwards noticed that someone had prised a stone loose at the far end so that the spirits of the dead would be free to come and go as they pleased.

The next expedition to the floe edge yielded five more seals. Beevee had already brought in the remainder of the deer meat which we had left just up the river. It seemed that everything started to go right at the same time, for as soon as we had a reasonably good supply of food and oil, a strong wind blew up, packing the snow down into a good travelling surface.

We planned to leave for home without delay. I had given four of our dogs to the camp and these animals, added to the few survivors they already had, would form a team of sorts for the remainder of the winter, which they could build up the following year.

Keeta came over before we left to tell us that her father had agreed that Aiyah should live with them, at least until the summer, when she would take any chance that might come to go back to her own home. She also told me that Padlu had held a meeting the night before during which he had told everyone that it was thanks to him that they had come out of this dreadful time, and that he could have managed it all without the white men.

The missionary too held a service in our snowhouse, at which he gave thanks to the Lord for having succoured them in their hour of need and brought so many of them through safely. It did seem to me that the Hudson's Bay Company might have come in for just a mention as having contributed in some way, but we got the best reward possible in the end. The camp turned out to salute our departure and, just as we were about to set off, Keeta came running over from where she was standing with Aiyah, to give me a little ivory carving wrapped round in sealskin. It was from her friend, she said, to thank the one who had come such a long way to help them.

PART TWO

Issumatak

VII

THE TIME HAD COME for Geordie to go for a holiday. He and Ooloo now had two children, a daughter having been born the previous winter, and their relationship seemed to have an air of permanence about it. Despite Geordie's party talk of starting a chicken farm down in Ontario, there was no doubt that he had settled in his mind for a long stay at Pangnirtung. Our manager was forty-six that year. He had formed no real ties anywhere else in the world, his only relative being a sister he had not seen for a long time, but there was every sign that he was much concerned about his children and possibly about Ooloo as well. Very likely, if it had been left to his own choice, he would not have taken a holiday at all, but the Hudson's Bay Company authorities did not approve of their employees becoming too much a part of the Innuit life, so insisted on regular visits to the outside world.

One day in the later summer, when we were expecting the ship to arrive at any moment, I was sitting at the table in the guardroom finishing off some bookwork when a furious altercation broke out in the kitchen.

This was of itself nothing unusual. Geordie and Ooloo frequently had noisy disputes which flared up, raged for while, then, as neither understood what the other was saying, died away again. I had never been asked to interpret what was actually said during the course of such exchanges, which was just as well, for while Geordie's remarks were the fairly normal expressions of an aggravated male, Ooloo's highly personal abuse ofted caused me to remove myself from earshot as soon as possible.

This time there was no escape. Ooloo rushed to the guard-room door and shouted at me to tell Geordie that she didn't care what he did or where he went.

There followed some very indiscreet comments on his abilities as a husband, but before she could go too far, I said, 'If you will speak more slowly and quietly, I shall be able to understand what you are saying,' thinking that this might defuse the situation somewhat. Unfortunately she started on me instead.

'I hear that you understood everything that girl Keeta said at Netilling. It is seen now that you prefer the women of the north to those here!'

This took the wind out of my sails completely. How on earth had this bit of malicious gossip reached the post? Beevee was no talker, nor was the man who drove the missionary's dogs. Then I realized that the clergyman had brought a young woman back with them to join her relatives on this side. Very probably the *angekok* had seen his chance to stir things up, so had made sure that the woman would have something to gossip about. I said with as much dignity as I could muster, 'Keeta was one of the few people with enough strength left to help. We could not do everything ourselves. What is it you are trying to tell me about Tooshinil?' – which was Geordie's Eskimo name.

Before she could answer Geordie broke in, 'What are you talking about now?' surmising that the conversation was drifting rather.

'She is being rude about me,' I answered, only too thankful that it would not be necessary to translate the earlier outburst.

Geordie thought that this was very funny and burst out laughing. Gradually the story came out. It seemed that they had been trying to discuss what Ooloo should do while the manager was away. He wanted her to move in with some friends during his absence and would give her a weekly allowance to be spent at the store. Ooloo was happy to accept the money, but she did not agree with the idea of moving out of the house. Why should she not remain where she was?

This was a collision point of two cultures. Geordie believed in monogamy, especially in the European fashion of that time, for women. Ooloo, on the other hand, while prepared to agree that a husband had certain rights of control over her activities, could not see why she could not, with his agreement, take up with another partner while he was away. As I had learned, this was quite an accepted procedure among her own people and had been for generations. The concept of a shared relationship was basic to the Innuit way of life as regards sexual matters and even the resulting children, but it had to be orderly, agreed and not promiscuous.

Fortunately, Geordie did not see the implications of Ooloo's desire to remain in the house, thinking probably that she just wished to be more comfortable.

It was obvious to me now what was in her mind. She considered herself to be the wife of a *kudloona*, therefore, if he was going away, she had every right to expect to be loaned, or even given, to another white man. Her angry remark about Keeta revealed quite clearly who it was she had selected for her next marital partner.

I knew Geordie was making his arrangements with the intention of seeing that she and the children would be cared for until his return. I could not tell him what Ooloo was really thinking. He would not have understood that she viewed the matter from a strictly logical standpoint: the relentless pressure of conditions had taught the Innuit that life was here and now, and that it was no use living for something that might happen in a year's time.

I told Ooloo that neither Alan or I would be permitted to keep her in the house as Geordie had done. Apart from that, it would not be right. Alan was going out to get married very shortly and I was expecting to be moved on. There was no truth in what she had heard about Keeta, who had simply been a very useful person in the difficult situation in which we had found ourselves. The women of Pangnirtung were as good as anyone. Something of this must have struck a chord, for she became silent and walked back into the kitchen. Geordie followed her and I heard the murmur of their voices start up again, though too faintly to be able to follow what they were saying.

The authorities dealt with Geordie's problem as sympathetically as they could. He had to go for a break, but they did promise that he should return the following year. Meanwhile, Alan was to take charge of the post and I was to be transferred and make the journey by dog team down to Ward Inlet at the top of Frobisher Bay in the early spring. I was also to call in at Blacklead Island, once a whaling station, later a company outpost, that had been abandoned, and shunned by the Eskimos, with a reputation of being haunted.

*

When I began to sort through my belongings before my departure there was not a great deal worth the trouble of such a long haul. The few clothes that had come with me were now in an advanced state of neglect. My 'colonial' outfit, which had been the pride and joy of my heart such a short time ago, had suffered badly from the years under my bed in the damp room. Practically the whole of the little outfit purchased with my £52 inheritance had to be abandoned, leaving me with less even than Jock Smith, my cabin mate on the first *Nascopie* trip.

Beevee was to be my travelling companion again, but this time we did not have to rush our preparations as we had had to do the previous year. There was time to make up a bagful of meatballs and Alan made us a good quantity of doughnuts and some biscuits.

At last all was ready, the boxes lashed on to the sledge while the dogs waited to dash down the hill with me for the last time. I was sad to be saying goodbye to my first northern home and to Alan, from whom I had learnt so much. He and Geordie must have had great patience to have put up with me so uncomplainingly for those years. I wondered if the three of us would ever meet together again and what would be the things we would remember if we did.

Beevee tapped the sledge with his whip, the dogs sprang up to rush forward for the first leg of the journey and we set off in fine style to the farewell shouts from the little company on the top of the bank. We were using the same large *komatik*, for besides my belongings and our own food, we had a pretty heavy load of dog food which was to last us as far down as Blacklead Island, where a break would be made for a seal hunt.

There had been a strong wind the previous week which had packed the snow into hard drifts so the going at this stage was excellent. The well-iced sledge slipped easily over the surface as we headed out of Pangnirtung fiord southward across the gulf, spending the day almost entirely on the sea ice on the way to our first overnight stop at Angmalik's camp on the far shore. It was a typical early spring day, the sun being visible, though the circle of false suns ringed round it, taken with the hazy sky, was not too promising an omen for the start of a long journey: somewhere along the line we were going to strike bad weather.

We made good progress that day, however, considering our

heavy load, and reached the camp just as darkness was falling.

Angmalik was one of the best hunters in the district, an alert and intelligent man. The conditions in his home bore testimony to his and his family's ability. The place was clean and tidy. The oil lamps burned brightly without smoking. The bed platform was covered with long-haired deerskins, while the women, perhaps expecting visitors, had put on their best parkas with cleverly worked patterns in greens, reds, blues and blacks using braid and beads.

It had been my intention to set up a separate establishment on the outskirts of the camp and to visit all the homes during the evening, but Angmalik's home looked so bright and attractive that I did not object when Beevee began to bring in our gear. There were no babies to share the pot with the stews either.

Beevee had caught a seal during the day's travel, which he now handed over to the lady of the house, who at once produced a large pot, very clean and shining, then cut the meat into chunks and in remarkably short time, considering that she only had the oil lamp to cook with, produced a stew of excellent quality. Her assistant at the other end of the platform took charge of the water for the tea.

It was amazing how many visitors called in while we were eating our meal. They all were invited to join us, but the meat gave out half-way through, so we produced our biscuits, which began to diminish rapidly, and another lot of tea had to be brewed. By the time the meal was finished, the home was full of people squatting wherever there was room. I thought they were being polite in bringing the conversation round to our trip to the starving camp the previous year, but despite my efforts to change the subject they kept veering back to it. They appeared to be fascinated with all the details and were obviously greatly impressed by the success of the venture. The Innuit do have a tendency to say what they think others wish to hear, but even allowing for that, there was no doubt that they gave not only the company but also Beevee and me a great deal of the credit for that rescue. Angmalik told me that my Eskimo name had been changed. Instead of 'Boy', it was now to be 'Issumatak', which meant 'one who thinks'. This was the name they would send down to Frobisher Bay with me.

The talk moved on to a discussion of the country ahead of us and the conditions we were likely to encounter, but my mind was still on the previous conversation. I took great pleasure in the realization that I had justified myself in their eyes and felt touched that my new title was bestowed as a farewell salute. Falling asleep at once, even the inevitable noise which must have accompanied my companions' slumbers failed to disturb me, a sure indication that I was graduating as a true northerner.

We had no visitors in the morning, but willing helpers had iced our sledge for us and put everything ready for loading, so as soon as we had rounded up the dogs we were ready to lash the last few items into place. A host of people came down to the ice with us for another lot of goodbyes, then off we went into the morning mist.

We stayed on the ice all day, but kept close to the land, almost at the edge of the barricade ice. The atmosphere was heavy. There was neither sun nor wind at the start so that it felt as though the weather had not quite decided what to do, keeping its options open until later in the day. In the event, the weather did not worsen for another two days and we were able to reach the next camp without mishap.

During the night of our arrival the wind got up, combining with the snow so that by morning there was a heavy blanket of drift – not quite a blizzard but certainly enough to keep all sensible travellers at home. The camp was one of those that had been passed over to the Pangnirtung post when the Blacklead

Island outpost closed down. As we did not know the people here very well as yet, I decided to visit round and introduce myself. During my first afternoon call I came across one of the most colourful Eskimo personalities that I was ever to meet.

She was an old, old woman, possibly of as much as eighty years, which was a really great age in those days, but she was in full possession of her faculties, quite at ease in dealing with white people and brimming over with memories of her youth. Her name was Tukulita and her face had more creases and lines than any I had previously seen. There was some sort of tattoo on her cheeks, though the pattern had nearly worn away, and there was great animation in her expression. She was clearly still able to look after a lamp, for the one in front of her was burning brightly.

The old lady began by telling me her name, spitting it out syllable by syllable, then, when she discovered that I could speak her language, she really got going. Probably her own people had long ago heard everything that she had to say, so it must have been a treat for her to find an audience interested enough to listen. There were many worse ways of spending a stormy winter afternoon.

Tukulita soon understood that I wanted to hear about their lives in the days before the coming of the white people, or at least before any of them came to live here. It would take far too much space and time to recount all that this old woman told me about the days of her youth, but one story about sickness and the people's attitudes to dying is worth repeating.

'Before the white men came to Blacklead Island,' she said, 'a ship from down there' – waving her hand in a vaguely southerly direction – 'was caught in the ice and had to spend the winter near an island on the other side of the bay. My father had his camp there and many of our people lived within a day's travel. That winter there was a woman at my father's camp who had the bleeding sickness very badly. The *angekok* said that her spirit had gone away, and though he tried everything he could think of, it would not come back again. There was nothing more to be done, so the woman's husband made her a snowhouse and moved her into it.'

'Did she have an oil lamp?' I asked.

'Yes, she had a lamp and some seal fat.'

'Did someone come to her snowhouse to keep the lamp going for her?'

Tukulita looked at me with astonishment, whether feigned or real I did not know, and said, 'The people left her in the house and moved to another camp.'

'With no one to look after her?'

'The dead do not require looking after. They care for themselves.'

'But you said that she was only ill, not dead.'

'She was already far gone from the people with the sickness. It could not be long before she was dead. The time had come for the camp to be shifted, for there was no more hunting to be done there. No good could come from taking her with us. There is not room enough on a sledge to take people in their beds.'

'Did she mind being left alone?'

'It was the way of the people. She knew this would happen.'

'So you never saw her again?'

'Yes, I did see her again. On the ship of which I have told you, there was a man who was not a missionary, but talked a lot about God. When he heard that we had moved camp and left this woman behind, he was very angry. My father tried to tell the man that she would be dead but he would not listen. He said that we must go and fetch her, for it was wicked to do such a thing and God would be angry with the Eskimo if they did not go back to her. My father agreed to go as the man was so angry, but hoped to be able to get away without doing so, for once away from the ship he need never return. Then the white man, seeing how unwilling my father was to go, said that he would go with him and it was agreed that I should accompany them, having been the woman's friend. This meant that my father would not have to enter the house of the dead, which was not a good thing for a hunter to do.'

'Did you find the woman still alive?' I asked.

But old Tukulita was going to tell the tale in her own way.

'The white man said that we would get off the next day, but there was a great storm which lasted many days. We could not travel until the storm was over.

'One morning the wind had gone. My father hoped that the white man would have forgotten about the woman, but no, for he came to tell us that we were to set off at once. We harnessed the dogs and the three of us travelled on one sledge. When we came to the place where we had been camped, we found that the snow had drifted over the houses so that they were buried beneath the drift and could not be seen.'

The old woman bent forward and cut off a piece of deer fat from a small supply she had beside her, chewing at this for a moment or two, perhaps to lubricate her tongue.

'Was the house lost beneath the snow then?' I asked.

She spat into the far corner of the cooking space before answering.

'No. My father dug his spear into the ground and very soon found one of the houses. By looking inside he was able to tell whose house it had been and so knew in which direction to look for the woman's home. The white man became very cross, because he thought that the one we sought might still be alive and that my father was taking a long time in the hope that we should not find her so.

'As I had often been across the camp to the sick one's home, we soon came to the place where we thought it should be. My father dug his spear hard into the snow and a block fell in, so that we knew we had found the house.'

'Was she still alive?' I asked again.

'Now that we had found the dwelling, my father moved away to a safe distance, for it would not have been well for a hunter such as he to have approached the place once it was open. The white man came forward to cut away some of the snow with his knife, making the hole large enough for him to climb inside. He spoke to the one within, but there was no answer. Then he spoke to God, so that I knew she was dead. After a while, the man called for me to look down at him. He had brought a candle in his pocket, which he had lit and was now holding in his hand. The door had not been closed properly after the last visitor so the snow had drifted inside, but the woman must have been alive then, because she had cleared it away from her head by pushing out with her hands, or so it seemed. Her fire must have gone out, for it looked as though she had tried to cut a piece of ice out from the pot where it had frozen, but she had not had the strength and the smooth surface was dented only where she had dug the knife in.

'There was a pipe by her head, but she could not have used it after the fire had gone out.

'The white man pulled out a skin bag from underneath her deerskin and reached up to put it on the snow beside me. When he put the bag down, some of the things tumbled out through the opening. There was a piece of ribbon for tying in her hair, some needles, thread and a funny-shaped stone which the *angekok* might have given her. I would not touch any of these things, for they belonged to the dead and only a very bad Eskimo would steal from the dead. I left the bag lying where it was on the snow. The white man seemed to understand that the dead woman's belongings were not to be interfered with by others. He reached up again to push the things back into the bag and replaced it under the deerskin.

'As he did so, he knocked another block of the snowhouse down with his arm, so I could see my dead friend more clearly. She lay as she had been when I left her, wearing an old sealskin jacket from which much of the hair had gone and a deerskin wrapped round her which had a big hole in one side. The bedding beneath her was old and worn, for it is known that the dead are happier with their old things, and the people did not then have enough skins for much bedding to be left behind in the place of one who would no longer be needing it.

'The white man tried to fold her arms over her chest, but she was frozen hard and he could not move them. He said some more prayers, then put the candle out before leaving the house. Afterwards, he cut some new snow blocks to cover the holes, then my father came back to help the man secure the place so that it would not fall in until the snow melted.'

'So, when the spring came and the snow had gone, the woman would be lying out in the open,' I said, thinking how callous it all seemed.

'What else could we do? We could not bury her before she was dead, yet we had to leave the camp for there was no more food to be had there. Even the white man saw that the snow was too deep after the storm.'

'Do you remember this happening to anyone else?'

'It was the way of the people. Even after the *kudloonas* had come with their wooden houses it was still done. Only since the missionaries came has it been otherwise.'

I had a feeling, though I may have been misjudging old Tukulita, that she still did not think it wrong to treat the sick and dying so harshly. To test her out, I asked, 'How would you feel now if your people decided to leave camp but said that you were too old to be taken with them?'

The old Eskimo was too wily to be caught by that one.

'Why,' she said, feigning astonishment, 'do you see many lamps burning more brightly than this one I am tending?'

To emphasize her point, she snatched a sealskin boot off the rack where it had been drying and started chewing it with great gusto, showing the yellow stumps of her teeth every now and then as she grinned at me. So, feeling that the question was one which was never likely to arise, I handed her a packet of cigarettes as thanks for her story then left to go back to my own snowhouse.

During the afternoon, the hunters came over to talk to me. The Blacklead Island outpost, only twenty miles or so west of this camp, had been a very convenient place for the men to trade their furs without having to travel any great distance. The severe depression had forced economies upon the company, one of which was the closing down of many of the sub-posts where it was possible for the people to travel to the main establishments. After having had a store so close, the hunters found the long journey to Pangnirtung very trying. Now they wanted to put their case in the hope that I might intercede on their behalf with the authorities. A deputation of four came in, evidently to raise a matter of some importance, but the conversation went in the usual roundabout fashion.

After the preliminaries, the man who appeared to be the chief speaker said, 'When the wind and snow come from the north, the fiord to the south is sheltered, so that the snow falls but does not get blown into drifts.'

'That is so,' chorused the others.

'It is not easy then to travel to the height of the land.'

I knew very well what they were eventually going to request, but played the game by pretending that each issue was a separate matter.

'There are no new camping grounds to which we might move from here to be closer to Pangnirtung.'

'The floe edge is often packed with drifting ice, so that we have to travel northward to the open water.'

'We had the sickness among the dogs this summer so that our teams are not strong enough to pull the *komatiks* far.'

'Our traps are set in a longer line this year so that we shall have more furs to trade.'

The conversation went round and round for so long that the talk became tedious. I told Beevee to boil the kettle. While they were drinking the tea and munching the biscuits, I said, 'I will ask the managers of the company to send a man to open the post on Blacklead Island again.'

I might just as well have added that they were about as likely to accede to this request as they were to send a man to the moon, but the look of jubilant surprise on the faces of my audience stopped me. The compliments started to flow.

'Here is one that thinks a lot.'

'He cares for the people.'

'We could do with such a one as he on the island.'

This was all going too far, so I warned them, 'I do not know whether they will take much notice of what I say, for my voice will not be heard very loudly down there.'

'*Ahmilak*,' they all chanted, which really means, 'That is so', but which I took here to indicate approval of my promise to help if possible.

Beevee went off with the men when they departed, so, once more alone, I got into my sleeping bag, propped myself up comfortably with some deerskin rolls and picked up the fine-paper edition of *Tristram Shandy* that I had brought with me.

That night old Tukulita's story kept going through my mind. That poor woman they had gone to find in the snowhouse. How did she feel when she heard them leaving the camp for the last time, knowing that she would never see or speak to any-one again?

What a way to die, too weak to keep the lamp alight, lying in the bitter cold without even a drop of water to moisten her lips, while the snow drifted in through the unsealed door and the draught cut through her threadbare garments. It was all very well to be a realist, but surely this was going too far.

My sleeping bag was under the air vent. As I lay gazing upward, thinking of these terrible things, it suddenly dawned on me that the stars were shining above me, that the drifting snow had cleared and that the moon had risen, for though it was not visible through the small hole in our roof, there was a pale glow over the piece of sky which I could see. All this meant that the weather was clearing. If the day was fine enough, Beevee could go off to the floe edge to replenish our supply of dog food, making a detour to drop me off on Blacklead Island for an inspection of the buildings, on which I had to make a report for the company. After the hunting, he could return to the island, where we would sleep, then we should be ready to set off finally the following morning.

The local inhabitants would not sleep on the island themselves. They said that the little people had taken the place over, the little people being a sort of Eskimo version of the gremlins. Whomever it was that frequented the place left footprints of a most unusual kind and were better left to themselves. I was not sorry that I should have Beevee's company for my night in the deserted house.

The next morning was clear and sunny. The hunters prepared for a visit to the floe edge while Beevee took me to Blacklead Island, where we unpacked the heavy load. Before he left he told me that he would spend the night with the other men so that he would have more time for hunting.

This seemed to me to be a crafty move to avoid spending the night among the ghosts. Whatever he thought before, it seemed that the stories of our friends at the camp had sunk in, giving him as little relish as the others for a stay at the old whaling station.

In his haste to abandon me Beevee forgot to unload my rifle from the sledge. I consoled myself that a rifle could only provide rather doubtful protection against ghosts. However, fresh bear tracks did rather cause me to hope that if the animal was still around it would not turn out to be hostile. I was not greatly encouraged to find during my tour of inspection that a bear had been trying out its strength against the walls of the storehouse.

It was in this cove that the whalers had had their station. It looked out over a limitless expanse of ice at this time of year, though I knew that the floe edge was only just below the horizon and that what seemed to be a cloudy distance was in fact the mist rising off the open water. The Eskimos were hunting big whales in the area of Blacklead Island long before the sailors came up from the south. They showed great daring in tackling these huge creatures with their very limited equipment, but the benefit of one kill was immense. One carcass would supply an entire camp's winter requirements of meat and fat, apart from giving them a valuable store of whalebone. This would save them many weeks of anxiety and hunger if the weather was bad or the hunting poor.

During the afternoon of my day on the island, a misty haze crept in from the direction of the sea, obscuring the sky so that darkness fell early, and with the darkness came the wind. Not a forceful blow but a light melancholy breeze, sifting past the deserted buildings rather sadly as though in search of the life that had once been here, swirling the mist without sufficient strength to disperse it.

The house, no doubt speedily built like many of the early northern residences, had suffered since the post was abandoned. The plasterboard ceiling had partially given way over the main room, hanging down so heavily towards the floor as to seem likely to collapse altogether before very long. The partition separating the kitchen could not ever have been very secure, for it was now tilted over at a lopsided angle, held from falling only by a small piece of the wooden support still remaining attached to the end wall. The small cooking range had rusted badly, but would have been usable had not the pipes been packed with snow. The bed frame was still intact, but the old mattress had been attacked, probably by lemmings, so that the interior stuffing was mostly scattered round on the floor. One wooden chair with a broken leg was pushed up against the wall. The only piece of furniture to have survived intact was the kitchen table. I had expected to be able to light a fire, for there was plenty of broken wood about as well as the coal stacked outside the door, and had hoped that an oil lamp would have been left behind for the use of possible travellers.

Seeing that these modest comforts were to be denied me, I dug out my candles to provide illumination while the Primus stove served for heating and cooking. Perhaps it was just as well that there was not going to be any great heat, for the gaps around the door and one of the windows had allowed little piles of snow to accumulate in various parts of the room, all of which would have had to be cleared away before they melted.

The candles fluttered with the movement of the air from the door to the window. No matter where they were placed, they would not give a steady light as they had done in the snowhouse. Even the flame of the Primus stove fussed to and fro. Eventually I produced a passable supper and, resigning myself to the in-evitable discomforts, settled myself for the night. From above in the rafters came the weirdest sounds of hissing and sighing, as though the ghosts were indeed limbering up for the night's activities, but surprisingly sleep came quite easily at first. Per-haps too easily, for I suddenly awoke long before morning with a dreadful certainty that all was not well.

The breeze had apparently died away for there was no sound from the rafters; instead there was a new and unsettling noise as of someone or something pacing round the house. The footsteps crunched past the door, faded round to the back of the house, past a window then up to the door again. Sometimes the circuit appeared to take longer than normal, giving hope that a new route, away from the house, had been chosen, but soon the steps would be resumed, so that I thought that whatever it was must in the end come right into the building. I tried to prepare myself for some ghastly confrontation, bitterly regretting the absence of my rifle.

The sound continued for about an hour, during which time I remained in bed gripped with fright, then suddenly it just stopped mid-circuit. It took me an hour or so to relax sufficiently to go back to sleep, but finally I drifted off and did not wake until morning. I never did discover any explanation for the footsteps, but did not tell Beevee of the incident, fearing that it might just serve to enhance further the rather unsavoury reputation of Blacklead Island.

The hunters had done well at the floe edge, having been able to give the dogs a really good feed as well as bringing a load of fresh food for the overland journey. Sadly, the predictions of our friends at the camp came true all too quickly. We travelled easily across the ice, but as soon as we turned into the southern fiord, we could see the surface stretching away right up into the hills with the same flat, unmarked whiteness that we had seen the previous year when looking down the approach to Nettling. The soft snow slowed us to a crawl. Beevee walked up just behind the dogs, spurring them on while I pushed at the back of the sledge.

It was to take us three long, hard days of travel to reach our destination. At times the *komatik* dug right down into the snow and the dogs, finding no solid ground to give them purchase, sank up to their chests. We would then put on our snow shoes and free the team to make their own way, which was as much as they could manage, while harnessing ourselves to the sledge so that we could continue to make some progress.

The night before we arrived, Beevee became quite expansive. We had travelled many miles together through all sorts of conditions, but had had a curiously formal relationship, our conversations usually being confined to the discussion of practicalities. But now that we were about to part company, my companion lit his pipe and began to tell me about when he was young and his family had lived up on the east coast, moving down to Cumberland Gulf when the whaling ships established a base there.

Beevee roamed up and down the coast with his memories for some time, but while we were drinking our final mug of tea for the day, he suddenly asked me what it was that I had said to the *angekok* at Netilling. When I told him, he said that Padlu had put it about that my interview with him had been for the purpose of asking his advice, which had been given and accepted, and that was why conditions had improved so quickly. I was not surprised to hear this after Keeta's words before leaving Netilling, but I was glad to have had this opportunity to set the record straight with Beevee.

The river course which we had decided to use for our descent to the shores of Frobisher Bay began at the foot of a strangely incongruous peak that dominated the otherwise flat plateau. A band of cliff, too steep to become snow covered, encircled the peak below the summit, giving a black landmark visible for many miles, especially in the clear weather we had been having. This had been a great help to us by pin-pointing our exact destination in the low and rather featureless surroundings, but the good visibility had given way to a thick haze by the time we opened up our snowhouse the next morning.

This meant that we should have to travel carefully, because in a mist of this kind it was quite easy to become totally confused, since the snow and the haze combined to form one continual expanse of whiteness in which all levels became one, so that it was quite possible to step off the edge of a hill into a steep drop.

While we were having our coffee break, the sun began to break up the mist and Beevee said that he was going to climb to the top of a nearby promontory in the hope of fixing our exact position. I went with him. We stood on a hillock peering into the distance as black shapes began to emerge from behind the snow haze. Then all at once the sun routed the mist completely so that the whole of Frobisher Bay appeared suddenly before us as though a curtain had been swept aside.

The sheer grandeur of the scene was awe-inspiring. Far away to the south the ranges rose upward, one ridge behind another like a giant staircase reaching up to the sky far above the lower cliffs and hills around the coastline. The bays and inlets shimmered in the now bright sunshine, while further away the coastal plain backed away southward towards Hudson Strait to merge with the mist still stretching along the horizon. Beneath us the river curved through a long slope down to the sea. This would be our route for some while, yet not until we had almost reached the coast would we turn off to come over the plain and climb the ridge that the post camp lay behind.

Along the northern shore the cliffs rose immediately out of the sea, black and unyielding but giving way to a softer valley a little further on, and then to a sheltered harbour. In the extreme distance, I thought I could see the sun sparkling on the Grinnel glacier, and began to understand how it was that Martin Frobisher had been beguiled from his purpose of finding the north-west passage into spending his summers exploring this then unknown bay.

We travelled with great dignity all day until coming down the very last slope behind the post house. There our lashing, probably because it had been chewed by one of the dogs, broke so that our load dropped quietly off to form a trail from the bottom of the slope right up to the post building. Jimmy Bell, another sturdy northerner who was the manager here, came out to greet us amid the jumble.

It seemed that the wheel had turned full cycle. There was only one bed at the post, so I was back on the floor again, but this time, in keeping with my more senior status, we were able to dig up a mattress to put underneath the sleeping bag.

Like most northerners, Jimmy was an easy chap to get along with. He was a fellow countryman of Alan Scott's, having left his home in Scotland to join the Hudson's Bay Company about five years previously, so in many ways it was just like taking up where I had left off at Pangnirtung. By the time I said goodbye to Beevee, my last link with the old post, Frobisher Bay had already begun to feel like home.

VIII

MOSTLY THE ARCTIC SPRING is cold and miserable, but that year it was lovely. In the evenings, Jimmy and I often walked over to the banks of a small river to follow the stream up its course to a lake not very far inland. The ground was soft and spongy after the winter snow and frost, but green and pleasantly sweet-smelling. There was a peaceful air about the post. The radio had given up the ghost some time during the winter, so we were quite separated from the world's news and would be so for a while to come.

We had our own disasters to discuss. The people of the bay had suffered two cruel blows of fate during the previous year. Jimmy had accepted these great misfortunes in his usual philosophical way, but his wry expression as he told of them indicated his sadness that such things, though he was in no way responsible, should have happened during his stewardship of the post.

The house and store had been built at the head of a little cove facing eastward, not very wide but sheltered by an island which stretched across the opening. Narrow channels on either side of this island gave access to the sea, so that the cove was almost landlocked, but the apparent shelter of the cove could sometimes be deceptive and it was this that caused the first disaster.

Early in the previous summer, a whaleboat full of hunters

coming into the post for supplies had been tacking up the cove under sail after passing through the narrows. They had had some difficulty outside the cove in Frobisher Bay itself because of a fresh gusty wind, but by patient manoeuvring had reached the island, navigated through the channel, then relaxed some-what after their efforts in the calmer waters of the little bay, keeping fairly well inshore to take advantage of the smoother water. As they came up towards the post they had to pass the mouth of a gulley which led away to the south-west, through which a fast river flowed down to join the sea. They came very close inshore here among the rocks and boulders of the reef line – not the wisest thing to do in the circumstances, though at the time there did not appear to be any particular reason for alarm.

A woman at the camp said later that she had watched them coming towards the post. She saw one of the hunters drop his pipe overboard. The others were laughing and joking about this when the chief man suddenly pointed up the river and shouted to his crew. The helmsman swung the rudder across to take them away from the shore. Two men pushed the boom over so that the sail would catch the wind in their new direction, but before they could clear the rocks, a powerful blast of wind came hurling out of the gulley to tear at the canvas. The centre board fouled a rock, the mast snapped and the boat capsized to fling all the hunters into the sea. The woman said that some of them were still laughing about the pipe as the wind caught them unawares. Five of the party were drowned; only two succeeded in clinging to the upturned boat until rescue came.

It seemed very strange that a people whose lives depended to such an extent on sea hunting should never have learnt to swim, but perhaps the coldness of the water and the hard rocky nature of the beaches accounts for this, and it has to be admitted that their skill in handling their various craft was such that accidents seldom occurred.

Barely two months later, a new and even worse misfortune befell the luckless people. The families had come into the post to set off for the annual deer hunt which took place up in the hills behind the cove. The people were in high spirits, the ice had gone early, the weather was good, and as the gulley led back quite gently, the women and children would be able to accompany the menfolk. Three days later a weary boy staggered into the house to tell Jimmy that his father, one of the best hunters in the whole bay, had died that morning and that another man was very ill. The boy hurried back to the post to ask what they should do. The manager sent the messenger back to tell the party to return at once in case the illness spread.

The returning party was hardly recognizable as the happy group of a few days previously. They had carried the dead man with them on a sled, then his friend had died on the way down, so they straggled into the camp in a long line, dragging the sled with both bodies behind the women and children. Several of the people took to their beds at once, complaining of violent pains and high fever. All of them, having seen what had happened to their relations, resigned themselves to the imminence of death.

There was no indication whatsoever as to what was causing this fatal illness, but Jimmy realized that if he did not act quickly he might lose them all. The surviving hunters told him that they had been eating trout caught from the river mouth as well as some ptarmigan they had shot on the way up. This all seemed very innocuous, but Jimmy continued to question the men very closely about their diet of the past days, until they at last admitted that they had brought with them a piece of whale meat from a carcass they had found on the beach near their home. He told them that this was to be thrown away at once, as well as all the other food which had been kept with it. Able-bodied hunters were to go off on a sealhunt and no one was to eat anything until they came back with fresh food. A big tent belonging to the company was to be set up for all the sick people. Those that were still well were to keep away as far as possible when they were not actually tending their friends.

By next morning, Jimmy was appalled to find that the 'isolation' tent now had twelve occupants who were either writhing in agony from their pains or lying motionless with seemingly no further interest in life. Three more died during the morning and a further two before evening. A boatload of people from another camp arrived to trade during the afternoon, but they were not allowed to stay. As soon as the trading was finished, they were told to depart for home before they became ill as well. This measure was effective for the sickness did not spread to the other camp.

That night the morale of the people sank to its lowest ebb. Four more died before morning. The tent was now crowded with fifteen sufferers. Jimmy did his best, serving up seal broth to those who could take it and reassuring the others as best he could, but the situation looked very black indeed. Miraculously there were no further cases and most of the other sufferers began to recover. But there had been eleven deaths among the thirty or so people; added to the fatalities in the boat incident, this meant that the post had lost sixteen out of a population of just one hundred in the two months of spring.

The Eskimos, perhaps from long experience, were able to absorb disasters of this kind. Widows would join up with relatives, or with widowers, or sometimes live by themselves with the help of a son. Any family would take the children in. The survivors would shake down and reassemble themselves. The bereavement was mourned loudly for a day or so because a familiar figure would not be with them in the flesh any more, but the spirit which had dwelt within their husband or wife, or whoever it was that had died, would not desert them, remaining at hand in case they should be needed. This was a comforting creed because it linked the worlds of the living and the dead in a simple way and did not even require an effort of faith.

Jimmy Bell sent out a full report on this epidemic and the powers that be decided that the dead whale had been the culprit. I was soon to question this rather facile conclusion, however, when the illness made a recurrence later that year and at odd intervals afterwards.

*

The long sunny days of early summer tempted me out of the house and away from the floor of the sitting room. I established a small camp for myself, setting up a tent on an enclosed corner of soft mossy ground in a bend of the river. Lying on the soft deerskins the first night, I resolved to rush out in the morning to plunge into the river, for there was quite a deep pool only a few feet from the door of my tent. My resolution was duly put into effect, but the briskness of the morning air, combined with the paralysing cold of the water, made it a less enjoyable experience than had seemed likely. Daily persistence with the routine modified the early shock, however, so that in a few days' time it became a pleasant exercise.

One night, my first arctic thunderstorm broke somewhere up Frobisher Bay. Lying in my sleeping bag, it seemed at first like the far-away rumble of a landslide, for the sound did not resemble thunder. The storm moved nearer; the rain began to patter down on the taut canvas while the lightning flashed brightly enough to light up every corner of the tent.

As the storm moved further away, I began to think about the St Lawrence River and the lightning on the hill. My thoughts moved on to the night of the wedding party and Laurette. She would be married by now no doubt. Would my life in the Arctic have done anything to make me less self-conscious in the company of girls and young women? Probably not. If I stayed too long, would it be to become like Victor – hardly able to bear being anywhere but among his woods, lakes and hills, with only scorn for the rest of the world? Did the commander's words hold true, here by this pleasant summer lake as well as in the valley of the blindness and the deep snow? But my questions remained unanswered as sleep overcame me.

Jimmy Bell had had instructions to take the year's merchandise by sea round the Lake Harbour on the southern coast of Baffin Island before the arrival of the supply ship, which did not call at Frobisher Bay. The night before the boat arrived he joined me for dinner at my summer palace. I had baked a fish in clay and he brought a bottle of rum which he had saved from his last year's supply. The fish was delicious and the rum stimulating as we sat far into the night discoursing upon distant hopes and aspirations, sawing the air with tin mugs from which we drank the potent liquid. What a world it might have been had our plans ever come to fruition, but alas these dreams are still drifting somewhere in the arctic air.

Jimmy left the post in fine style the next morning, leaning nonchalantly against the mast of the Peterhead boat used for these journeys. We had loaded the furs aboard in the morning, and then, just before midday as the tide was on the turn, the engineer galvanized the diesel engine into life, spasmodically at first but with gathering strength and rhythm as the gears were engaged, and pounded off towards the narrows.

My life quickly settled into a routine after Jimmy's departure. The post people had gone off for a few days' hunting, taking their families with them, so that I was quite alone. The continuous silence was somewhat unsettling, for there was no radio or gramophone to bring any sound into the quiet house. I began to hold conversations with myself about the most ordinary, mundane matters to prevent my mind from setting up a fantasy world of its own.

Fortunately, there was plenty for me to do. The house needed painting outside. Inside, too, some repairs and redecorations were essential. The kitchen had suffered damage one day when we had decided to thaw out some tins of fruit which had been left to freeze in the store by mistake. We put the tins in the oven, then promptly forgot all about them, only to be somewhat noisily reminded when the oven door blew off, embedding itself in the wall as bits of the fruit sprayed over the walls and ceiling.

Each morning I had my dip in the river. Though the temperature of the water had probably risen only very slightly, for the snow was still melting up on the hilltops, the cold never again seemed as formidable as it had at first. It even became pleasant to lie floating for a minute or two listening to the rather plaintive call of the ducks coming from the lake above me. Then a quick rub down before lighting the Primus stove, on with my clothes and out with the pan to fry a couple of gull's eggs. These were eaten with a hunk of my own freshly baked bread while the coffee percolated gently, the pleasant aroma drifting up the deserted river bank.

Before commencing the morning's work I had to equip myself against the mosquitoes. The pests swarmed everywhere for a couple of weeks or so, but at that time they had not reached as far north as Pangnirtung so this was my first experience of them since that summer journey up the Labrador coast. By making use of a good supply of netting and wearing a pair of gloves, it was possible to press on with the painting of the building.

One day, to my surprise, a whaleboat appeared tacking through the far entrance to the harbour. The hunters were not expected to be back so soon from their trip, so probably these people were from another camp further down the coast. This supposition was soon proved wrong, however, for it was indeed our own people returning with bad news. They came ashore just below the tiny jetty, talking away at the tops of their voices. They seemed to be arguing as to which of them should come up to tell me their news, then one of their number, a man by the name of Kudlu, detached himself from the group to come up to the house.

As usual it took several minutes to get to the heart of the matter, though it was quite simple. Two of the hunters were ill. Kudlu eventually told the story and his despairing tone indicated that he was thinking of the previous year's calamity. He looked at me questioningly as though he had some hope of my being able to perform a miracle. No doubt he had heard the tale of our Netilling success and thought that I might be better able to deal with the situation than Jimmy had been. It was my turn to prolong the conversation while considering everything that I knew about this strange malady.

Prompt action was necessary. Any hesitation on my part would convince the sick men that they were doomed and once they had turned their faces to the wall to await death my task would be considerably more difficult.

After Kudlu had gone down to tell the men that I was coming, I got out my attaché case, which still looked quite impressive with my initials stamped on the side in gold letters. The first-aid book had little to say on the matter. The assumption was that the men had been afflicted with some kind of food poisoning. The suggested remedy was short and to the point. 'Give an emetic,' it said, 'and if the symptoms persist, send for the doctor.' This was apparently the only illness in the book requiring the attentions of a doctor.

My first patient, a man named Kuperachu, lay on his back groaning.

'I am going to die, am I not?' he said when he saw me, then relapsed into long trembling groans of a most unnerving kind.

The people sat along the edge of the platform gazing at me expectantly. Despite his ghastly appearance, he did not seem to have a fever, which hopefully ruled out a repeat of last year's death toll. I was undecided but covered up by shuffling through the contents of my attaché case. My hand came in contact with a tin of mustard which I had put in at the last moment. The book had said 'Give an emetic' and that was just what he was going to be given, particularly since to implement the second part of the advice and send for a doctor would involve a delay of at least two years.

Everyone in the tent watched my preparations with the greatest interest. I borrowed a mug, then mixed up the most ghastly concoction imaginable. The sick man's wife propped him up as I forced the liquid unmercifully, sip by sip, into the unwilling patient's mouth. His expression suggested that death might even have been preferable. But he swallowed it all manfully. No doubt in days gone by the *angekok* had stuffed in equally unpleasant mixtures in the hope of forcing the devils to withdraw. I warned his wife as to what was likely to happen next, then hastily departed for the next tent.

Nukertou, the other sick man, was in a similar condition but had not given himself over quite so completely to despair. He watched my preparations with a sort of vague interest which I felt encouraging, then he swallowed the mixture without any protest. He had hardly finished the draught when cries of distress came from the direction of Kuperachu's home, so back I went.

The man had been violently sick all over the bedding. The home was in a shambles, the smell beyond description, while Kuperachu looked worse than ever. Every now and then he let out a sort of shriek, and though his eyes stared fixedly at me as if he wished to say something, he was evidently incapable of speech. I told the women to clear the place up while I completed Nukertou's treatment.

My other patient, having absorbed the emetic, lay as still as death, but did appear to be breathing normally, so it seemed best to leave him as he was for the time being in order to attend to Kuperachu. The women had cleaned the tent, but the man really did not appear to be doing too well. Lying facing the side of the tent, he was breathing with shallow, rapid gasps and yet there was something about him that made me suspect he was not really as ill as might be supposed.

A more impressive demonstration of the wonders of medicine might help him to recover, and quite suddenly it came to me how this could best be done. I opened my case, took out a hypodermic syringe, turned the man over so that he could see what was happening and made my arrangements right under his nose, uncorking several bottles to make what appeared to be a most complicated mixture.

Silence fell, even the groaning ceased. So closely were they all watching me that I almost had to descend to sleight of hand in order to ensure that what really went into the syringe was a very weak solution of aspirin and water. I bared the man's arm, wiped it over with some ether in a most professional manner, then quickly made the injection, taking care to see that the bulk of the liquid dripped harmlessly down into the deerskins. They all thought that the injection had gone in to be absorbed into Kuperachu's body and gasped in astonishment. For some unknown reason the man started to go very red in the face, little beads of perspiration came out on his forehead and he started to groan again.

'Give him a drink of water,' I said to his wife in as careless a manner as possible, hoping to convince everybody that this was precisely what I had expected to happen. I closed my bag firmly and went off to the other tent aware that Kuperachu's case was now in the hands of the Almighty.

Nukertou still lay silently on his side, having presumably

absorbed the strongest emetic in the book without any apparent effect. There was nothing for me to do but leave him as he was, but as a last thought I left an aspirin tablet behind with his wife, telling her to give it to him with a drink of water when he woke up. I knew this would do nothing for him medically but it might possibly have some quite reassuring psychological effect.

Later in the afternoon, back at the house, Kuperachu's wife appeared unexpectedly before me.

'My husband has sent me,' she said. 'I am to ask whether he is not to have a little white pill like the one you gave to Nukertou.'

For a moment I couldn't think what she was talking about. Then it dawned on me that this man who had thought himself close to death this morning, must be considerably better to be even thinking about pills and I gladly gave her an aspirin tablet.

The emetic never did have any effect on Nukertou, apart from apparently sending him to sleep. The people attributed his cure to the white pill, for he was very much better the next morning. As for Kuperachu, having once got over the hump of that dreadful day, his recovery was nothing short of miraculous. Within a couple of days, both men tottered out into the open air, weak and ravaged looking, as well they might, having literally returned from the gates of the happy hunting ground. At that moment in time, I could have set up my tent as a practising *angekok*.

One night a wind blew up and with it the rain came spraying straight up the river course. My camp had no shelter in this direction, while the wooden door that I had fitted faced down that way so that it rattled and banged, although it had been tied on the inside to keep it from flying open. From time to time during the night I awoke to listen for a minute or two to the windy noise, then fell asleep again.

The sounds became part of the night, which was probably why Innukpowak could not at first wake me when she came knocking at the tent door. She must have been there for some time before she started to call.

'*Kudloona, kudloona*, do you hear me? It is I, Innukpowak, who must speak to you.'

Her voice penetrated through my sleep but my first thought on waking was that it could not yet be morning and if it was then it was a very dark one. Innukpowak called again.

'*Kudloona, kudloona*, have you not woken yet?'

I eased myself out of the sleeping bag far enough to untie the door fastening. The woman must have been crouched right up against the wood, for as it was released she almost fell in. I lit a candle to see who it was wandering about the camp in the middle of the night. At once the woman spoke loudly into my ear, as though afraid that I might still be half asleep.

'I have come about my daughter, Kooleang. She is sick in the same way as the men were.'

'Kooleang?' I queried, not recognizing the name.

'Sometimes they call her Suzhie,' she replied. I remembered the child, a very lively little girl of about seven with a flat oriental face and the shiniest black hair who darted about like a sparrow.

'Yes, I know her. What is the matter?'

'She has pains inside,' said Innukpowak, 'and she talks a lot. It is not she who is speaking though, for it is the sickness that makes her do this.'

I feared that the evil spirits would be harder to dislodge from young Suzhie than from the others. If what Innukpowak had described was delirium, it would seem that the child had a high fever, which meant a serious illness.

'I will come when I have put some clothes on. Which tent are you in?'

'In the one nearest to the boat above the jetty,' said the woman, pushing her way out into the wind to pad off home.

From what Innukpowak had said, it appeared that this was not the same affliction as the two men had suffered. Children ran high temperatures much more frequently than adults, I knew, so there was just a hope that some minor complaint had caused a fever. In any case, it was essential for me to fetch my attaché case, still full of bottles, from the house.

Innukpowak had two oil lamps going, both newly lit by the look of things. The tent was not very large and was becoming insufferably hot, so I asked her to put one of the lamps out. Suzhie was sitting up among the deerskins, her face flushed and a wild look in her eye.

'Who is he, mother? Who is this?' she cried clutching her mother's arm.

'It is the *kudloona* who gives you the sweets,' replied Innukpowak.

'Has he come now with the sweets,' gabbled the little girl. 'Where are they? Where are they?'

'He has come to help you go to sleep, my little daughter,' said Innukpowak.

'But why should I go to sleep in the daytime?' asked Suzhie.

'It is not daytime yet,' replied her mother, looking over at me.

I moved on to the platform, sitting between the sick girl and her father, who lay awake but had not so far spoken. He made room for me to sit beside him.

I gave Suzhie a tiny bottle of coloured pills to hold and put the thermometer under her armpit, not daring to put it in her mouth for fear that she might break the thing. The child did not like having to keep her arm by her side, but fortunately the pills fascinated her as she turned the bottle over and over to watch them tumbling from one end to the other.

The thermometer read somewhere between 104° and 105° as

far as I could see. Even allowing for the warm tent this was pretty high. I sent Innukpowak up to the house to fetch my kettle of boiled water and a cup. When she came back with them, I crushed half an aspirin into the water, sat the girl up and helped her to drink it slowly. Holding her in support, I could feel the bones of her body sticking out quite sharply and wondered how so slight a child was usually so full of energy.

Her father said that he would go to the river to fetch water if it was wanted. This seemed a good idea, for if they bathed Suzhie's head with the clear cold water, it might help to calm her down so that she could get some much-needed sleep.

When the man came back, Innukpowak brought out a piece of material to begin the bathing of her daughter's forehead. The child quietened down, lying very still as her mother gently dabbed her head with the wet cloth. There did not seem to be anything more to be done at the time, so I made my way through the now slackening storm to my tent. I lay awake for a long time, trying to work out what could be the matter with the child and thinking back to the remedies our own doctor had used to quell our childish fevers.

In the morning, Kudlu came up to say that he and the other hunters were going to set off for a short distance inland, as they thought that they might find some deer at the top of the valley and the wind was still rather strong for going in the boat. He inquired whether I thought that Suzhie's father should stay at home as the girl was ill. I said that the man would have to decide this for himself. There was nothing that he could do apart from helping his wife with the invalid. He evidently decided to go with the other men, for when I went down to see the girl, Innukpowak told me that her husband had accompanied Kudlu.

Suzhie had slept for a while during the night and the wildness had gone from her eyes. I had no trouble taking her temperature for she lay quite still. The reading had come down to 102°, but though this was an improvement, I did not like the look of her. Her eyes seemed glazed when the previous night they had been glittering, while her face had gone a yellowish colour. She had an anxious expression as though she did not understand what it was that was happening to her.

I crushed up some more aspirin. She drank very slowly, her eyes closing as soon as I laid her down, but her mother seemed to think that the child had improved and was more cheerful. I went to see my patient again at about noon. Her face had gained a little colour, which encouraged me to give her a drink of milk. We had some cans of evaporated milk in the house, so I fetched a tin, boiled some water to dilute the contents, then sat Suzhie up to help her to drink the liquid. She swallowed some of the milk, but then I saw that tears were running down her cheeks. The silent crying was unnerving and I asked her what the matter was but she didn't answer. Innukpowak put her arms around her to comfort her.

The child said something about pain, then the next moment the milk that she had drunk gushed back out of her mouth, dribbling from her chin down on to the bed. Suzhie lay still and quiet with the tears still wet on her cheeks.

The rain had stopped early in the morning, but the wind was scuttling the empty clouds across the sky when I got out my paint pot, determined to press on during the absence of my enemies, the mosquitoes, and I made good progress that gusty afternoon. My patient seemed neither better nor worse in the evening, indeed she had hardly changed her position. Suzhie drank a little more aspirin mixture, then her mother sponged her face so that she managed to raise a rather thin, wan smile. Innukpowak said that this was the first time she had smiled since the illness began, so we felt encouraged.

That evening, I took down my tent, shifting my belongings,

cooking gear and the like back to the house. The boat was due to return from Lake Harbour at any moment, with the possibility of my having to move on. Also the weather was less settled, so that it would be better for me to be in the house, especially since the bed was now available.

I debated with myself as to whether to visit my patient again, but decided not to in case she was asleep and made a cup of tea instead before going off to bed. That night I dreamed that one of the deer hunters had hurt himself and had had to be carried back to the post, where the others had come into the room to call me, for someone was shaking me by the shoulder and saying, '*Kudloona, kudloona*, come at once.'

My eyes opened to see a dim shape standing by my bed, so still thinking about the injured man I said, 'Where is he?'

'It is Innukpowak who is speaking to you.'

'What is it, Innukpowak? Is Suzhie worse?'

'I am frightened. She is strange.'

'Go back to her. I will come.'

One glance at the sick child told me that Innukpowak had not come up to the house without good reason. Suzhie was propped up on a pillow. In the glow of the oil lamp her face was like parchment. Her mouth had fallen open and her head seemed to pump up and down with each rapid breath. Every now and then she made what seemed like an involuntary noise, as though the air had to pass through an obstruction coming in and out of her lungs.

I went over to the platform to sit beside the child, lifting her slightly in an attempt to ease her breathing, but her head fell limply into my lap. I pulled the deerskin across to make her comfortable, supporting her head against my chest, and motioned to her mother to pass me the water and cloth so that I could set about bathing her head. In a few moments, the noises ceased and her head stilled, though her breathing remained very shallow and rapid. We sat like that for several minutes.

Innukpowak poked the fat together behind the wick of the lamp. The flame flared up once or twice. By its light I could see that the little girl's eyes opened slightly now and then, but it looked very much to me as though she were going off into a coma. I rested my head against one of the tent poles, trying to think of anything else that I could possibly do.

Innukpowak spoke again. 'Have you no medicine like the white pills you gave to the hunters?'

'No, Innukpowak. The little pills that the men had are what she has been drinking in the water.'

'What about the small spear with the medicine behind it which you put into Kuperachu's arm?'

I dared not tell her that that had just been a trick and wondered how doctors would get on if every minute detail of the treatment they gave their patients became immediate public knowledge.

'This is for grown people only, we cannot use it for children.'

Innukpowak looked at me silently as though willing me to produce some new medicine which would cure her daughter. I felt guilty and wanted to shout out that I was really only a fraud, knowing nothing whatever about people's illnesses but marching about with my little attaché case as if God had given me some special power to cure the sick. The *angekok* had just about as much chance of success. What about God though? Could he intervene at this late stage? I closed my eyes and made up a little prayer.

The woman said, 'Are you asking God to make her better?'

'Yes.'

Surprisingly, Innukpowak leant across to touch my hand. Perhaps she understood my distress, but she dropped her head sadly, realizing now that there was nothing more that we could do. This made me feel more futile than ever.

The child's head started to move again and an awful rattling noise came up her throat as if something had come loose. I put the girl face down on the platform with one arm under her forehead and applied gentle pressure to her back. It was hopeless. Suzhie took a few shallow breaths, coughed twice, inhaled deeply once more, then her body went limp. Innukpowak turned her face quickly away so that I should not see her streaming tears. I laid the child gently back on the deerskins, closed her eyes and walked slowly out of the tent.

A long cloud hung motionless just below the summit of the cliff face, but wisps of the mist drifted down across the cove, giving cover to the occasional seals taking advantage of the night quiet as they broke water to breathe. Coming from somewhere beyond the inlet, the rhythmic beating of an engine was distantly audible, heralding the approach of the boat, my old friend the *Ungava*, bringing our supplies round from Lake Harbour Post. Though my anxiety to receive the year's mail was as great as ever, I did not wait for the men to arrive, flopping down on the bed instead from sheer nervous exhaustion. There was something dispiriting, almost humiliating about my total inability to help poor Suzhie. Coming so soon after the dramatic recovery of the two hunters, Innukpowak had felt certain, I knew, that the white man's magic would cure the child. My only consolation was that I had done my best, but that could not stop me from thinking how this slight, happy child had been left virtually unaided in her extremity.

It was just as well that I did not wait up for the mail to arrive that night, for sleep overcame me more quickly than had seemed likely and the sun was streaming through the window by the time the opening of the outside door awoke me in the morning. One of the men from the boat had left a packet of mail on the kitchen table. I got up to bring the package back into the bedroom, tearing the wrappers off on the way. There

were several envelopes with the red flag of the Hudson's Bay
Company in the corner, but I pushed these to one side for later
perusal in favour of the family news from the other side of the
world.

One of my brothers had been married the previous year, now
the news was that he had a daughter. My sister had become
engaged. They had survived those dreadful first years as immi-
grants to a country in the grip of its worst ever depression and
were digging their roots into the sunny land of the South Pacific,
settling down so well that they wanted me to join them.

I made some coffee, then gathered the official letters together
to look them over while sipping the hot liquid and eating a
thick chunk of bread and marmalade.

The first letter drove all thoughts of breakfast from my mind.
It was a short official note saying that Geordie had died very
soon after arriving at St Johns, Newfoundland, the previous
fall. It didn't seem possible that he could be dead. By this time
he should have been on his way back to his fiordland home at
Pangnirtung. Now Ooloo would be left after all to make her
own arrangements for herself and the children.

I sat, holding the letter in my hand, gazing out of the window
for several minutes thinking of Geordie as I had last seen him,
rather dolefully leaving the security of Pangnirtung for the
uncertainties of civilization. I began to glance mechanically
through the remaining mail. Another surprise lay in store. One
of the official letters was from the district manager telling me
that Jimmy Bell was not returning to Frobisher Bay as they
had decided to take him out for a holiday. My apprenticeship
days were over as I was to take charge of the post forthwith.
I was to manage the post for one year, after which time I would
be moved to Southampton Island in Hudson's Bay.

My head whirled with all the news and the conflicting emotions it provoked. As my thoughts gradually crystallized I

remembered Geordie that day he had come aboard the *Nascopie* so amiably drunk, hands stuck in his braces, the ridiculous smile, the wide hat and striped shirt. I decided to walk up the hill and keep his company for just a little while longer.

The sun had gone behind the clouds as I started off across the flats to my camp site. I turned up the river bank along the route Jimmy and I had taken for our evening strolls, stopping for a breather by the side of the lake from which the fish had now all gone down to the sea, then continued on a stiff climb to the top of the hill.

The view was superb. The whole bay stretched out before me with all its coves and inlets, while over to the south, only just visible, lay the plain where Frobisher himself had camped more than three centuries ago.

A flight of ducks rose suddenly from the lake below me to swing along the river bed, over the tiny white buildings of our post, then out across the bay towards the beckoning hills on the far shore, green and inviting now that the clouds had slipped away from the sun. I watched the birds disappear into the distance on their way southward to the mainland and thought of my family's wish for me to join them in far-off New Zealand. But a warning from one of President Roosevelt's winter fireside chats came into my mind. Our generation, he had said, had a rendezvous with destiny. Already, the distant roll of drums was sounding the first faint call to arms. What better place to await the horror of war than here in this harsh but quiet and honest place?

I hurried back down the hill towards the jetty where the Eskimos were laughing and shouting as they unloaded our supplies for the coming season.

IX

THE AFTERNOON AFTER Suzhie passed away, Innukpowak
came up to the house. I saw her open the kitchen door, then
close it again, as though she had thought better of whatever
impulse it was that had prompted her to come. When I went
out to see what had happened, she was staring up at the
clifftops.

'Did you want me for something, Innukpowak?' I asked.

She hesitated for a few moments, then replied nervously, 'My
husband sent me to ask if we can have some pieces of wood
from the boat to make a box for Suzhie.'

There was a fair amount of spare wood on the *Ungava*,
mainly planks which had been used to separate layers of cargo.
No one would miss the one or two planks needed to make a
coffin for a little girl, so I said that they could help themselves.
Innukpowak thanked me, but made no move to set off home.
Apparently she had something else on her mind. We were silent
for a minute, then it came out. They wanted me to act as the
missionary in a burial service. This puzzled me rather, for it
was meant to be a Christian burial. I wondered why they had
not asked the catechist (an Eskimo appointed by the mission)
instead of getting me to take over the role. I felt pleased to have
been asked. Perhaps they wished to let me know that they
appreciated my concern for Suzhie and that they did not hold
me responsible for their little girl's death.

After she left, it suddenly came to me that my bible and prayer book, given by my godmother to accompany me on my travels, were still up at Pangnirtung. Fortunately, after a rather frantic search, I found a very tatty book of mission hymns and verses. Mostly they were inappropriate, but on the last page there was a child's prayer, 'Now I lay me down to sleep'.

This seemed fitting for the melancholy occasion, and although the Eskimos could not have understood much of what I was saying, for I did not translate the words, they must have found it quite moving because Innukpowak and one or two of the others wept during the reading. Afterwards, the family came back to the house with me for tea and biscuits, but very soon went home, perhaps to perform some ceremony of their own. I could only hope that little Suzhie would rest peacefully, under the rocks in a bend of the river.

I spent the following days sorting through the new supplies, entering them in the stock-book and reading through some of the circulars. Some of the goods, in particular a very dowdy selection of men's suits, looked like unsaleable throwouts from the bay stores in the Canadian cities, which I could not imagine any Eskimo having the money or inclination to buy.

One very welcome item of stock, however, was a new battery for the wireless. I listened to my first programme since leaving Pangnirtung and was pleased to hear the old favourites like *Amos 'n' Andy* and *The Honourable Archie* were still going strong.

Soon after the departure of the *Ungava*, some of the Eskimos proposed a deer hunt. Innukpowak's husband, Askhut, came up with two other hunters, Evi and Nikoo, to ask if they could have credit for a small outfit. Their previous expedition had not been successful as they had only shot one small doe and apart from the ever present need for meat, the skins were now urgently required so that the women could start making the winter clothes. Normally, the men would only be permitted one allowance of summer debt, but for an important hunt like this, I decided a second advance was justified.

Over the following weeks I completed much of the season's trading. A party of hunters from a camp near Niuntellik Island in Warwick Sound arrived, having sailed nearly the whole distance in a rather ancient whaleboat because they had run out of petrol. Mingumai, the spokesman of the party, told me that they had run into a heavy ice pack coming through the inside passage behind Gabriel Island. Without an engine to give them manoeuvring power, it had been no easy matter to work their way free, but they slowly eased their way through the passage into clear water for the rest of the journey.

These people had not done any trading since the early winter last year, prevented first of all by soft snow at the end of the season and then by the pans of heavy northern ice which had swung into the bay from Davis Straits earlier in the summer to block the entrance to their harbour. As a result they had almost half of last season's furs to trade as well as an assortment of sealskins and deerskins. It was to be one of the busiest days in the store for a long time to come.

They arrived with their bags of furs and rolls of skins just after breakfast. One of them, Annawa, had two flour sacks of fox pelts. He told me that he had set his traps round an old whale carcass with excellent results. The only drawback was that the furs, being very greasy from the whale blubber, required a lot of cleaning. He was very pleased with himself because it was not an especially good fur year, yet he felt sufficiently affluent to have offered to pay an extra share towards the cost of a drum of petrol which the men bought between them, which would last them all summer.

When all had eventually been completed more or less to everyone's satisfaction and I had returned to the house for my lunch, Annawa came very uncertainly into the kitchen. I asked him what he wanted, but he shuffled from one foot to the other, hesitating with his eye on the door for so long that it seemed likely he would go out without even speaking. At last his grievances burst out of him. He wanted to complain, he said, about the behaviour of the hunter Savik, a man from his camp who had not made the trip with the others. Not wishing to become involved in a personal dispute between the men, my response to this was non-committal, but once launched, Annawa was determined that I should hear the whole story.

Apparently, Savik had recently taken to spending the night propped up on the sleeping platform beside Annawa and his wife. This in itself was distracting enough to prevent them from getting a good night's sleep, but to make matters worse, Savik had now begun to sing whenever he suspected that the couple were about to engage in a martial embrace. The song, if such it could be called, was a long recitation of the more dubious aspects of Annawa's sexual affairs, delivered in a droning monotone.

My immediate reaction was to burst into laughter, but managing to suppress this impulse under cover of a coughing fit, I attempted to appear seriously concerned about the man's dilemma. He was unable to offer any explanation as to why Savik should behave like this, but I promised to give the matter some thought, while privately deciding to question some of the other people as to the real cause of the upset.

I had found that the Eskimo women were often readier to discuss domestic situations than the men, so I asked Innuk (which is what her friends called her) whether she knew why Savik should be subjecting Annawa to this treatment. She was silent for some moments as she considered what she should say very carefully, then said, 'The men had agreed to change wives, but one of the women has gone away.'

Whether Innuk believed this to be an adequate explanation for Savik's actions, she did not say, but she was clearly reluctant to discuss the matter any further. Shortly after Innuk left, Mingumai and his wife, the only woman to have made the trip with the recent arrivals, came in to give me the details of the two births and one death which had occurred at their settlement since they last had contact with us. The Innuit had become used to the idea that records should be kept of births and deaths and were keen to have the information written down in the official book.

When we had completed our business, I made some tea, and as we sat at the kitchen table drinking from the tin mugs I seized the opportunity to raise the question of Annawa's marital problems. Mingumai at once became evasive and professed not to know anything about the affair. When I pressed him to tell me what he thought the explanation might be, all he would say was that Annawa and Savik had some sort of agreement. Judging by the expression on his wife's face, it looked as though she would be happy to fill in the missing details. I thought it best not to pursue my questioning for the moment, but hoped instead for a private word with the lady before the Eskimos returned to their camp. Sure enough Mingumai's wife, Meelai, came in the next morning with a pair of boots to trade which she said she had overlooked the previous afternoon.

No longer restrained by the presence of her husband, Meelai was positively jovial, quickly disposing of her boot money so that she could get down to the real purpose of her visit. Our conversation was for once reasonably direct as well as being surprisingly informative.

Meelai began by saying, 'The man Annawa himself caused the trouble of which he has spoken to you.'

'How was that?' I asked.

'Annawa's wife, Peeta, who is the daughter of my husband's

brother, was wife to Savik for one winter before she took up with Annawa. Although she is our relative, we know that she is a lazy girl who does not sew well, but the young men think much of her. After Peeta had gone, Ali the daughter of my sister went with Savik. She is a person who thinks much about the young men but works well and the older women find her useful in the home.'

Meelai paused for a moment to stare at me as though wondering whether I understood what she was saying, then continued, 'After one winter, Annawa became dissatisfied with the woman Peeta and told Savik that it had been bad of him to allow his friend to take up with such a person without warning him of her failings. The men had a long talk and agreed that they would exchange their wives at the end of the next summer. But that spring, Ali suddenly left Savik's home to go to the home of her father who was ill.

'When she had been gone for several months, Savik, who had need of a wife, went to Annawa to say that although it was not quite time to exchange their women as agreed, as his friend had found Peeta to be unsatisfactory, he, Savik, would now take her back. Annawa thought about this, but because there was no other woman to be his wife, would not agree to let Peeta leave. Savik tried to persuade his friend to allow his former wife to return to him but failed and the two men became angry with each other, each of them thinking that the other was in the wrong.'

Meelai lapsed into silence but to my mind there was one important query.

'Why has Ali not returned from the other camp yet? Is her father still sick?'

'He is now dead.'

'But she has still not come back?'

'She remains at her former home.'

It seemed to me that Meelai was now becoming as evasive as her husband had been the previous evening.

'What is she doing there?' I asked.

'She is helping in the home of her mother.'

'But why does she have to help in her mother's house now that her father is dead?'

'There are others in that home.'

'Do you mean that there are young children there?'

'No. My sister has no young children.'

Meelai, who at first had been so informative, had become defensive, having perhaps decided that any further revelations might be discreditable to her own family, but a suspicion as to what had really happened had taken root in my mind and I felt that we had been beating about the bush for long enough.

'Has Ali taken up with another hunter?' I asked.

For a moment it looked as though Meelai would go out without replying. She had already opened the door and it was not until she turned to close it behind her that she looked back at me to say, so quietly that she might almost have been speaking to herself, 'In my sister's home the hunter Kopenoak also lives.'

The woman obviously had no intention of answering any further questions, for by the time I had absorbed this piece of information she was out of the house, hurrying back to the tent where she and Mingumai were staying.

Reflecting on Meelai's rambling account of this marital tangle, I resolved to stay on the sidelines of the dispute as much as possible, though I would be ready to separate the main parties if it should come to that, or to offer impartial advice in the event of a major row developing.

A gale blew up during the night with the wind storming almost head-on into the inlet from the south-west, driving the sea in great mounds right up to the ledge below the Innuit homes. I awoke in the middle of the night to the noise of the wind thundering round the house. A tremendous blast against the end wall caused such a trembling of the building that about thirty tins of condensed milk, my reserve supply, banged down to the floor one by one with a sound like a rattling machine-gun. Geordie's story of the terrible experience that night up at Pangnirtung when the roof of the store blew away, and three of them huddled underneath the table until morning, came into mind, but I did not get out of bed, believing that if the roof was going to be ripped off, by no means an impossibility, it would sail away behind the house somewhere and not collapse on top of me.

The sea spray, swept before the wind, spattered into the window beside my bed like a hail of small stones. At times I thought that if the window broke, the sea itself would come swirling over me, but that thought paled into insignificance with the onset of a new, ominous rending sound coming from above my head, suggesting that at least a partial collapse of the woodwork up there was imminent.

Rigid with apprehension, convinced that some major disaster was in the making, I lay unable to take my eyes off the ceiling, which in the darkness seemed to be billowing like the waves of the sea, until quite suddenly the plasterboard holding things in place above the bed gave way and a shower of books of all shapes and sizes cascaded around me.

For my bombardment by books I had no one to thank but myself, as it had been my bright idea to gather all the volumes scattered about the house together and to store them up in the roof space.

A small pile of heavier books fortunately landed on the bed head, so I managed to extricate myself from the debris of lighter works, having suffered nothing worse than a couple of bruises on my head. The sudden removal of the protective layer of books and boards between the room and the roof exposed me to the storm, because right overhead a little block of about four tiles had now been blown away, with the result that a steady stream of rainwater was splashing into the bedroom. I struggled out of bed to find my trousers and a parka and await the next disaster.

Unexpectedly, the door suddenly crashed open as a number of Eskimos, mostly women and children, burst into the house. Some of the children were crying and the rest of them all talking at once, so it took me some moments to discover the cause of this invasion.

An older man, whom I did not recollect ever having seen before, came over to explain the situation to me. He said that the people now in the kitchen came from two tents which had apparently been pitched too close to the water's edge so that the sea at high tide, with the powerful wind behind it, had swept right into their homes, swamping everything and terrifying the children. Before they had had time to recover from the first great surge of water, another giant wave rushed in. Realizing they would have to move the children as quickly as possible, but knowing there was not enough spare room in the other tents, they had hoped to be allowed to stay in my house until order could be restored in their own places.

Meanwhile, the storm showed no sign of slackening. The roof was still protesting with alarming creaks and cracks giving warning that the situation here might be even more dangerous, but the unsettling sounds did not appear to alarm the people in any way. In fact, the children, some of whom had never been inside the house before, quickly forgot about the misfortune which had struck them and were soon gawping round at all the things which were new to them, the tables, chairs, the row of pots and pans, the cupboards fixed to the walls and not least, the huge old iron range sputtering quietly to itself in the middle of the room, which astonished the children by pumping out heat in their direction without any visible fire.

The people had come sparsely clad, having just pulled on whatever they had at hand, two of them having arrived with only a deerskin wrapped round themselves, so I brought out some old skins and blankets which had been stored in a little room off the kitchen and a very striking-looking girl of about eighteen or nineteen took charge, spreading everything out on the floor so that they could continue their night's rest.

When the gale seemed to be moderating for a brief spell, the old man went out to see if he could devise any method of preventing the sea from swamping their homes again. Encouraged by the apparent lull, I tidied up the books, moved the bed over to the window to avoid the watersplash from the leaking roof, and lay down with my clothes on, covered by an old eiderdown. The soft noises of slumber coming from the kitchen were quite comforting until a very alarming, roaring noise boomed down from the hills behind the post. The storm was gathering on the plateau high above our settlement, as it prepared to thunder down from the north through the river gulley to strike us with all the force it could muster.

The thought had hardly passed through my mind before the onslaught began. The building stood up well to the new buffeting, shielded to a certain extent by the low hills and the store, which helped to absorb the main blast gusting down the line of the river bed, but a powerful eddy swirling along the backs of the houses gathered up a piece of wood with enough impetus to dash it into our end window and smash the glass.

Glass and rain sprayed into the room through the sizeable hole, showering over the partition wall which divided off the kitchen. The smaller children, hardly settled from their previous disturbing experiences, began wailing again, but were taken in charge by the older girl, who soothed them down very firmly by telling them that it was only the wind playing one of its tricks. Then she and another woman, whom we called Polly, came into the room to assist in repairing the damage. Between us we managed to fix a piece of board cut from the lid of a tea chest right across the lower half of the window, tacking it to the woodwork of the frame to hold it in position.

Polly and the girl, Nyla by name, worked most efficiently, keeping up a sort of running commentary on our progress so that the people in the other room should know what we were doing. I knew Polly already as she was Nikoo the hunter's wife. The two had no children but were known to have performed some quite spectacular hunting feats. Jimmy had considered them to be the most reckless people he had ever come across. I had not met Nyla before but she quickly proved herself to be a most able worker as well as being a fine-looking girl.

By the time we had finished the work, the night had quietened considerably. We all settled down once more, but sleep had deserted me. I decided to make myself a mug of tea and read for a while. Creeping carefully into the kitchen, I managed to avoid stepping on any of the sleeping bodies, but having got that far, just as I was pushing the kettle into position, Polly's voice said, 'Could I also have some tea, Issumatak?'

This startled me rather, not because of the request, but this was the first time anyone down here had used the name given to me latterly by the people of Pangnirtung.

Polly's plaintive request for a drink of tea stirred everyone but the smaller children, so down came the largest teapot for me to serve up a midnight feast of tea and biscuits. Now that they were fully awake, the Eskimos became quite talkative. This was the first time that I had ever really 'gossiped' with the women of the camp. What surprised me most was their obviously intense interest in the activities of the few Europeans known to them to be resident in their homeland. They had heard about Geordie and Ooloo, she having a reputation among them of being a fiery-tempered and occasionally violent person. The tales of her exploits had evidently become greatly exaggerated. Polly asked me if it was true that once in a fit of rage she had smashed the house door, but the women seemed almost disappointed to hear that Ooloo, though quite capable of vigorous self-expression, was not such a fury as they had been led to believe.

Looking back over the years, it is clear that much of her anger was justified. The girl had not come into my mind since the news of Geordie's untimely death reached me, but the questions these people were asking stirred my memory of her, not without a certain degree of guilt and unease. It might seem that she was a figure of fun because of her sometimes extravagant behaviour, but her outbursts had only been very occasional and were quite possibly due in part to the insecurity of her position. She and Geordie had had two children, a son and a daughter, for whom there would now be no security unless Ooloo could find herself a husband.

When their questions about the Pangnirtung post had been answered, the talk dwindled. The room had become warm because of the number of people packed into the space and drowsiness overcame them all, so I damped down the fire and returned to my bed in the other room.

When I awoke, my friends had gone, but had noiselessly tidied up the kitchen before they left. Everything was as it was before they came. The whole thing might just have been a nightmare but for the boarded window and the collapsed ceiling, which confirmed that the storm had been a reality. I remember wondering that morning about Nyla, the girl who had helped us so efficiently, and how she had come to be so quick and practical, especially at such unusual work.

The day began quietly, the storm having been as fast moving

as it was sudden and violent. Very likely, Mingumai and his crew would be getting ready for their return home. Nothing had yet been done about poor Annawa's disturbed nights, though Meelai's information gave me the impression that nothing really effective could be done unless one of the hunters had a change of heart. Nevertheless I decided there would be no harm in making an appeal to Savik's good sense to give up his nightly vigil.

As luck would have it, later that very day Savik's brother Kudlu came in to trade an ivory carving his old father had made, but the man claimed that he did not know anything about the argument over the wives. Feeling that further intervention on my part would serve no useful purpose, I confined my action to the writing of a note in the syllabic suggesting to Savik that it would be more suitable for him, as well as for everyone else, if he were to spend the night sleeping in his own home.

Mingumai and his party did indeed leave the next morning. Some of the men came in to say goodbye before they left. I asked Mingumai why they were not waiting to see their friends, who were expected back from the deer hunt that same day, and was very surprised to hear that the party had already returned. Normally they would have come straight up to the house to let me know how they had got on. All Mingumai would say was that things were 'not good'. Quite obviously, something had gone seriously wrong, but I could not have anticipated the awful misfortune about to befall us. It seemed that the dreadful affliction that killed so many the previous year had returned.

Three families were already affected, so there was little hope of containing the infection. It did not seem practical to isolate the victims and we had no evidence that the illness was infectious rather than being caused by eating contaminated or poisonous food.

The symptoms were pretty much the same in each case. At the onset there was a severe headache, then a sore throat developed with fever and pain in the joints. Two of the older people were suffering from excruciating spasms in the neck, but all the victims were in dire straits, and it seemed one or two could not last much longer.

Looking back to the starving camp at Netilling, I thought that at least then we knew the enemy we were fighting and had the remedies at hand. This time I had no idea as to the cause of the people's suffering, nor did I have any remedy, not even so much as an aspirin tablet. Everything had been used the previous autumn and was not to be replaced until the following year. There was nothing I could do to help, and yet, faced with all these stricken men and women, whose faith in my ability to cure them seemed so strong, I felt compelled to make every effort to assist and reassure them.

My first quick look round the homes left me in no doubt as to the scale of the disaster. Poor Innuk's husband, Akshut, was so badly affected that only a miracle could save her from a second bereavement in less than a month.

I longed for medical advice, but because we had had no contact with the *Nascopie* even the previous year's outbreak was yet to be discussed with a doctor. Although the manager of the ship had heard about the misfortune, there was no mention of it in his annual letter, so obviously a recurrence was not expected.

I went back to the house for the medicine chest and studied the book, but after reading through all the sections I came to the conclusion that nothing in the box was going to be of the slightest use to me on this occasion. Then suddenly I remembered a small case at the back of the kitchen cupboard marked 'Dr Parkinson's Painkiller'. Who 'Dr Parkinson' was, or had been, neither Jimmy nor I had the faintest idea – indeed, we had had a good laugh about him, supposing him to have been some sort of travelling quack. However, his moment of truth had come at last, for his cure-all was about to be put to the test.

I also managed to find a largish bottle of cough mixture and put this in my bag together with a thermometer and some pills selected at random to make my outfit look slightly more businesslike. I had already poured two bottles of the painkiller into a glass flask, which looked quite impressive besides containing enough of the liquor for several doses.

I had the misfortune to enter Innukpowak's home at the very moment of Akshut's death, which very nearly undermined my resolution completely. A stunned silence greeted my entrance, almost as if the two events – my appearance and his death – must have some sort of supernatural link. Poor Innuk was overcome, but as there was clearly nothing that could be done now, I touched her on the hand in sympathy, then moved on to the next home.

There were two victims here, both of whom, though seriously ill, were able to take a dose of the medicine. A boy of about twelve grasped my bag just as I was about to pick it up and announced that he was going to accompany me into the other homes. This small gesture of support gave me a considerable boost after the earlier calamity, the implications of which, apart from the blow to the general morale, sifted through my mind while I attended to the other victims. Akshut and Innukpowak, having worked with company people for some time now, were accustomed to their ways and peculiarities, which meant that they had provided not only the necessary help, but also an element of companionship not easy to replace. It would have been an added difficulty and sadness for me if Innukpowak, now without a husband, decided to move away from the inlet.

My assistant, an intelligent lad, quickly picked up the routine.

First, the thermometer was taken out of its tube and wiped with cotton wool ready to be inserted in the sick person's mouth or under the arm, then wiped again and replaced after the temperature had been noted in my little book. Next came the medicine, dependent upon the state of the person.

My last patient that day, an older woman, was in a dreadful state, breathing with awful rattling gasps, well beyond the point where my ministrations could be of any real help. So that her relatives should not think she had received no proper attention, I poured a dose of the cough mixture carefully into a tin mug, then handed it to the woman who was tending the lamp, with instructions that her friend was to drink the mixture when able to do so. An overwhelming feeling of helplessness threatened to engulf me at the sight of Akshut, now dead, and this woman, who was surely not going to last more than a few hours at the most. This transformation, so swift and merciless, from their former healthy, active selves, emphasized the sinister nature of the affliction that we were being forced to fight with such meagre resources.

One of the families gave me a hindquarter of deer meat and I still had some green vegetables left from the small supply sent round on the *Ungava*, so was able to make a nourishing broth for those who were well enough to eat. My assistant carried the meat up to the house for me, and much to his delight I rewarded him with a chocolate bar before starting my preparations for the caribou stew. Polly came up to help with the preparations, as Innuk was of course in no fit state to be working, and proved to be an able and efficient helper.

During the evening, some time after eight o'clock, I went the rounds again, serving out my stew with a small follow-up dose of the painkiller for those requiring medication, reduced somewhat from the previous dosage because of the limited supply available.

It was a blow to find that the woman who had been so poorly earlier that day had passed away. Thankfully no one else seemed critical, but several people were in a fairly desperate state.

Those that were able tucked into my stew as if it had been manna from heaven, though whether they were just being kind to me or genuinely enjoying the food was hard to tell. Nearly everyone had at least a small ration, but many were difficult to persuade because of their disinclination to eat and the soreness of their throats.

It was quite dark by the time I returned to the house to find that there was no oil in the lamp, so it was supper by candlelight. Fortunately I had left a plateful of stew to keep warm in the oven.

I took the candle and my supper over to a little table beside the wireless, expecting to eat my meal while listening to a band from 'downtown Chicago', but the first voice to come out of the loudspeaker was that of the radio operator on the *Nascopie*, saying that he hoped that I was listening because the district manager had a message for me. This was almost too good to be true. I felt sure that they had had time to read about the events of last autumn, and would now be in a position to discuss the symptoms and at least give me some advice as to what steps should be taken to keep the outbreak within limits.

Those hopes were at once completely dashed, for the manager, realizing that the *Nascopie*, now steaming north through Davis Straits, was almost directly opposite the mouth of Frobisher Bay, had decided to take the opportunity to give me a short lecture on the trials of living alone in such an isolated place and how best to overcome them. To the best of my knowledge, the man had never lived anywhere by himself. His homily was devoid of anything that could have been remotely useful to me in the situation in which I found myself.

Thankfully, the wireless officer must have thought that something less heavy was in order after the manager's pompous effort, for he next summoned an old friend of mine, Charlie Stephens, to the microphone to let me in on all the latest northern gossip picked up during the *Nascopie*'s journey through Hudson's Straits and round the bay. Charlie's voice was as welcome to me as my hotpot had been to the people here. It was the first news of its kind to reach me since ship-time the year before at Pangnirtung. There would be no more until the middle of next summer, apart from the possibility of a message during the late Saturday-night arctic broadcasts from the CKY station in Winnipeg.

Charlie gossiped on for about ten minutes, telling me how the short arctic summer had been a good season for romance, with three marriages and two engagements in the space of four weeks. Then, with suitable expressions of regret and commiserations, he returned me to the silences of Frobisher Bay. I brooded that the following night they would be too far north for me to receive the broadcast and would instead be turning their attention to John Cormack up at Clyde River. By the time they came south again, they would be too far over towards the Greenland coast for me to hear them.

It took a real effort to bring my mind back to the situation confronting me at Ward Inlet and certainly the sight of my supper debris in the flickering light of the candle, combined with the image of the *Nascopie* moving away northwards, did nothing to create any new surge of confidence. I resisted the temptation to disturb everybody by making another round of the camp, turned off the wireless and went to bed.

A new, disturbing thought dampened my appetite for breakfast. What if our recent visitors should develop the dread disease back in their own camp to spread the germs through a whole settlement of people who had had no contact with the illness last year? Mingumai and his friends probably mixed quite freely with the stricken hunters, and if the thing were infectious, which was a definite possibility, it would almost certainly develop among the Niuntellik families.

I did not go straight down to the tents after my meal. Part of me wanted to go right away to see if my ministrations had had any beneficial effect, but the rest of me dreaded what I might find, so it was mid morning before I left the house. One bit of good fortune came my way, though, when I found a half bottle of aspirin stuck at the back of one of the kitchen drawers.

My first calls of the day brought me a degree of relief. My worst fears, that it might be necessary for us to spend the day burying the night's dead, were not realized as no one else had succumbed to the onslaught since the previous day, but ominously there were two new victims, both of whom had been out with the deer hunters. Although this development did not by any means prove that the outbreak resulted from an infection rather than from poisoning, I decided to attempt some form of segregation to separate the sick from the healthy as far as possible. Nikoo and one of his friends, fortunately both still fit, bustled into action once they understood what needed to be done, setting up two tents to be used for the unaffected people then arranging for skins and bedding to be brought over. With fewer people in the homes, the patients could be looked after more easily by the one or two women left in charge.

There was very bad news in the last tent of the morning round. Nyla, who had helped to repair the bedroom window on the night of the storm, had somehow contracted the disease. She was lying in very thin deerskin bedding, shaking from head to foot because of a very high temperature, almost 104°. Her eyes were full of tears, which trickled down her cheeks and dripped on to her long hair, but she made no sound. When I did my best to comfort her, the tears increased, though a flicker in her eyes showed that she recognized me, which strengthened my resolve to keep her alive. The girl took a few sips of water, swallowed two aspirin tablets then drifted off to sleep.

Nyla's case struck new fear into my heart. Surely she could not have been infected and have developed the disease in the short space of time since the deer hunters had returned. The germs must have been here in the camp all the time. If this was so, how many more of us were to be struck down? I wondered if there could be some connection with the illness the two hunters went down with earlier that summer. Certainly Suzhie's death was something different, but the men's symptoms were similar. Nyla had also been working in quite close contact with me on the night of the storm. Up to now the thought of going down myself had not entered my head.

That afternoon we took Akshut to the river to be buried. Innuk had found me in the store and asked me to go with them once again. Our little group walked slowly over to the bend of the river. Three hunters carried their dead friend, while ranged behind were Innukpowak, her older daughter, myself and three other women of varying ages. I hoped that I would not be thought to have overstepped the duties of a post manager, but read the little poem again, which seemed to please everyone.

The sun broke through the clouds to lift the gloom a little just as we completed our doleful task, but walking home beside Innukpowak and her daughter, Koolie, I could not help wondering how many more of our shrinking numbers would be lying beside the river before the plague released us from its sinister grip.

The afternoon round was not encouraging. Some temperatures had risen since the morning and two of the men, though not exactly in their death-throes, had sunk into a listless state from which it was going to be hard to arouse them. Others were still in considerable distress.

I asked one of the women if she thought another of my stews would help, and she responded quite favourably to the suggestion, so Nikoo went out to cut off a joint for me. While my concoction was simmering gently on the back of the range, to keep myself occupied and prevent my mind from sinking to the same low level as the others in the camp, I went over to the store again to do some tidying up.

Nothing had been done since Mingumai and his crowd were being dealt with. The furs, mostly white fox, were still in a heap on the upstairs floor waiting to be sorted. Annawa's pile alone would require a lot of attention before they could be packed because the London warehouse did not like being sent greasy furs. This was work for some of the women, who cleaned off the fat as far as possible with the aid of sawdust or cornmeal, then hung the pelts outside on fine days for a good blow in the fresh air.

A couple of hours in the store helped to revive my normally optimistic spirit sufficiently to face the evening round. It was hardly to be expected that the sick would greet the appearance of the food with anything but indifference, but with a great deal of effort we managed to persuade most of them to swallow a little of the soup. Nyla was unchanged. I took two of the deerskins from our stock in the house to replace her threadbare bedding. Although she was clearly too ill to show much animation about the change, she did drink nearly a cupful of broth and certainly looked more comfortable.

That night, somewhere between two and three o'clock in the morning, I awoke to a hammering at the window pane beside my bed.

At first, in my drowsy state, it seemed as though a polar bear was trying to break in, then a young boy, desperate to arouse me, pushed his face up against the window, so that a squashed nose appeared in the centre of the pane, while at the same time the child endeavoured to shout a message through the glass.

I pulled some clothes on over my pyjamas and went out to see what the trouble was. The boy gabbled something about his uncle, then rushed off into the darkness. Any doubts as to just where the boy had gone were quickly settled by the level of noise coming from the tent nearest to the house, inside which an unexpected and bizarre scene confronted me.

A naked Eskimo, a half brother or some such relation of the hunter Evi, was kneeling up on the sleeping platform, brandishing a dangerous-looking snowknife in his right hand. He did not appear to have any aggressive intentions towards his friends, but judging by from the strips of deerskin lying beside him, he seemed to have been occupied with cutting up his wife's bedding. He was making a loud and continuous moaning noise as if he were trying to say something but had lost the power of speech. This weird, discordant sound, combined with the wild glitter in his eyes, had sent the women cowering to the back of the platform.

The man was clearly delirious, but it was likely that his relations believed this to be the manifestation of an evil influence.

I attempted to calm the man, but though he relapsed back into his bedding he would not give me the knife until, quite suddenly, his eyes closed. Whether this was in sleep or a coma of approaching death I could not decide until the knife fell out of his relaxed hand and it became clear that he was unconscious. All we could do for the hunter was to bathe the perspiration from his forehead with cool water.

There were three more deaths during the night. The hunter responsible for the nocturnal disturbance died without regaining consciousness, while the two other men who had been deteriorating also passed away.

The bodies were wrapped in old sealskins together with each

man's worldly treasures, then carried away to the rock cache on the river bank below the bend where Suzhie had been laid to rest. The only faintly hopeful sign that morning was that Nyla showed a slight improvement.

After lunch Innuk came up to the house. She said, 'Would you like me to make some bread?'

I must have looked a bit astonished for she went on to ask, 'Do you not wish me to work for you now that my husband is dead?'

It had not occurred to me that Innuk would be prepared to resume her duties so soon after her bereavement and her question caught me unawares. I had not yet considered whether it would be wiser to release Innuk now that Akshut was dead, or to accept a greater degree of responsibility for her welfare as she had no hunter to depend upon. Something of my dilemma must have shown in my face. Innuk, noting my hesitation in answering, asked rather dolefully, 'Am I to go then?'

She looked so dejected that I hastened to reply, without any further thought, 'No, we will continue as we are for now.'

After my awful night and morning, her company was most welcome, for upon hearing the news that she was to stay, she brightened up considerably, took off her parka and set about her preparations in a most businesslike manner.

When Innuk had completed the preliminaries, she sat down on a chair opposite me and looking straight out of the window, as though talking to someone out there rather than to me, said, 'Evi says that the sick people are going to die.'

This announcement left me momentarily speechless. Up to now, Evitook had been helpful in several ways, without giving any impression that he thought our activities to be a waste of time. In our present state, such an expression of hopelessness could have catastrophic results, especially after the previous night's dramatic episode had ended in the man's death. Perhaps this was just a private opinion. I asked, 'Is he just saying this in his own home?'

'No,' replied Innuk, 'he speaks like this to the others also.'

I looked at my companion inquiringly, hopeful that she might expand her answer. I appreciated the fact that, in talking to me like this, Innuk had taken a very big step indeed, for she would not normally discuss any of her people in this way with the company man. It struck me that although she was now a widow, with one of her children already dead, she could not be very old herself, probably under thirty. She had accepted the calamities that had befallen her with the usual Innuit stoicism, but her eyes sometimes had a far-away look about them and there was a line across her forehead which gave her a quizzical appearance. Innuk had been at the post ever since my arrival at Ward Inlet, but she had not impacted on me to any extent until her daughter's illness. It seemed as if she had now decided that it was time for me to take notice of her as a person, and for this reason had allied herself to me with the revelation concerning Evi's conduct. My friend did not volunteer any further information but waited for me to question her. I began, 'Does he think that by saying these things he is helping people?'

'I don't know what he thinks. He says that the medicine which you pour from the bottle is only nasty-tasting water.'

This cynical approach to my efforts in dealing with the sickness floored me for a moment, not in small part because of the degree of justice in Evi's comments, but I reassured myself that the Parkinson's mixture did appear to give limited relief to the patients. Innuk waited patiently for my next question.

'Does Evi know of any medicine which might be better than mine?'

'He does not know of any medicines like yours.'

'What does he think should be done?'

Innuk hesitated for a few moments before answering this question, looking at me rather doubtfully as if she was fearful of being laughed at.

'He says that it is time for the people to follow their old Eskimo ways because the *kudloona*'s water is not helping them.'

Innuk's words brought to mind Padlu's behaviour at Netilling the previous winter.

'So Evi is an *angekok*.'

My friend did not answer my statement, but was undoubtedly relieved that I understood without need of further questioning. I fully appreciated Innuk's efforts, however reluctantly she may have embarked on them, to let me know what was really happening among the people.

We had had quite an intense few minutes, so as the kettle was bubbling away on the back of the range, I made a pot of tea, then, unwisely perhaps, brought out two doughnuts, part of a batch produced during a short cooking spree that morning from a recipe of Alan Scott's. Innuk welcomed the tea but looked very doubtfully at her doughnut. Not wishing to offend me, she took a mouthful, though the expression on her face would have done credit to one of the early Christian martyrs on his way to the stake. Gradually, her natural good manners overcame her reluctance to sample my cooking and she relaxed sufficiently to encourage me to continue with my questions.

'Has Evi said what he can do to help the sick people?'

'He began last night.'

'What did he do?'

Innuk took another half-hearted bite at the doughnut but did not answer the question. I tried to prompt her.

'Tell me what he did, Innuk, because it's no use my trying to help the people who are ill during the day if Evi comes at night to do something different.'

Very slowly my friend replied, 'Evi talked to the man you went to see during the night. He said that as you had not done anything, he would help.'

'How did he talk to him?'

Innuk hesitated again, then said quietly, 'He talked loudly, in the way of *angekoks*.'

I wondered whether the hunter had regained consciousness after my departure.

'Did the sick man speak to Evi?'

'No. They said that he remained asleep.'

This seemed to indicate that Evi had been either commanding a bad spirit to depart from the patient or calling on a good one for assistance. Whichever way it was, there was apparently a considerable amount of noise involved.

'Was that all that happened?'

'No. Evi had brought some food which he wanted his friend to eat, but nothing came of this because he would not open his mouth.'

The chances were that the patient had not been conscious of Evi's attentions at any stage during these proceedings, having lapsed into the final comatose state of the illness.

Apparently, Evi did not shrink from taking on the people who were at death's door, for two of his other 'patients' had also died. The question really was which of our methods was likely to be most successful in containing the scourge. I had to be honest and admit, to myself at least, that neither of our efforts was achieving the desired result, but it did not seem feasible to me that shouting at a patient in the middle of the night and trying to force him to eat unpalatable food could possibly be beneficial, unless it were by some mysterious spiritual means beyond the range of my experience. On the other hand, my potions, though they may have given only minimal relief, were certainly not harmful.

227

Innuk had been most useful and informative, but was clearly discomforted by some of my questions. After completing the first phase of the breadmaking, she hovered at the doorway of my room looking nervous and ill at ease.

'Evi will be very angry if he hears that I told you about him. The others might think it bad of me also.'

I tried to reassure her.

'I am not going to speak to anyone about this. Because some people have died after taking my medicine, others may think that the *angekok* is better able to help them in the old way. They must do as they wish, for all of us want to cure the sick people as soon as we can.'

My main concern was that Evi's denigration of my efforts would wear down the people's confidence in my ability to help them. Their faith was at this stage central to the victim's recovery.

I was relieved to find there were no further deaths over the next two days and my spirits lifted a little as two fairly doubtful cases, though still very shaky and haggard, began to improve. Sadly the tears continued to run down Nyla's cheeks, but she did manage a cup of hot soup each day.

One evening after Innuk had gone home, I sat listening to the wireless. Roosevelt was giving a talk, then there was some soothing music which lulled me off to sleep. By the time that I woke up again, the station had closed down for the night, so it must have been late, but in the quiet a distant but vaguely disturbing noise reached me from the direction of the camp.

Outside everything was very still, so that the little bursts of faint sound drifted towards me with the mist gliding up from the sea. I set off towards the settlement to solve the mystery, but had not gone far before it became evident that the cause of the disturbance was not people talking but one person shouting. Evi was performing again. Here was my chance to confront him while he was actually at work, and to settle Innuk's fears that people might suspect her of betrayal.

There was no plan in my mind, as, guided by the sound, I made for the tent where the *angekok* was operating. Someone who had just emerged from an adjoining home went in ahead of me, masking my entry sufficiently to enable me to squat down close to the door without anyone seeing me for a moment or two. Evi was in the process of 'talking' to a man lying in the deerskins when one of the women noticed me and let out a shriek.

The effect of my sudden appearance was to freeze the action into a sort of grotesque charade. Since I had not lit my lamp after Innuk's departure from the house, the people no doubt believed me to be in bed asleep. Now all eyes turned toward me with varying degrees of astonishment as if they did not believe the evidence of their sight. Evi's confusion was almost comical. A look of bewilderment settled on his face, as though he could not understand how he had somehow conjured up the wrong spirit. In his right hand, he was holding a rather unpleasant handful of food, while his left hand was pointing towards the door.

During my years in the training corps, we had always been taught to make the maximum use of the element of surprise. At the moment, the initiative was firmly in my grasp, giving me an excellent opportunity to considerably deflate the *angekok*. We stared at each other in silence for a few moments while I decided what to say and Evi remained too astounded to be capable of speech. Finally I said, 'You have interfered with my sleep, Evi, and you are disturbing this man's rest. It would be best if you go to bed yourself now.'

With that, I turned to make my departure as sudden as my arrival had been, hoping that this would be a more effective method of dealing with the situation than allowing myself to be drawn into any discussion as to the relative merits of our treatments of the invalids. I was also conscious of the fact that I must not humiliate or ridicule Evi. He was only doing what all good *angekoks* had been doing for centuries past and any attempt to make fun of him would almost certainly unite the whole camp against me.

The following day I behaved as though nothing had happened. My boy assistant woke me, playing outside my window, and we went the rounds exactly as before, armed with the painkiller, the last of the aspirin and a big pot full of soup made up out of canned extract. One man had died during the night in the home where Evi had been performing. I was tempted to use this in my favour, but it seemed wisest to remain silent.

Nyla had made some improvement. Her temperature was down a degree and she was hungry enough to take a bowl of soup without too much difficulty, which was encouraging, though she was still in considerable pain. As I left the girl's home, Polly followed me out. She had evidently decided to join Innuk in keeping me informed as to behind-the-scenes developments, for when we were out of earshot of the others, she said, 'Last night after you had gone home, Evi came to this house.'

'What did he come for?' I asked, rather foolishly because the reason for his visit was quite plain.

'He had said that your medicine is not strong enough to cure the people.'

'Did anyone ask him to come?'

'No, but he came to the door and asked if they would like him to help them. He said that the medicine you have been giving out is only coloured water which cannot do any good for anybody.'

'Did they ask him in?'

'Yes. He talked first to Pikaluk, the man in the corner of the sleeping platform. Afterwards he tried to talk to Nyla, but she turned away from him. Evi became angry and said that she was a wicked girl who would bring more misfortune to the people, but she took no notice, saying that you were helping her and that she would get well again with the medicine.'

'Was Evi very angry about this?'

'We thought that he was angry, but he did not speak much after that except to say that some of the people had forgotten their old ways by drinking the *kudloona*'s dirty water.'

I felt pleased that Polly had thought it right to tell me what had happened, and thanked her, adding, 'It is very difficult for me to help the people if others are saying such things about what I have done. The medicine which has been given out is not just dirty water as the *angekok* has been saying, for it helps to stop the pain so that the people can rest and get better. It will do Nyla more good than to have people shouting at her.'

It occurred to me, however, that any argument about this remedy was shortly to become academic for the supply could not last much longer.

Having missed out on breakfast because of sleeping late, my insides were protesting hungrily by the time the round ended. I had not eaten a hen's egg for nearly a year, so decided to visit the store on my way home, open the case of eggs which had just arrived and cook myself an egg feast of some kind as a treat. Someone in the order department had slipped up when it came to processing our order, for though a case of eggs had certainly been delivered, they turned out to be the very smallest pullets' eggs, which would need to be cooked at least six at a time to make even the basis of a meal, so I scrambled up about eight of them, toasted a couple of slices of Innuk's bread (which had turned out very well), made some coffee, opened a packet of chocolate biscuits and afterwards felt rather ill for an hour or so.

To work off the effects of my unusual lunch, I felt the necessity for some gentle exercise, so got out my small rifle and set off walking towards the river bank in the hope of coming across a hare to make a change of diet for me. My route took me right up to the river, past the little flat where we had buried Suzhie, up to the next bend where my own first camp had been, then over in the direction of the hills where Jimmy and I had strolled. There did not seem to be any hares about in my vicinity and I began to dwell upon my inability to control either the spread or the severity of the illness.

While this was going through my head I had been steadily ascending the slope in a fairly aimless manner, certainly without giving the surroundings a hunter's scrutiny, so that it was something of a surprise when a little group of children emerged from the cover of some rocks just below me. It turned out to be Innuk's daughter, Koolee, and two of her friends, a boy and a girl. When they saw that I was waiting for them, they came up to me and their chatter and the mere fact that they had come to keep me company helped to restore me to a reasonable state of mind. I was so pleased that on our return home together I rewarded them with half a chocolate bar each.

Going through the official mail that afternoon, which I had not given more than a cursory glance until now, I came across a shaky epistle sent to the head office in London by an old man who had been the first mate on a whaler, operating at the entrance to our bay at the beginning of the century.

One long ago summer's evening, the correspondent claimed to have seen a very odd-looking rock, the tip of which rose clear of the sea at low tide and was surrounded by a luminous green haze which showed up quite clearly in the gathering dusk. The mate reported his sighting to the captain, who at first thought so little of the matter that he did not even record the experience in the logbook. A few days later, the mate sighted the rock again and this time drew the captain's attention to its luminous qualities, but the skipper, though astonished, once again failed to record the strange sight.

The old sailor had now managed to convince the company officials of his story and had drawn a very rough map of the area where his find had been located, but was vague as to the precise spot where the rock had been seen to emerge from the water.

There was a possibility that the green haze indicated the presence of uranium deposits, and if this were so, an area must be staked out and claimed on behalf of the company. Several close-typed pages gave full instructions as to the procedures to be followed in carrying out these orders and the expedition was to set off as soon as possible. It was immediately obvious that the journey would have to be delayed until a larger number of the camp were in good enough health.

There was one other hitherto neglected letter, which gave us the details of an eclipse of the sun expected to be total in our area. We were warned not to stare too fixedly at the sun while it was apparently covered with the moon's shadow, for the light coming from the edges would be harmful to the naked eye, and therefore dark glasses should be worn for protection.

The day was well on by the time I had finished sorting the letters and circulars and was ready to visit the sick. My helper, who was usually waiting outside for me to emerge with my paraphernalia, was nowhere to be seen. I feared that his parents, not wishing to appear to be in open opposition to Evi, had kept the boy at home. It made no real difference to me whether the boy came or not, but as an indication of a growing division within the settlement, his absence made me uneasy.

Late in the evening, when it had become clear that no one was going to come up to the house, I collected my things together to set off for the routine visit. Little gusts of fine cold rain were billowing in from the sea, then drifting gently up the slope behind the house to merge with the mist already slipping down the cliff face. Soon our cove would be enveloped in a wet fog which would thicken as night fell.

It may have been my growing apprehension, but it seemed as though people's attitude to me had changed from friendly cooperation to one of almost total indifference, accepting their potions with reluctance, as though no good would come of it. Evi was sitting in his own home looking very smug, but he said nothing, not even to voice an objection to one of his relatives being given a dose of the 'dirty water'. The only person to show just a flicker of interest in my visit was the faithful Nyla, who was rewarded with the last of the aspirin tablets. Otherwise the round was made in almost total silence.

I walked slowly home as the fog swirled around me, hardly aware of the now increasing rain. There was just one less than gloomy thought in my head, which was the fact that there had been no further deaths in the past twenty-four hours.

X

JUST WHEN THE SITUATION in the camp, not to mention my own resolve, seemed to have reached an all-time low, events took on an unexpectedly positive course.

I woke one morning to find Kidlapik, a native catechist in the pay of the Anglican mission, seated at the kitchen table. The man hardly waited for me to enter the room before explaining the reason for his presence. Rising rather solemnly to his feet and waving his arm in a generally southerly direction, he said, 'Because there is so much sickness here now, the missionary at Lake Harbour would wish me to gather the people together to pray to the Lord for assistance in this time of trouble and for the souls of those who have died.'

Kidlapik had not been very active since I arrived at Ward Inlet, but he obviously felt it was time he earned his keep. What my part was to be in the gathering was not, however, very clear. I said, 'Perhaps you should do as the missionary would wish then and get all the people together.'

The catechist was visibly pleased at my ready encouragement for him to hold his meeting, so came quickly to the point of his visit by saying, 'As there are no big tents at this camp, perhaps we could gather the people together here in this house.'

It was one thing to give modest assistance in a campaign to keep the Lord on our side, but it would not do to play a leading role in the matter. To my way of thinking, an open-air meeting would be the most suitable arrangement, particularly as the murky conditions we had been experiencing had this morning given way to clear skies and brilliant sunshine, which was presently streaming through the window. Not wishing to be unhelpful and seeing that Kidlapik had set his mind on an indoor service, I offered the store building as a possible site, a suggestion immediately accepted by Kidlapik, who went straight off to tell everybody.

I had hopes of making myself a cup of coffee to help me start the day, but the catechist had gone about arrangements in such a rush that people began to drift across towards the store right away, so there was just time for me to wash the sleep out of my eyes before going over to get the place ready for a service. The first arrivals helped me move the cases about to make room for everybody. So many people came up that I was concerned there would be no one to look after the invalids, but Nikoo assured me that they would not be deserted.

We had just had time to get everything organized when Kidlapik reappeared with a last group of stragglers, mostly older children whom he had gathered in from the beach. He asked me, perhaps out of politeness, how he should begin such a service. Should they sing a hymn or say a prayer? Having already decided that the proceedings should be conducted entirely by Kidlapik as the accredited representative of the church, I said simply that he could tell the people that tea would be served at the house afterwards. The man was quite happy to accept the preparation of the refreshments as the reason for my non-attendance.

Back in the house with my delayed coffee and toast, the question still uppermost in my mind was whether this new attempt to limit the suffering of the people would amount to anything more than a diversion. A sobering thought for me was that after this day I would, to all intents and purposes, become powerless against the infection, for though the church would still have prayer as its main bulwark against these misfortunes and the *angekok* his spirits, my stock of painkiller would be exhausted.

I had prepared for the ending of the service by filling the two big kettles. They were hissing gently on the front of the stove, ready for the tea to be made, but the service went on for nearly an hour. Evidently the catechist, having once gathered everybody together, was making up for lost time.

Eventually the store door burst open and my guests streamed up towards the house. Innuk was the first person to come through the door. Whatever Kidlapik had said, it had undoubtedly raised my friend's spirits, for she looked a different person as she bustled about to take charge of the refreshments, quickly organizing people, then producing mugs from all sorts of places round the kitchen until everybody was sipping hot tea and munching biscuits.

Looking out over the inlet from the sitting-room window, I could see the sunshine sparkling along the wave tops as the rising tide urged the water gently up the beach, rustling away again after each surge as though repelled by the rocky shoreline, then creeping back ahead of the rolling waves but losing momentum as the sea dispersed along the shore.

'Would you like some tea, Issumatak?' inquired Innuk from the door, where she was standing watching me.

Although the coffee had hardly had time to settle inside me, I nodded my head (a gesture which the Eskimos understood but did not use themselves). My employee was making so determined a move to re-establish herself as a useful helper under the new conditions, that it was only fair to give her as much encouragement as possible, so I accepted my tea, amused to see it served in a proper cup and saucer together with a buttered biscuit on a plate.

I was unsure what sort of relationship would develop between

Innuk and myself. She and her husband had worked for Jimmy Bell for the last two years in a fairly straightforward arrangement as married employees. My friend had made it clear that she saw no reason why she should lose her employment because her husband was dead, but this would mean that our association would be on a more personal basis. She was a pleasant person both by nature and in looks, and although she was a few years older than me, I considered her a very suitable person to have around the house.

The sea looked so bright and calm that it suddenly came to me that we should seize the opportunity to take the fit people out for an afternoon in the sun, which would be bound to raise their morale a notch or two. I said to Innuk, 'Would you and the others like to go out to pick berries this afternoon?'

The response to this simple suggestion amazed me. Innuk positively sparkled with pleasure, and without even answering the question rushed off to the kitchen to spread the good news, at once setting off a general chorus of approval. One problem that occurred to me was that it was not going to be possible to get all these people into my boat, but Nikoo came into the room just then with the answer, for he had a whaler of his own which we could tow behind.

Before we departed, I went on the rounds, giving out the last of the patent medicine. With the aspirin already gone, this left only the cough mixture as treatment. I was deeply dispirited to find that Nyla was not so well. There were no specific symptoms of a worsening of her state, just an overall impression that her eyes were slightly glazed and her face a fraction greyer. There was nothing left for me to give her except moral support, so for lack of any other inspiration, I sat with her bathing her forehead with a deerskin sponge. Kidlapik agreed to watch over her while we were out in the boat, which I hoped would protect her from Evi.

Innuk was waiting for me at the house, surrounded by all the young people of the camp as well as one or two older hunters. Some had hunting equipment, others had sealskin bags in which to bring back the blueberries we hoped to find further down the inlet. Despite the seriousness of the illness which still had our settlement firmly in its grip, there was a holiday atmosphere in the air.

It is difficult to describe the astonishing degree of enjoyment that so simple an expedition brought about. We set off to a crescendo of laughing and shouting when it was discovered that two of our number had fallen into the water while pushing Nikoo's whaler off from the shore. We circled back to pull them into our boat, but although they were thoroughly soaked, they got no sympathy from their friends as no one was going to miss the opportunity to make a joke at their expense.

At last we got away up the harbour towards the narrows where the two arms of our cove came together; there was only a quarter-mile strip of water between them. With their ribald jokes and coarse exchanges, the party made enough noise to frighten off any lurking seals, so poor Nikoo, who had hoped that he might line up one or two, had to put his rifle back in its cover.

Most of the young people leapt out of the boat as soon as we arrived at the chosen spot to rush up the beach towards the hillside without so much as a backwards glance, leaving five of us to take care of the boats. Now that the noise had subsided, the seals were once again rising cautiously to the surface and we brought Nikoo's whaler in to the beach so that the older hunters could go off in the company boat to try their luck. Nikoo wanted me to go with them, but I said that it would be best for me to remain and see that his boat did not go aground as the tide fell, which would delay our departure later that day. Innuk and Koolee stayed with me near the beach with the intention of picking the berries on the nearby slopes. The fruit was plentiful and my two companions got straight down to it, gathering in the small berries with amazing speed. My inexperienced efforts were pretty pathetic. At least Koolee evidently thought so, for she shouted to her mother, 'He doesn't know what to do. Shall I show him?'

The girl came over to give me a demonstration, flicking the berries into her bag with one simple motion, but my fingers were not supple enough to follow her movements, so I gave up, saying, 'You and your mother are too quick for me. I am going to walk up the river bank.'

The girl gazed after me as though debating whether to come with me or not, but in the end resumed the fruit picking as I went over to climb a grassy knoll beside the river.

From the top of the knoll there was a good view of the island which provided shelter for our harbour. On this western side of Ward Inlet there was a narrow channel between the island and the mainland. It was somewhere in this vicinity that the boating tragedy had occurred, but looking out over the calm sea in front of me, it was hard to understand how such a thing had happened.

As I looked back over the disastrous events at Ward Inlet over the past fifteen months – the boat tragedy and the terrible affliction which struck the people the year before and now again this summer – I saw there was good reason for the Eskimos to believe that evil influences were working against them and so to call upon the *angekok* for his assistance. I also considered the ominous possibility that the number of active hunters had fallen to a level at which the continued existence of a trading post might no longer be thought economically sound.

It would be a sad day if this bay, with its many forgotten footnotes to arctic history, were to be abandoned and the brooding mountains, deep fiords and sheltering coves returned to the silences first disturbed by Martin Frobisher over three hundred and fifty years ago. I reflected that life in these parts had changed little since those first sailors probed into our bay. In the quiet of that summer's afternoon in a place so far removed from the bustle of everyday life as I knew it, where so little had changed for hundreds of years, where no sound of motor car had ever disturbed the lonely peace of the majestic hills, it was easy to imagine the intrepid sailors in their tiny craft of those long-ago days, tacking down the bay, searching for the route which would bring them through to fame and fortune.

A sound coming from beneath me broke into my reverie. Looking down from my perch on top of the knoll, I saw Innuk and Koolee standing at the bottom, gazing up at me with a rather comical air of bewilderment, as though they half-expected me to take off like a bird and disappear into the blue sky. In fact Koolee shouted, 'He looks like an owl on top of a rock. Are you going to fly away, Issumatak?'

'No!' I shouted back, then rushed suddenly down, swept the girl into my arms, held her over the river bank and threatened to drop her into the water. She screamed with laughter but grabbed hold of my clothes for safety, so I put her down by her mother, who said, in a slightly reproving tone, 'The others are coming down the hill. Shall we make the tea?'

So we filled the kettle with water, got out the Primus and in a few moments were joined by our friends as they ran back from the hillside.

Everyone was more subdued on the journey home. A rising easterly breeze chilled the warmth of what had been an unusually mild early fall day, catching us head-on at first, then swinging more or less behind us as we made our way up Ward Inlet with the last of the daylight. We had had a very pleasant outing, our bags were full of berries and the hunters had secured a couple of seals.

Harsh reality awaited us at home. Two men had not fared well during the day. One had been vomiting. Nobody said anything, but the sheepish way they told me of this made me suspect that the *angekok* had taken a hand in the matter. The hunter was in a bad way, well past the stage where my limited efforts could bring any hope of a reversal of his condition, even if my supply of painkiller had not given out. His friend, though he had not actually been sick, was in great pain and was showing signs of the breathing troubles that were usually the beginning of the end.

It was a relief to find Nyla exactly as I had left her. According to the old lady, she had slept for most of the day and now drank half a cupful of warm milk, which was about the only thing left which could be of any use, except possibly our care and attention.

I walked slowly home through the camp, quiet now after the excitement of the afternoon expedition. The breeze, colder as the night settled round us, was drifting across me from the hills on the opposite side of the river,. The thoughts which had encouraged me on the way home could not sustain me against the certainty that the pall of death had not yet lifted from our sorely tried settlement.

Back in the house it had been my intention to write up my diary. I brought the table over so that I could sit beside the range and warm myself up a bit, for not having been very heavily clad, the trip home had been rather chilly. Then going round the homes had not helped, but with the heat of the range on one side aided by the warmth coming from the lamp on the other, my body temperature began to rise sufficiently for me to begin my writing. I had not progressed very far before Innuk suddenly appeared before me. My friend really did have an uncanny ability to enter the house almost noiselessly. She examined my arrangements with a look of concern, then cross-examined me as to why it was necessary for me to sit so close to the stove. Was I cold? Were my clothes not warm enough? Should she make me a new parka? It was as though it was a personal affront to her for me not to be adequately clothed. I managed to persuade her that it had been carelessness on my part in not putting on a warm enough jersey for going out on the sea and that it would not be necessary to make me any new clothes until it was time to start on the winter deerskins.

When she was satisfied as to the state of my wardrobe, my friend went on to ask me whether I had had a meal, but without giving me time to answer, she said, 'The old lady has cooked some deer meat at home. Would you like me to bring you some?'

I had no idea who the old lady was, perhaps it was the one who had been tending the lamp the night that Suzhie died. How did Innuk know that I had not had any supper yet? Was there anything the Eskimos did not know about what was happening in the house? Probably not, but while all this was going through my head, Innuk was looking at me very strangely, genuinely puzzled as to why it should take me so long to reply to such a simple question. She said, 'Have you already eaten?'

I pulled myself together.

'No, Innuk, I haven't, and it's nice of you to come over to ask me. I would like some meat, thank you.'

While she was out of the house I opened a tin of mixed vegetables, put them on top of the range to boil and laid preparations for the meal out on the table.

I had very much wanted to ask my friend about Evi's activities, but she was so pleased by my welcome on her return that it would have been unkind to subject her to questions which she would find difficult to answer.

Nikoo came up to see me after supper. Our conversation, though roundabout, was confined to practical matters. The hunter began by saying, 'We shot eight deer at the top of the gulley the morning after we left on the deer hunt.'

'How much meat did you bring back with you?'

'About three carcasses. The rest we left in a cache at the top of the hill.'

While this little talk was going on, I was trying to puzzle out the real reason for Nikoo's visit at this time of night and fervently hoped that it did not mean that someone else had had a seizure. In fact, Nikoo had come to propose that they use the post boat for a hunting trip. There was a great need for seal fat and meat for the families of the sick hunters.

With so few fit men in the camp, success was much more likely using the post motor boat, so I put Nikoo's mind at rest by agreeing without any more talk. Nikoo waited for a few moments, got up as if to go, then hesitated by the door. To save him from embarrassment, I said, 'You can use our petrol as long as you bring me some meat.'

There was still something holding the hunter back. He finally admitted that he did not have any cartridges either, which did not seem right to me.

'What about the box you bought before the deer hunt?'

'I gave half of them to Komanak as he did not have any of his own.'

This man Komanak had not been allowed further debt because he owed too much already. Although he was quite a successful hunter, Jimmy had said that he never liked settling his debts, always having a ready excuse for not paying as much as he ought to have done, with the inevitable consequence that he had reached the limit of his credit and could only obtain a further advance for the most urgent of reasons. The hunter had come up to the store with the other men before the deer hunt but must have understood the situation because he had not asked for any supplies. Nikoo continued, 'If I use more now there will be nothing left if we have a chance to hunt walrus.'

I knew that walrus hunting was important whenever the opportunity occurred because the meat provided a supply of good dog food, vital for a trouble-free trapping season. To my way of thinking, there was one easy way out of this little difficulty, which was to issue another box of cartridges to be charged and added to Komanak's debt. Nikoo's mouth dropped open with astonishment when he heard my suggestion. He thought he had not heard me properly, for he mumbled, looking decidedly uneasy, 'Komanak?'

'Yes. Komanak.'

'But he is dead, he died yesterday.'

It was my turn to look astonished. I had got into a muddle over names, for he was still alive according to my records. It was time for a swift reappraisal of my plan.

'I had not realized that Komanak was one of the dead. In that case we will supply the cartridges.'

Regretfully, I have to admit that what was concerning me most at that moment was the thought of the sizeable and irretrievable sum which would have to be written off as a bad debt. Nikoo made more purposefully for the door this time, his doubts about the seal hunt having been resolved.

Still somewhat shocked by the revelation that our principal debtor had passed away, I said, 'Tomorrow, in the afternoon, the shadow of the moon will cover the sun and there will be darkness.'

Once again, Nikoo's mouth dropped open in astonishment, but this time he did not know what to say, so he just gazed at me. I cannot think what prompted me to give the man this bit of news, perhaps just a pressing need to say something after my blunder over Komanak's death. Hurriedly attempting to make this strange prediction easier for the hunter to understand, I confused him still further by using my hands to illustrate what was going to happen, saying, 'The sun and the earth and the moon come into a line with each other so that the shadow hides the sun and the day goes dark.'

I realized this was woefully inadequate as an explanation as, completely mystified, all the Eskimo could do was to mumble, 'Dark?'

'Yes,' I explained. 'Dark for a little while in the afternoon.' Then, seeing poor Nikoo's discomfort at this strange talk, I added, 'But the darkness will not last long enough to stop you from hunting.'

With obvious relief at now being able to change the subject, Nikoo took the opportunity to ask if he could take the cartridges and petrol at once so that they would be able to set off early in the morning. I fetched my lantern from the porch, then we went over to the store to get the ammunition and to the oil shed to fill a can with petrol for him to top up the tank.

*

The afternoon outing in the sunshine went some way to restoring my morale and supplied me with renewed energy to face the days that followed. All did not go well. We lost three more hunters in the space of four days and poor Nyla was hanging on to her young life literally by a thread. She looked so wasted it seemed that if the deerskin coverings had not been holding her down she might have floated up towards the roof. The one small ray of light shining through the dark hours was that there were still no new victims.

Evi was also at work again, this time right out in the open. Some time after my return home from a sick-round, what seemed to be a disturbance broke out on a piece of ground between the house and the Eskimo homes. At first sight it looked as if a fight was taking place down there, but when I opened the door to see what was going on, I saw Evi addressing a small gathering in a very loud voice.

The group must have seen me come out of the door, so I had little choice but to take some kind of action. I closed the door carefully behind me, then walked, outwardly with confidence, towards the gathering. As I approached, Evi's strident tones faltered somewhat, while two or three people at the back of the meeting disappeared back into their homes, but what silenced the *angekok* completely was my sudden decision to pass right beside him on my way to the tents beyond.

This manoeuvre of mine was not the result of any deep thinking on my part or indeed of any thought at all, being the consequence of a sudden wave of indecision which came over me on reaching the meeting place. I had been quite unable to think of anything suitably crushing to say without being abusive, so could only proceed in a dignified manner, right through the assembly as if there were no one there, aiming for the nearest tent some distance beyond.

No carefully thought-out plan could have been more successful, for Evi's address petered out at once and several people, though all women, trailed after me down towards the camp. As it was not my time for visiting, I had brought no equipment with me, but fortunately the two invalids in the home I entered were sleeping, apparently peacefully, so it was enough for me to say a few words as to how much better it was to allow the sick people to rest quietly than to disturb them with unnecessary noise. A general murmur of approval greeted my words, but no doubt if Evi had come in to raise the roof with his routines, the family would have been equally approving.

There was no real need for me to visit the other homes as there would have to be an evening round in any case, so I made for home. On my way came the darkness caused by the eclipse. I wondered if Nikoo had understood my muddled explanation of the previous night or whether I had simply succeeded in making the whole thing more mysterious than it would otherwise have been.

My supper that night consisted of shrimps on toast, which turned out to be a very unfortunate choice, for during the night I was taken violently ill with terrible griping pains accompanied by vomiting and diarrhoea which continued until morning, by which time I was prostrate and must have looked an awful sight when Innuk came up to the house. She called out from the kitchen, then when there was no reply came into the bedroom to gasp with horror as she saw me sprawled out on the bed.

'Issuma! Issuma!' she cried despairingly, no doubt convinced that death was about to intervene in her affairs once more.

I did not reply. Perhaps this was childish of me, but at the time, feeling too weak to engage in lengthy explanations, it seemed that my best course would be to feign sleep in the hope of being left alone.

Innuk went out almost immediately, but did not remain absent for long, returning shortly with a friend. They stood by the bed, presumably examining me before deciding what course of action to take.

'He looks very bad,' said Innuk.

'Is he the same as the others?' asked her friend, whose voice I recognized as that of Nikoo's wife, Polly.

There was little point in my becoming involved in a discussion with the women, far better to continue to be 'asleep' in the hope of being left alone to rest. This hope was not to be realized, for my friends showed an unexpected determination to take action of some kind. Polly, no doubt recollecting my insistence that all the sick should be given plenty of liquid, sent Innuk to fetch a glass of water, then proceeded to prop me up in bed while she endeavoured to pour the drink into my mouth.

With great difficulty, I managed to remain apparently asleep while swallowing a few sips of the water. Polly held me in a strong grip and appeared satisfied when the water began to run back out of my mouth. The women mopped me up, then had a brief talk as to what they should do next, eventually agreeing that they would leave me for a while and return later.

Some time must have elapsed before my nurses reappeared. A deep sleep had helped to restore me to a near normal condition after my dreadful night. It seemed that the sheer violence of the attack had cleared my system of the poison that had caused it. In a few moments, a sponge was being applied to my forehead. It had been my intention to 'awake' before the treatment began, but it was really quite pleasant to receive these attentions from the women while their soothing scent, a combination of deerskins and blueberries, drifted into the room. Then a very interesting conversation took place, which began with Polly saying, 'Why don't we fetch Ookoo?'

'We can't do that. He is not pleased with Evi and the *kudloona* do not have *angekoks*.'

'But he was only cross with Evi because of the noise. Ookoo is a quiet person.'

Innuk did not reply to this, but continued with her sponging, giving me time to think. Ookoo, who I presumed to be a woman, must be the female type of *angekok* whom I thought had more or less died out since the coming of the missionaries. Whether these women ever acted in the capacity of full-blown *angekoks* or simply fulfilled a minor role was not clear, but there did not seem to have been any prejudice against them simply on the basis of sex and they were certainly called upon in times of sickness.

What poetic justice it would have been if my illness had been serious and a cure had been effected by an *angekok*! There was no reason for me to pretend to sleep any longer, so quite suddenly I opened my eyes. Innuk was in the process of examining me closely, her head only a few inches from mine, giving me a close-up vision of a pair of startled, jet-black eyes.

My friend backed away but continued to regard me rather doubtfully, as though I might yet slip out of her grasp. I reassured her, 'I shall be all right now. Thank you both very much for coming to look after me, you have helped me greatly.'

There was silence for a few moments. Polly's expression indicated great puzzlement, so I said, 'Did you want to ask me something?'

Polly looked over at Innuk, as though asking permission to question me, then could restrain herself no longer.

'My husband Nikoo said that you told him that there would be darkness yesterday while he was seal hunting. How did you know this?'

The tone of her voice sounded as though she rather suspected that I had somehow caused the eclipse. Rather foolishly, I brushed her query aside by simply telling her that the ship people had told me about it, an explanation that did not really satisfy her curiosity. Later, I was sorry not to have given Polly a full explanation about the eclipse. I had not intended to be so mysterious about a perfectly ordinary happening and certainly did not want to give her the impression that I was capable of some form of magic.

My main concern at this point was for the patients I had been forced to neglect. I insisted that my two reluctant guardians set off home while I prepared to visit the sick. During my rounds I discovered that Polly had taken it into her head to bring Ookoo for a visit to Nyla.

Ookoo was a beaming, pleasant-faced Eskimo woman whom I would never have suspected of being an *angekok*. I had seen her about before and always thought what a kind-looking person she was. As I entered the home Ookoo was talking to Nyla in a quiet, rather low voice. What she was saying did not seem to make much sense to me, but there was a hypnotic quality about it that made the words irrelevant. The strange quality of her persuasive voice had affected not only Nyla but also the others in the tent, so that the woman in charge of the lamp had neglected to check the wick and the flame flickered unevenly, adding an unearthly dimension to the scene.

I sat myself down on a box by the entrance. Ookoo wavered slightly at first then continued on with her talk. Nyla, looking more peaceful and relaxed than when I had last seen her, was already half asleep. A rising wind rattled at the tent door and tugged at the dry skins of the roof, but Ookoo held the people silent with her soothing voice. It was like being beside a summer river on a warm day with the water rustling endlessly away to the sea. There was none of the shouting normally associated with the *angekok*'s business. When Nyla was quite asleep, Ookoo rose suddenly to her feet without warning, stepped over to the door and was gone.

The others showed no surprise at her quick departure. They sat silently, as though spellbound. Polly gave me a searching look, as if she were estimating the effect upon me of her proté-gée's performance. Evidently satisfied by what she saw, she followed Ookoo out of the home.

The 'treatment' Nyla had just been given could not have done her anything but good, but it was a new experience for me. I had always assumed the *angekoks* to be people whose dealings with the spirit world invariably involved a high degree of disturbance. It had now become necessary for me to revise my previous judgements. So that the people should not assume either approval or disapproval from my actions, I tried to behave as though nothing out of the ordinary had occurred. It would not do for the report to get about that a company manager had shown too much approval of an *angekok*'s ceremonies, but if Ookoo's efforts resulted in the slightest improvement in

Nyla's condition, I would certainly not discourage her in any way.

A brisk wind coming off the sea urged me homeward. Cool enough to hint that summer was already giving way to the fall, it did not yet cut with the icy edge to be expected in the later months, but in my weakened state it was penetrating enough to send me home in stumbling haste over the rough ground.

Innuk and Polly had heartened me considerably by the real concern they had shown for my welfare but foremost in my mind was the growing reappraisal of my attitude to the *angekoks*. It was clear that Ookoodlea, to give her her full name, had a definite ability to give assistance to people, judging by the effect she had produced in Nyla's home. I wondered if it might also be possible that Evi's more strident incantations could aid a patent's recovery at least as effectively as my provison of painkillers. It had been my assumption that such a raucous approach to a sick person must be harmful, a view reinforced by the fact that most of the people treated by the *angekok* had died. Perhaps, instead of automatically opposing Evi's spells and chants, a more conciliatory attitude might have had better results for the patients, which after all was the end object of our attentions.

Enough time had now elapsed since our last newly afflicted patient to conclude that the epidemic was over. It was quite possible that not all the present sufferers would recover, but life did begin to return to a sort of normality, within the limits imposed by the sudden removal of so many hunters. The fear that other camps might also have been affected had receded, for we should have heard about it by this juncture.

At last I began to feel that we could look beyond the next twenty-four hours. We could even start on the now urgent plans as to how best to organize ourselves for the winter after the loss of yet another group of hunters.

One morning around this time I woke to the sound of my bedroom door opening. A childish voice betrayed the fact that it was Koolee.

'Can I go and look at Issuma?' she asked her mother.

There was no audible reply to this, but heavy breathing coming from just beside the bed indicated that the girl had come straight in and was probably subjecting me to a close scrutiny.

I lay so still that Koolee called, 'Is he dead mother?'

This nearly caused me to burst out laughing, but fearing I might frighten the child unnecessarily, I opened my eyes slowly, took hold of her hand, which was right beside my face, and said, 'No, Koolee, I am not dead, but am very thirsty. Will you ask your mother to make me some tea, please?'

After the tea and my morning ablutions, Innuk helped me to work out our exact 'casualty list' and how the families had been affected.

Up to now, eight people had died, six men and two women. Three others we expected to recover, but they would not be fit for some time yet. There were two other men in a very shaky state and Nyla was still hovering between life and death. This meant that, including the last year's tragedies, we had suffered 24 deaths out of a total population of 121.

The worst realization was that eighteen of the twenty-four dead were hunters out of a total hunter population of forty-two. Most of these men came from around the post area or near by, so bearing in mind the number of people who would not be able to undertake full hunting duties for a while yet, we were going to be in a parlous state at Ward Inlet with a lot of mouths to feed and lamps to keep alight and very few able bodies to provide the wherewithal. We only had a couple of months left in which to make what preparations we could to ensure at least a minimum stock of the essentials needed to carry us through the winter.

I still, of course, had the camp rounds to attend to, but these had become much more pleasant than had seemed probable. To my surprise everybody was quite affably disposed towards me, and my offerings of nourishment were accepted with every show of gratitude. In Nikoo's home, one of the best in the camp, Polly was looking after a relation of some kind, who was now making such good progress that a complete recovery was to be hoped for.

She followed me out of the house after my visit and said, 'My husband and the others have gone to fetch the deer meat from the cache up in the hill.'

I did not reply to this, feeling reasonably certain that she had not come out of her home to give me a piece of information which she could easily have passed on inside. Undoubtedly there was something else on her mind. The woman remained silent for a moment or two, waiting in vain for me to speak, then said, 'The people are asking how it was that you knew about the darkness that fell on the day that Nikoo went sealing with Powlussie.'

'The little box which stands on the table in my room told me about it,' I replied.

Polly looked as though she did not believe this explanation, which was unsurprising since it was completely different from the one I had given her the other day. She let the matter pass, however, because she had another mystery to solve.

'The people say that you must know more than we do because the illness left you so quickly.'

'That was because it was a different illness,' I replied, thinking it best not to go into a lengthy discourse as to the cause of my upset.

Again my friend was unconvinced.

'You looked the same as the others,' she said doubtfully.

I was trying to think up a conclusive explanation which

would damp down Polly's curiosity when I noticed more practical matters had taken a grip on her mind. Polly was studying the harbour, paying particular attention to the narrow area on the eastern side of the island in the mouth of the bay. Her jolly face had assumed an air of professional concentration as she took a sighting over the sharp peak of a rock sticking up out of the reef straight ahead of us.

In a moment, my companion relaxed somewhat and said, 'Kikitukjuameot.'

She had observed a boat approaching and had already identified it as belonging to the people who had been staying at a camp on a large island down towards the mouth of Frobisher Bay. Although my eyesight is very good, the craft was not yet visible to me. I said, in English, 'You've got eyes like a hawk, Polly.'

Her face broke into a happy smile. Heaven only knows what she thought I had said, but she obviously considered it to be something complimentary, and since she was unused to compliments, for Eskimo men do not normally indulge in such niceties, this was almost tantamount to my flirting with her. We suspended our little tête-à-tête so that she could dash off to inform the camp of the approaching boat.

There were two boats as it turned out, both well loaded with men, women and children, for the whole camp had made the journey, but also with a good weight of walrus meat to trade. This pleased me greatly, for we would not be able to do much walrus hunting by the time we had got a crew together and carried out the search for the uranium, which had been lurking at the back of my mind.

Our visitors set about establishing temporary homes right away, but as the tide was half down, they had to carry their gear a fair distance, which delayed their appearance at the house. When my door opened, expecting to see one of the newcomers,

I was surprised to find that it was Nikoo already back from the hills.

The hunter did not look at all happy.

'The meat had nearly all gone,' he said, without any of the usual preamble, indicating the seriousness of the loss. What was even worse, the skins, so badly needed for the winter clothing, had been spoiled as well.

Under the strain of bringing the sick people home as quickly as possible, the hunters had not constructed the cache as carefully as they should have done. The skins had been left behind so that the unaffected people could give their sick friends all the help they needed. In nine years out of ten, no harm would have resulted, but in this jinxed year a wolf pack had made one of its rare appearances. The animals had broken open the cache, so that even after they had helped themselves, the foxes could follow on to steal most of what was left, an opportunity which the scavengers had not neglected.

Before we had time to get to grips with this added problem, which was bound to call for decisions from me since any new hunt would have to be financed with credit, the visitors made their belated appearance. The good news was that none of the bad luck, seemingly inescapable at Ward Inlet, had affected them.

The men had had a very successful walrus hunt on a nearby island, then afterwards had only to journey a short distance inland before coming across quite a large herd of caribou, which they were able to follow for some miles, eventually securing ten of the animals. Later, they had gone for a second hunt. Now they were here to trade the skins from this second hunt together with a few sealskins and various other wares.

The main spokesman for these people, a man called Koojesse, who was one of the most efficient hunters in the whole of Frobisher Bay, said that they had also seen several big whales down in the vicinity of the old whaling station. They had even thought of going after one of them, but lacking the experience of earlier generations in hunting these huge creatures without the proper equipment, they had decided against risking their spears and lines in what might be a fruitless quest.

Koojesse's people had had good sealing too and they had brought enough meat of all kinds with them to help us out of the doldrums into which we had been sinking. He also quite unknowingly gave me one or two ideas as to how to set about making some sort of a comeback after the misfortunes of the past weeks.

The evening after Koojesse's arrival, my walk home was punctuated by two claps of thunder, which was most unusual for those parts. The heavy black clouds had banked up from the western side of the bay, to edge their way slowly across our inlet without shedding their load of moisture until they reached the long high ridge, which runs the whole length of Frobisher Bay. Unable to cross the cliffs so heavily laden, the clouds released their load, so that soon the hills disappeared behind a thickening mist of rain, which drifted back to isolate the post house from the rest of the settlement and to hasten the fall of darkness.

I was sorting through a box of books that had arrived with the *Ungava* when I heard the kitchen door open.

An old man and a younger woman were hovering uncertainly by the door when I came out to greet them. Much relieved to see me, the old man said, 'My name is Ninguapik and this is my daughter Koomuk. You are known to us because of my other daughter, Kuni, who was starving with the people at the Kevitou camp when you and Beevee brought them food from across the hills. Kuni said that many people would have died without your help and this has been much talked of by the people of that place.'

The old man's little speech both astonished and pleased me, though our journey had been fairly routine and should not have been thought of as anything other than a normal rescue operation. I said, 'We heard that the people of Kevitoo had no food. On our way over to assist them, we came across a herd of deer, so were able to bring them meat as well as the other things from the post.'

The old man gazed at me as though he had forgotten what he had come for. Koomuk leaned forward to whisper in his ear, whereupon Ninguapik produced a bag from under his parka and shook the contents out on to the table. It was a model dog team with sledge and driver; twelve little ivory dogs were each connected by a thin skin line to the sledge on which the driver was seated, his whip poised for action.

'What a good carving,' I said, not quite sure whether the old man had brought the set in to trade or not. Ninguapik pushed it all over towards me.

'It is for you,' he said. 'My daughter asked me to make something as they had nothing to give you.'

'They did not need to give me anything. We were glad that we were able to help most of them before it was too late.'

'This is what Kuni wanted.'

I was extremely moved by this beautiful gift and gratified to know that the Eskimo families, their realism always at work, had appreciated our practical assistance in their hour of need, despite their readiness to call upon the spirit world.

After the father and daughter had gone, I sat in the kitchen in the darkness thinking about our situation at the post. At present, food was reasonably plentiful, especially since the arrival of the boat from Kikitukjuak, but the testing time would come in the cold dark days of winter when the weather would often be bad and the hunting difficult. How could we arrange things so that the hunterless families would have enough fat to keep the lamps burning as well as the increased amount of food necessary to sustain life during those bitter months?

The wind had risen as the daylight faded, brushing quite gently round the house at first, then gathering enough strength to rattle at the door and sweep the rain against the window in gusty spasms. This background noise combined with my mental preoccupation completely absorbed the gentle sound of Innuk's entry into the room, so that I did not realize that she was standing almost beside me until she spoke anxiously into the darkness, 'Issuma, are you here?'

'Yes, Innuk, I have been sitting here since Ninguapik and Koomuk left and must have fallen asleep.'

My friend would know about the visitors and probably about the carving they had given me, but she would have been puzzled as to why anyone should sit in the darkness thinking. To avoid confusing her, it seemed best to take refuge in sleep once more. She accepted this explanation quite readily.

'Shall I light the lamp for you?'

'It's in the other room somewhere, but there is a candle here on the window ledge.'

I found the matches with the candle and in the fitful light, for the wind was seeping into the kitchen in little bursts, saw that Innuk, dressed in a sealskin *artigee* with the hood up over her head, was standing beside me.

Every now and then, a flicker of light from the candle lit up her face framed in the hood. She was spattered with rain, but I thought what a pleasant person she looked and was. Producing my pail rather diffidently, she said, 'I have brought you some seal meat in case you have not had anything to eat yet.'

'Thank you, Innuk, but you should not have come out in all this rain.'

She did not reply, but looked at me very intently as though

she was saying something to me without speaking, then at last she asked, 'Would you like me to stay with you?'

Instinct told me what the answer to this question ought to be, but never having had a lady friend or indeed never having been alone with a girl other than my sister in my life, fright seized me so that I said quickly, 'No, Innuk, you must go and talk to your friends.'

I hoped that she would not think of this as an insult, for it was certainly not my intention to infer that, as an Eskimo, she was in any way inferior and therefore unacceptable. A slight smile came over her face when she heard my answer, however, as though she had divined the reason for my sending her home and could not understand why I should be afraid of her.

When she opened the door to set off home, the rain was very heavy indeed, so I fetched my sou'wester to give her some extra protection. This appeared to amuse her, but she was looking very pleased when the tiny strip of light from the candle caught her face as she passed the window.

The storm rose to a crescendo after Innuk had gone, but because it did not have the sheer violence of the previous onslaught when the people's tents had been flooded, the creaking of the rafters and the rattling of the rain on the roof were not quite as alarming. After eating supper, I lay in bed listening to the wireless without undue concern even though a steady dripping sound coming from somewhere up in the roof space indicated that water was penetrating into the house. This careless attitude was to cost me dearly.

In the morning, I awoke to the familiar sound of the door being opened. Once again I kept my eyes closed until the sound of heavy breathing coming from close by my head suggested that my visitor was Koolee, who once engaged in her newly acquired pastime of 'looking at Issuma' was unlikely to be deterred by my feigning sleep.

A strange apparition appeared before me as I opened my eyes. Standing by my bed was what appeared to be my headless sou'wester jerking about, waiting to confront me, though one dark eye peering out through a buttonhole confirmed that it was Koolee concealed within the garment. Pretending alarm, I cried out, '*Kinaluk una?*' ('Who on earth is this?') and dived beneath the bedclothes.

There was silence for a few moments, then a quavery voice said, 'Come out Issumatak, it's only Koolee.'

I emerged cautiously from under the bedclothes with an expression of relief. The girl was staring at me curiously with the oilskin draped round her shoulders. She wanted to know if I had eaten all the seal meat that her mother had brought me the previous evening and why it was that *kudloonas* did not sometimes eat uncooked meat *innuktetoot* (in the same manner as the Eskimos).

I said, 'Because we have big fires like the one in the other room. With plenty of wood and coal to burn it is very easy for everything to be cooked quite quickly. You Innuit only have your lamps to help you prepare your food. Nearly everybody else has some quick way of cooking, so very few other people eat raw meat, that's why the Indians, who live near you, called you Eskimos.'

'Indians!' interrupted the girl with a scornful wave of the hand.

'We call you Eskimos too,' I added.

Koolee made a great effort to pronounce the word and came out with something which sounded like 'Echeemo', so I sat up in bed to show her how to say it.

'Ess–Ess–Ess,' I mouthed to demonstrate how to place the tongue and teeth to produce the sound.

'Ech–Ech–Ech,' piped up my companion.

'No. No. Not like that. Like this,' and I opened my mouth

to point out the position of my tongue. While sitting up in bed with my mouth wide open mouthing these ridiculous sounds, I saw that Innuk had joined us and was standing in the doorway watching the proceedings with an amused smile, as of one watching children at play.

'I was teaching your daughter to speak English,' I explained rather lamely.

'Yes,' said my friend, coming into the room, still with that rather patronizing smile. 'Would you like some tea?'

So I lay in bed sipping my tea and eating the biscuit Innuk had brought me while my thoughts went back to the previous evening, first of all to the pleasant and totally unexpected surprise Ninguapik and his daughter had given me, then to Innuk's offer to keep me company during a dark and stormy evening. It was clear that my refusal had not upset her in any way.

Mother and daughter retired to the kitchen, giving me a chance to regain my dignity, but when I stretched across the bed to turn the wireless on in the hope of hearing the morning news, no sound whatsoever came out of the machine. A brief investigation revealed that, during the night, the water leaking in from the roof had run along a cross-beam in the roof space, then down one of the uprights before splashing off a shelf into the back of the wireless, soaking the components so thoroughly as to render the apparatus completely useless.

I gasped with the full realization that there was no possibility of replacing the equipment.

Hearing my distress, Innuk came running in to see what had happened. Her woebegone expression when she heard that my wireless was now defunct showed that she appreciated what a blow it was for me. She stood gazing at me sadly, until, pulling myself together sharply, I recollected the harsh blows my poor friend had had to withstand during the past month and the stoicism and endurance which she and the others had shown in bearing their terrible misfortunes. It would not do for her to see me shattered by a minor mishap like this.

'*Ionamut!*' ('It can't be helped!') I said. 'And it will mean that I shall have more time to teach Koolee English.'

Nevertheless, this attempt at light-heartedness could not dislodge the thought from my mind that this meant the end of all outside news and music as well as the Saturday-night messages.

XI

I HAD THE GREATEST ADMIRATION for the ability of the Eskimo people to adapt to the circumstances that surrounded them and to make the best of hard times. With this in mind, it occurred to me that a general spirit of cooperation between the affected families would substantially improve our prospects for the winter, particularly if I took the lead in the form of supplies. We needed to organize a hunting expedition, but first of all the air of resignation which had been hanging over the camp since the start of the illness had to be completely dispersed. The arrival of Koojesse and the others had begun the process, and I decided we needed to build on the fresh spirit they seemed to be injecting into the camp. I managed to persuade Kidlapik to hold a 'thanksgiving' meeting for those of us that had survived the ordeal. When I then remembered it would soon be my twenty-first birthday, we combined the two events into a day-long celebration.

The supply ship had brought me a large birthday cake from my mother, which was still sealed up in an airtight tin. I hoped it had survived the long journey from New Zealand intact, to be produced and washed down with mugs of tea during the party.

I knew some of the invalids would not be well enough to attend the gathering. In general the men were still in need of gentle recuperation and Nyla still worried me greatly. The girl's progress was very slow, so slow in fact that it sometimes seemed as though her constitution had suffered an irretrievable setback. I was pleased, though, that Ookoodlea had taken Nyla under her wing. She was often in attendance talking to the girl and her generally helpful and calming influence was invaluable.

The preceding evening, I was drawing up a list of events for the party, when Koojesse came up for a chat with Nikoo and a couple of other hunters. They said that they would go out in the morning to see if they could get seal meat for our gathering. I took this opportunity to show Koojesse the map the office had sent me with their letter about the green rock which seemed to be located somewhere in the vicinity of Warwick Sound. They were all totally mystified, having never themselves seen or heard of such a rock.

The hunters said that the whaling ships, of which there had been at one time a great number, cruised up and down the bays and sounds which indent the coastline all the way from the station at Cape True along the east coast as far as Cumberland Gulf. If the old man could not accurately recall where he had made his sighting, the rock might have appeared anywhere along this very long stretch of coastline and we would have very little chance of success unless we were prepared to undertake a long hunt. I had no intention whatsoever of journeying into Davis Straits at any time of the year. The post boat would simply not be up to coping with an autumn gale out there, so our investigations would have to be confined to the area around Warwick Sound. I explained that this trip fitted in well with my plans to organize a hunting expedition, because we should then be able to charge the whole cost of the trip to the London office as the journey would have been made primarily on their behalf.

The two hunters, both highly respected in their communities, were interested to hear about these plans, so while they were at the house we discussed the camp's predicament. We were all agreed that unless we could work out an effective organization fairly quickly, there would certainly be shortages of food, fuel and clothing materials during the winter months. The few hunters remaining in the local camp would hardly be able to keep themselves going, let alone assist the widows and orphans of the hunters who were dead.

Nikoo proposed that for a start he and his friends could set out the seal nets at present lying unused at the back of the store. Innuk had told me that the men had used them quite successfully last year, so with any luck, with our need now even greater, we would be equally fortunate.

We also decided that as the caribou skins were still in good condition at this time of year, the securing of deerskins for the women to make the winter clothes ought to be the first priority. We would travel out to the area at the head of Frobisher Bay near the big fish river, an extensive stretch of flat land that was much favoured by the caribou for late summer grazing. The other, equally serious hunt, to ensure a supply of winter meat and fuel, could then take place. As this second hunt would mean travelling in the opposite direction, I told Nikoo and Koojesse that we could combine it with my search for the strange green rock. This meant it would have to be underway before the autumn gales set in.

Unfortunately, credit limits had already been extended beyond strictly permissible levels because of the failure of the first deer hunt. The only alternative was some form of relief venture using the post boat, the expense of which would also have to be borne by the company. It was much better that they be assisted in this way rather than falling back on handouts later.

When Koojesse first mentioned about the whales he had seen this summer, the idea of setting up a full-scale whale hunt had passed through my mind, but I discouraged it on account of the general lack of equipment and experience. While sorting through a pile of old stock at the back of the store, however, I came across a large, unmarked box which contained a Norwegian harpoon gun, together with 'bomb' ammunition and a big coil of strong rope. By the look of it, the weapon had never been used, but the method of operation seemed quite simple. I felt certain that the Innuit hunters, never unwilling to accept a hunting challenge, would be prepared to undertake a whale hunt armed with this equipment.

*

The party was a resounding success. Kidlapik officiated at a simple service, which was followed by an afternoon of sports. The kayak race caused some delay because we had too many entrants to get them all off at once so the hunters had to be divided into two heats, with the first two in each heat qualifying for a place in the final. Eventually, we got everything under way to the enthusiastic appreciation of all present. A young hunter from among the visitors was the clear winner of the final, thus saving me, as judge, from the embarrassment of having to pick the first man home in a close finish.

A crowd of women and older girls contested the potato and spoon race, so we had to pack them all together, which resulted in a considerable degree of good-natured jostling. Ookoo had both her spoon and potato knocked out of her hand by a passing contestant and the whole race came to a temporary halt while the other competitors enjoyed a hearty laugh at her expense. The women covered the rough ground with remarkable dexterity. As they approached the winning point, the front five or so looked as though they might finish in a dead heat, but Polly suddenly burst out from among them with a last rush of speed, after which they all sank to the ground for another round of hearty laughter.

The children soon grasped the idea of sack racing and in no time were bouncing across the stony ground as if they had been doing it for years. Koolee and a visiting boy were neck and neck for most of the race, with the other children not too far behind them, but the girl succeeded in manoeuvring her opponent off on to a very bumpy part of the course at the last moment and edged ahead to win the race.

The weather worsened after the tea break, with a thin drizzle hastening the approach of twilight. This might have been a good moment to call a halt to the proceedings, but foolishly, as it turned out, I decided that we should have a three-legged race and that the women should have the right to choose their own partners.

Polly took immediate advantage of this free-for-all to select me as her partner, which did not appear to displease her husband in the slightest. In fact he chortled with amusement as our legs were secured together. Happening to glance over at Innuk, however, I saw that the idea had been a great blunder on my part, for it was obvious that she was not pleased. It was too late to draw back, as Polly, having clearly set her mind on victory, set off at a determined pace, dragging me somewhat unwillingly beside her.

We won the race, but by then Innuk was nowhere to be seen.

The day had dwindled and the mist, suspended down at the harbour mouth all afternoon, now began to roll slowly towards us, hovering at first along the line of the reef, then spreading gradually over the rocky foreshore enveloping us like a damp blanket. It was time to gather our belongings and go off for the seal supper provided by the efforts of the morning. Everyone had been able to participate in the fun and there was still the dance to come.

While the rest of the camp finished their supper, I prepared the 'dance hall' for the evening entertainment.

Nikoo came up to help me push some of the boxes to one side to provide an open space down the centre of the store. We hung my two gas lanterns from the rafters at either end of the room to give sufficient illumination and organized a seat up by the counter, from which the fiddler could call the steps and provide the music, for this was not to be a traditional Eskimo dance but the set dances and reels of the type introduced by the sailors of the whaling ships.

As the thickening mist began to creep into the store, an old man carrying a fiddle appeared, leading behind him, like an Eskimo pied piper, a line of would-be dancers. In no time at all, he had tuned up and was scratching out the first dance.

I saw Polly at the other end of the line but was forced to retreat behind a pile of boxes when she caught my eye as I needed to sooth Innuk's ruffled feelings and bring her back into the fold.

Koolee had come across but could not say whether her mother was to follow her or not. She thought it unlikely because her mother seemed rather cross about something. This was pretty much what I had expected and it was up to me to put things right again.

My progress through the foggy night was perilous in the extreme. The darkness was complete and a slight breeze had sprung up, not sufficient to disperse the mist, but enough to swirl the fog and the drizzle together into vague ghostlike shapes which disorientated me to such an extent that I thought I might miss my destination altogether and finish up wandering off along the north shore.

Fortunately, some dogs began barking, enabling me to correct my course, but in changing direction I tripped and grazed my hand against a rock, so that when I entered Innuk's home my hand was bleeding.

My friend's annoyance dissolved at once into concern over my injury, which looked very much worse than it was. Nyla, who had moved from her old home, was sleeping peacefully in the middle of the sleeping platform, while the old man and woman were looking after things at the other end, so Innuk then came back to the store with me to join in the dancing.

After two or three reels up and down the line, I decided to rest for a while on a box at the back. Koojesse joined me in a moment or two and we got to chatting about the hunting, so I showed him the harpoon gun. The hunter became quite excited at the thought of trying the weapon and said that there would be no difficulty in getting a crew together to operate the gun from my boat. As we had discussed, however, the first priority was to get the deerskins for the winter clothes, so I resolved that night to get an expedition to the head of Frobisher Bay underway as soon as possible.

Unfortunately, another frosty encounter with Evi the next day left our hunting party rather slight. Polly informed me that Evi had been collecting payment for his recent services. At first I sensibly decided to ignore her rather eager information. However, Polly, clearly aware as to which of her revelations would be most likely to aggravate me, kept the titbits till last with the disclosure that two of the men had had to give up cartridges and a third his .22 rifle. What made me angry was that both the men had obtained the cartridges as part of their debt allowance. Underwriting payments to the *angekok* was definitely not part of the company's function.

Without pausing to consider what the eventual outcome would be, I stormed off to interrogate Evi. The man was obviously surprised to see me, for we had not actually spoken to each other since the night of my dramatic appearance in the sick man's home. He seemed amazed at the degree of my anger over what, to him, must have been quite a small matter, and on calmer reflection I too felt that the strength of my reaction had been excessive.

As it was, Evi handed back the ammunition without any protest, but the hunters did not show much pleasure in the return of their gifts. During the afternoon, some of the hunters who had previously shown an interest in taking part in the Frobisher Bay expedition, came up to the house to tell me that they had after all decided to try their luck nearer home. Everyone felt that the deer would still be grazing at no great distance from the Kikitukjuak camp, and if this were so it would give them an opportunity to do their hunting on the way back from the post instead of having to spend time going round to the fish river.

As, one after another, they came up to tell me of their altered plans, I realized that this was Evi's reply to the humiliation he had undergone in having to give back some of his pay. My party dwindled until it became clear that the planned trip would have to be abandoned, at least in its original form. The last man to come up to the house was Nikoo. At first I assumed that he also wished to withdraw from the party, but he surprised me by casually suggesting an alternative grouping. He and another hunter, Powlussie, were going to remain. If I joined them and we took the women, Innuk and Polly, both of whom had often gone on the annual deer hunt, there was no reason why we should not have a successful outing. It was unusual to say the least for the company man to go hunting in a mixed party, but it was certainly a simple solution to our problem.

Apart from Nikoo and Powlussie, all the hunters were leaving together. The group remaining at Ward Inlet would include Innuk, Koolee and the old man and woman who lived with them, Ookoodlea, her two children, Nyla and an orphan boy. Powlussie's wife would leave with the others on the understanding that Powlussie would be returning to his family after the hunt.

Innuk and Koolee came in after the men had gone and were

apparently well pleased at the prospect of an outing. When Koolee had gone out to play with her friends, I asked Innuk why so many of the men had changed their minds about the deer hunt. She was reluctant to say anything at first, but after some cajoling I discovered that Evi had told them that it would not be good to go hunting again in this area so soon after the summer deaths.

The Kikitukjuak and Twerpukjuak parties departed the day before us. When everything was ready, they came up to say goodbye, some of them a trifle sheepishly. I was careful to part on amicable terms with everyone, even managing a few civil words with Evi. As so many people would be down or near Warwick Sound, Kidlapik decided to go with them in the hope of being able to muster a reasonable congregation for his services.

Before they left, we made a definite arrangement with Koojesse to go whaling with the harpoon gun on the day of the next full moon. One whale carcass would give us a sufficient stockpile of meat and fat to ward off any serious shortages during the winter months. The timing was of some importance because the tides would be at their highest over the full-moon period, which would help us to beach the carcass well up on the shore for the cutting-up process.

The sea was quiet and patches of mist were clinging to the surface of the water as we set off from the harbour the next morning. Polly was at the helm, steering us skilfully through the reef and on towards the western side of the narrows. Her expertise surprised me. Although the Innuit women had at one time been prominent boat people, it had been my experience up in the gulf that this was no longer the case, partly because of the widespread use of engines. In days gone by, when the Innuit had to rely almost entirely upon their own resources, much of the sea hunting was done in *oomiaks*, or 'women's boats', which were rowed and steered by women to leave the men free to use their hunting equipment: rifles if they had them, or spears and lances.

Looking back from the narrows, about three miles or so from the post, I could see that the mist had formed into a strip stretching right along the shoreline. The post house appeared like a window in a cloud hanging above the surface of the sea, overshadowed by the heavy black cliffs which ringed both sides of the inlet, reaching towards each other from either side to encircle the harbour. The hunters were very patient all morning, accepting my decision that there should be no shooting until we had passed the island of Nuaktualuk off the tip of the Beecher Peninsula. They became more restive as the mist drifted away to allow the seals to start showing themselves at no great distance from us.

It was not in the nature of my Innuit friends to deny themselves the chance of shooting a seal simply because they were primarily engaged on a deer hunt. Centuries of hard living had taught them that no matter what the pressures on their journey time might be, a present opportunity should never be neglected. A potential food supply at hand in the morning might not be obtainable at all later. However, by forgoing the hunting opportunities which were present in Ward Inlet, we made good speed, which was important if we were to get back in time for the whale hunt.

We kept close to the peninsula coastline until we came to what seemed to be a point of sharply rising cliffs, which stood out prominently ahead of the flattish land we were now approaching. Nikoo corrected my first impression that this was part of the mainland by informing me that there was a sea passage on the eastern side of the cliff, but that it would suit our purpose best to pass to the west as we were making for a harbour on a straight course ahead of us.

Soon after, we reached the lowlands, which were so much more gentle than the steep surroundings to Ward Inlet and the greenest place I had yet seen on Baffin Island. I thought that this would have been a far pleasanter site at which to establish a trading post amid the waving grass and a few low hills, but perhaps other, more important reasons influenced the eventual choice of Ward Inlet.

Polly, who had apparently decided that our day's journeying should now be concluded, directed our course towards the western headland of a small bay which had opened out in front of us. Just behind the very tip of the land, our navigator headed in towards the shore, aiming for a camping site which everyone seemed to recognize.

We had a splendid supper of seal stew, a wedge of Innuk's bannock and mugs of tea, then afterwards settled ourselves among the deerskins to while away the evening. Polly produced a piece of string to demonstrate her version of a cat's-cradle game in which she made intricate representations of deer, whales, walrus, seals and polar bears. Koolee joined in with her length of string, so that shortly they were vying with one another to achieve the fastest fingerwork, eventually appealing to me to judge between them as to which was the champion 'string twister'. Being slightly afraid of Polly and not wishing to hurt the young girl's feelings, I took the path of diplomatic cowardice by declaring them joint winners. Then Koolee brought out a bagful of ivory bits and pieces, roughly carved as ducks, birds and the like, to form the basis of another game, but they were all much too quick for me, so I retired to read a few pages of my book.

After a half an hour or so of good-natured banter among themselves, the carvings were put away and Nikoo asked me about my book. He seemed to think that it was the Bible, but as it was actually a Thomas Hardy novel this was pretty wide of the mark. However, to enter into the general spirit of entertainment, I offered to tell them a *kudloona*'s story and the enthusiasm with which they accepted the offer astonished me.

I decided to give them a version of the Snow White fairy tale. The women were quite carried away when I came to the 'who is the fairest one of all' part. Polly actually rummaged in a deerskin bag she had with her to produce an old piece of broken mirror. Staring into this fragment of glass, of course, she could only see herself, which caused her to utter shouts of approval, but when she passed the mirror over to me, I angled it so that she could just see Innuk sitting at the far end, and she cried, in disbelief, 'It's Innuk!'

At that everybody burst into laughter. The noise was certainly sufficient to alarm any deer feeding in the vicinity on that quiet, frosty night, so to calm things down I told them a tale, with apologies to Lewis Carroll, of a walrus and a 'carving man' who went to sea in a funny boat and had a curious conversation with a passing seal. In the Innuit storytelling tradition, animals and men frequently converse together, so my tale was listened to with great attention and was not even considered to be silly or unlikely. Powlussie then told us a tale of his grandfather's about an ancestor who had been befriended by a polar bear. As this was quite a long story, by the time he had finished we were all ready to retire to our deerskins.

We ranged ourselves out in a rough semicircle, with Innuk on one end and then Koolee next to me, my other neighbour being Powlussie alongside Nikoo, and Polly on the other end.

Nikoo was the only snorer, but quite made up for that in the volume of sound he produced. Fortunately, I did manage to sleep in between the louder outbursts, so got enough rest to prepare me for an active day's hunting.

In the morning, all was business as we prepared for an early start. Innuk demonstrated her familiarity with the normal traders' routine by cooking up a pot of porridge, followed by a brew of tea. The others then finished off the seal meat from the night before. I contented myself with a couple of ship's biscuits as it was my intention to take a Thermos of coffee and two doughnuts in my pack to keep myself going during the day. The people watched my arrangements with interest, but nobody said anything. Even Polly remained silent, though her expression suggested a strong desire to cross-examine me. Innuk favoured me with one of her indulgent smiles.

The plan of campaign was quite simple. Powlussie was to head straight across towards the higher land behind the coastal lowland, then turn westward. This would bring him into a position on the far side of the feeding grounds from where he could prevent the deer escaping in the direction of the high hills and hopefully move them towards the rest of us. Nikoo and Polly were to proceed up behind Powlussie, ready to deal with any deer moving in their direction, while my role was to police the territory nearer the coastline which would be the probable route of escape.

The morning was cool and cloudy when we set off just as the dawn was turning into actual daybreak. Powlussie moved off at a great pace over the easy slopes, closely followed at the start by Nikoo and Polly, leaving me to take the lower path over the flats. I could not resist the excitement of the chase, half expecting to come across the unsuspecting deer over the brow of every hillock.

Instead, several small animals appeared and disappeared again. Two hares dodged about despite my proximity, a weasel darted purposefully through the grass and some fox cubs made as if to investigate me, but their mother, peering very suspiciously at me from the safety of her lair, barked a warning to summon her young back to their den.

The morning quiet was suddenly shattered by two distant

shots. Powlussie had sighted our quarry. I stopped, waiting to see if Nikoo and Polly would get a burst in, which indeed they did, for a fusillade of shots broke out from much closer to hand than I had anticipated. The deer were going to cross my path very shortly if our deductions had been correct, and there would be little, if any, time for me to compose myself or make a mistake.

The sudden, frantic appearance of ten or so deer charging straight towards me as I crept cautiously over the brow of the nearest hillock almost unnerved me, but those sharpshooting procedures so constantly drilled into me in the school training corps saved the day.

Confronted by my bombardment, the mob swerved off at an angle to the line of the shore, giving me another brief chance to take aim. Seconds later they were gone, thudding away from danger at top speed, leaving four of their number dead or disabled behind them. Three of them were quite dead, but the fourth, hit as it was swerving away, was still alive so would have to be dealt with promptly to save it unnecessary suffering. I was steeling myself for this unpleasant task when, as if by magic, Innuk and Koolee appeared and my friend went straight over to kill the struggling animal with a quick blow from a knife.

We skinned the carcasses straight away. Then I got out my Thermos flask and persuaded my companions to share my food. For the coffee, I had a tin mug. And Innuk drank hers from the cap of the Thermos, while Koolee had to be content with the little inner cap. This time Innuk did accept a piece of doughnut, but with some restraint, her natural good manners battling with a disinclination to partake of my strange food. Koolee nevertheless ate hers with positive relish which so pleased me that I gave her an extra piece, half of my share, as a reward.

The men arrived just after we had finished our lunch. The

people were certainly impressed with my bag, and to tell the truth so was I. Powlussie had managed to shoot two deer as he headed them down in our direction, while Nikoo and Polly had four between them. We had secured a total of ten in all, a really excellent morning's hunting, due in no small part to our well-planned attack. My friends soon reduced the carcasses to a neat pile of meat and skins, and then Polly, who had stayed behind to work on the other deer, joined us for a consultation as to what our next move should be.

Nikoo was all for going back to the boat so that we could move down the coast to confront our intended victims from the other direction, but on reflection we decided to complete our work there by getting the skins and meat down to the camp, where there was an old, empty cache for us to use. We packed all the skins neatly, reorganized the cache to take most of the meat and had everything cleared up by mid afternoon.

The hunters went off in their kayaks to try their luck on the water, while the two women and Koolee accompanied me on a walk, bringing bags with them for berry picking. Though not a sunny afternoon, it was pleasantly warm, so I lay on the reindeer moss. When I closed my eyes, Koolee came over and demanded to know why I was always pretending to be asleep, at which both Innuk and Polly, being within earshot, laughed very heartily.

The hunters returned just before dusk with one seal between them, so as we now had a reasonable supply of oil, Innuk set up her lamp. The others were going to eat seal meat again, but when I said that I would cook myself a deer steak on the Primus stove, Innuk insisted on doing that as well. She cooked for me very nicely a huge steak which would really have been enough for two people, but I struggled it all down, not wishing to hurt my kind friend's feelings.

After supper, I lay propped up on the deerskins and in the

warm, soothing glow of the oil lamps we spent a quiet evening chatting. They had heard of my arrival at Pangnirtung, apparently young enough for the people to refer to me as 'the boy', which puzzled them rather. The Eskimos, being very family orientated, could not understand why someone so young should have to leave the family group, unless it were to join other relatives or because of severely bad behaviour. I hesitated, thinking they would not understand the family circumstances leading to my departure. Then I remembered that the Archdeacon of the Arctic had at one time been the resident missionary at Lake Harbour and had visited Frobisher Bay, so I told them about his visit to my school. I said that the pictures he had shown us of the Innuit and their country had interested me to such an extent that I had written to the Hudson's Bay Company to ask them to send me to one of their posts, with the result that I had been accepted for Pangnirtung.

Inevitably my story generated many questions, especially from Polly, who wanted to know if the archdeacon was my father or some other relation and also had other fairly pertinent inquiries before the matter could be dropped. By the time I had finished the evening was well on and we settled down for the night. I was asleep before Nikoo got going with his nocturnal noises, but woke again very early in the morning, when all was reasonably quiet. I turned over carefully to avoid disturbing my neighbours, and saw that Innuk was watching me with a strange expression on her face. She held my eyes for a moment or two, so I smiled before settling back to sleep again. A slight feeling of unease passed through my mind at the possibility that I was drifting into a relationship with Innuk which I had been trying to avoid, not because of any fault with my kind and respectable friend, but because of the moral questions such an association would raise.

There was no reason for delay in the morning. With the boat

already loaded, we could set off straight away on the short journey towards the head of the bay. Seals were quite plentiful, as were the ducks, but not wishing to cause too great a disturbance this early in the day, we had decided once again not to do any unnecessary shooting.

We were soon approaching the mouth of a big river. The Innuit called it the fish river because of the very large numbers of fish to be found there in the early summer and fall. The sound of the water rushing down to the sea could be heard distinctly above the noise of our engine, and then, to my surprise, Polly leant over the side to catch up a dipperful of water, which she proceeded to drink. She laughed loudly at my obvious astonishment before explaining that it was fresh water and passed the dipper to me to test for myself. Plainly this was a river of considerable size that could throw out such a large volume of fresh water for so great a distance against the tide. Presently we reached the estuary, which was literally swarming with fish, much to everyone's delight. Whatever else happened, we were certainly not going to go hungry.

We wasted no time in establishing ourselves on a point of land which formed the western arm of the mouth of the river and prepared our plans for another round of stalking. Nikoo and Powlussie manoeuvred their kayaks across the river so that they could make their way up the east bank. I started out with Polly, then set off along my own course. Innuk and Koolee were going to organize our temporary home before following on behind me in case their assistance should be needed. I did not hurry at first, for the scenery was quite the most beautiful I had seen in the district. The river was quite tame for half a mile or so from the mouth, then there was a sharper rise, where the water rushed down over rocks, dropping probably as much as sixteen feet in less than a quarter of a mile. Boulders lined the banks for the first two miles, then became interspersed with grassy patches. Some way up from the sea, a plain opened out, growing wider and wider as it extended back towards the mountains.

Although the signs of deer were numerous all the way up my route, I saw nothing but old carcasses covered with grass or earth as evidence of past successes. I peered long and hard through my glasses, but there was nothing moving anywhere within my range of vision. There was no point in wandering on and on even in this pleasing place. I thought we might have better luck if we moved across the head of the bay to the banks of the smaller river.

Innuk, who had arrived with Koolee while I was sitting on a rock pondering our next move, was less than enthusiastic about crossing the head of the bay. She had once lived in this area and was concerned about the awkward mudflats as well as the tidal difficulties which we would probably encounter navigating among the small islands and large rocks strewn across the mouth of the river. On his return, however, Nikoo was of the opinion that we should be able to cross the bay without too much risk.

The two men gave a great display of boat handling, leaping out among the rocks and mud to push us clear of the obstructions with great skill. Even so, we took several bumps, scraped our bottom badly at least once, then grounded on a mudflat as we neared the shore. We had to wade across a patch of soft mud to reach a grassy patch suitable for a campsite, but the boat was stuck high and dry until the tide came well up again. Innuk, whose advice I would treat with considerably more respect next time, set about establishing our home with Koolee once more, while the rest of us spread out on either side of the river. This time, Nikoo crossed the water to the far bank with Polly stretched out on the kayak in front of him, so that they could make their way up the west bank. Powlussie and I were to strike inland from the camp area, with me taking the inside track by the river.

My route led me up past a very bulky rock, beyond which an attractive waterfall came suddenly into view with an assortment of river birds jostling about and enjoying themselves at the base. The fertile plainland was well grassed and rose slowly into quiet hills leading back in the distance to the inevitable brooding mountains. On all sides, there were more signs of animal life than there had been beside the other river and the bird population was as profuse as it was varied.

The first stage of my walk was interesting but uneventful until sudden bursts of shooting blasted out from both sides of the river, followed by the swift thudding sound of rapidly approaching deer. A mob from Powlussie's direction arrived first, aiming to escape along the river bank, but sweeping off in disarray when they came under my fire. As soon as the first wave departed, another group charged down the bank towards me, giving me time for a couple of shots before they took a wide turn to gallop off at an angle to the river.

The sudden pandemonium had been dramatic and overwhelming. Amazed that the frightened animals had not trampled me underfoot in their panic to get away, I retired behind a rock to recover my equilibrium before going to inspect the outcome of my shooting.

At that moment, Polly appeared before me on the opposite bank so unexpectedly that she might have materialized out of thin air. She was real enough and very welcome too as she hitched up her parka and crossed the water in five or six huge leaps, springing from rock to rock. If her intention had been to startle me, she certainly succeeded, but there had scarcely been time for me to wonder what I should do if she fell into the river before she had arrived beside me, her eyes sparkling, her cheeks glowing and hardly even out of breath.

'Good heavens, Polly, you're as agile as a mountain goat,' I said admiringly in English.

I swear my friend blushed with pleasure at my tone of voice, and feeling herself to be on safe ground she inquired what it was that I had said to her. She would probably only have had the vaguest idea as to what sort of animal a goat was, so I toned this part down to a general approval of her jumping skill. Polly positively beamed and proceeded to astonish me by asking why it was that I had no Eskimo wife. Did I not like the women of Frobisher Bay?

I mumbled some sort of a reply like an embarrassed school-boy, but was saved from any more intensive questioning by the arrival of Powlussie. Both my friends looked at me in dis-belief at my inability to tell them how many (if any) dead deer there were in the vicinity. Powlussie had shot two. Polly said that she and Nikoo had accounted for three more, but when they looked at me, all I could do was to point up the bank and hope there would be at least one prize on the other side of the slope. In fact there were three, which caused Polly to jump about with pleasure, whether in acknowledgement of my suc-cess or simply because we now had a really good tally I could not tell.

Our efforts to get everything back to the shore camp as soon as possible were hampered by a steadily increasing downpour. When darkness began to fall it became clear that we would not get everything down to the camp unless we were prepared to stay another day. The hunters would have been quite happy to have done this, but my thoughts were switching to the forth-coming expedition to Warwick Sound. The increasing danger of bad weather as the season progressed would threaten our chances of a successful whale hunt.

Nikoo and Powlussie did not put up any great opposition to my plans and cooperated wholeheartedly in gathering the skins together and caching as much of our surplus meat as possible, so that little more than the carcasses would have to be abandoned. We could start for home in the morning.

I had carefully calculated the time at which we would have to leave Aggoun, which was the local name for the area, in order to give us the maximum amount of water, so made sure that everybody got going in good time. Even though the tide was still well up, our journey along the Kingnite coast was hazardous to say the least. Innuk's misgivings proved to be only too well founded. We had travelled somewhere between four and five miles when I genuinely believed that we might be wrecked. The tide at this point, for some hard-to-fathom reason, rushed in and out with great violence, causing areas of swirling currents and whirlpools, while the sharp rocks, distinctly visible not too far below the surface of the water, lurked ominously close to our keel.

My companions were alarmed but kept commendably cool. Nikoo and Powlussie stood ready in the bows with boathooks to fend off the rocks. Polly was at the helm, now assisted by Innuk, who had the most recent experience of travelling in these parts. Koolee was busy bailing out the water which had slopped over the side into the bilge while it was my job to control the engine as necessary to avoid the dangers. We suffered one or two bumps, fortunately not heavy enough to cause serious damage, but we were all truly thankful to be able to move away from the mainland coast.

With a favourable tide, we took an oblique course across the bay, heading for the high island which we had passed just before making our first encampment. Before long the seals began to appear. Our hunters shot two quite quickly but were in agreement that our first priority must be to get home without too much delay. We had four seals by the time we came to Nuaktualuk, where we made a brief stop only, and then, satisfied with our overall catch, we put the rifles away and went full ahead for the post.

Our hunt was entirely successful. The skins we obtained, together with those traded by Koojesse and the other hunters, were sufficient for the much-needed clothing without any call for further expeditions, while we had kept within the time limit for us to be able to meet up with Koojesse on the day of the full moon.

Good news awaited us. Nyla had progressed during our absence. She was dressed and sitting up on the deerskins if still looking decided frail, but the old lady said that the girl had been eating quite well. So far she had not been outside the home, but her strength was slowly returning.

XII

WITHIN DAYS, with not a little excitement, we set out on the whale hunt which was to be rounded off with a search for the green rocks. Innuk and Koolee remained at the post to take charge of things in the event of a visit from one of the other camps. Innuk had the keys and my full confidence in her ability to cope with any situation which might have arisen. Both Nikoo and Powlussie closely examined the whaling gun before we left and considered it to be in full working order. It was unlikely that either of them had actually used this type of weapon before, but the Innuit were very quick to get the hang of any implement which was relevant to their own hunting methods.

Polly came with us to help with the steering until the other hunters joined us, but did not come on the whale hunt itself.

As we reached the entrance to Ward Inlet, we came upon a cape of black cliffs with huge piles of rocky debris scattered around their basee. There was nothing soft about the coastline beyond the promontory either, which consisted of a high and uninviting brown rock face, in all bearing little resemblance to the pleasant lowlands of the last journey. Numerous small islands straggled the coastline, while further out to sea a few larger ones stretched over towards the Kingnite side. These were spaced out sufficiently for us to hold a steady course towards the Kikitukjuak area.

Although the day was reasonably calm, we had seen no seals

close enough to distract us, so we had managed to keep on schedule, until a polar bear appeared from behind the rocks on an island already astern of us. I would happily have left the animal to its own devices, but the quiet was immediately shattered by cries of 'Nanook! Nanook!' while the boat was whirled round to retrace our passage. Nothing seemed to arouse an Eskimo's hunting passion to such a pitch as the appearance of one of these huge but largely inoffensive creatures.

While my friends were bustling to get their rifles at the ready, Polly had begun to look rather uneasy at the steering wheel. Not for the first time it occurred to me that there might be some sort of restriction on women's participation in certain kinds of hunting. Being able to deal with both engine and steering for a short period, I offered to take over. She agreed at once, and then sat very meekly on the engine cover with her back to the proceedings.

We had returned to within about a quarter of a mile of the island before the bear came into view once more. This time it was lying down, but, startled by our noise, it raised itself on its haunches and after carefully surveying our approaching craft decided to depart forthwith with all speed.

The two hunters, seeing their prey make a strong bid to escape, began shouting with an awful wailing sound, causing it to stop and turn round for a further observation. Almost at once the bear, deciding that we could not possibly be friendly, whipped round to gallop away. We aimed the boat towards a point of land which seemed to be more or less in the path of the fleeing animal, so we were not surprised when it came rushing along the point to hurl itself into the sea.

This was not a wise move. On the island there had been cover behind rocks or in one of the hidden gulleys, but escape was most unlikely in the sea, where it could not compete with us for speed. Our prey still had one or two tricks up its sleeve, however, the first of which was to put a small island between itself and the boat. In response, the men redoubled their shouting with the object of delaying their victim long enough for us to close the gap. At the next sighting we were definitely closing in on the swimmer, so the men renewed their cries with even more vigour, causing the animal to wheel round and observe the source of this new disturbance. Quickly realizing the ever-increasing danger of its position, the bear suddenly changed course in the hope of escaping to more open water, but by so doing condemned itself to almost certain death.

With his first shot, Nikoo wounded the swimmer in the head. Enraged, the bear cast all caution to the wind by swinging round in the water to do battle with us, thus enabling the men to take aim at an almost stationary target for a quick finish.

It had been my intention to proceed as far as possible along the coastline before camping for the night, but we now had to tow the bear ashore for the skinning and cutting-up process. We could still be in time for our rendezvous with Koojesse if there were no further delays, but it had become clear to me that my attempt to adhere to schedule was quite ill-advised.

We decided to aim directly for the shore because we were practically abreast of a small encampment where we would be able to spend the night without having the bother of setting up our own shelter. There were five homes here in quite a pleasing little cove on the sheltered side of a narrow cape.

These were people who had recently been with us at Ward Inlet but who had decided to come home to do their deer hunting. It was not easy for me to stifle a surge of satisfaction on hearing that the hunt had not been up to their expectations. I said nothing, but Nikoo rubbed a certain amount of salt into the wound by describing to them in some detail the splendid results of our journey to the head of the bay.

The bear was skinned and dismembered very quickly. Some

of the meat was dispersed among the people of the camp, part of the remainder would be shared round the families of our whaling crew, while a sizeable hunk was reserved for immediate consumption. The lady of the house produced a pot and soon our supper was bubbling nicely over her lamp.

While the food was cooking, the men discussed the bear hunt at some length and Powlussie told me that it had always been the custom to inflate the bladder of a newly killed bear and hang it in a prominent position either in the boat or the home.

We all had to split up to sleep because of the limited space available. Powlussie and I remained where we were, while Nikoo and Polly retired next door. My host and hostess were fine-looking Eskimos with two very pretty daughters, both of whom had thick black hair and sparkling eyes. I thought what a stir they would cause in a year or two if it were possible to transport them to the south and take them suitably dressed to some city social function. It seemed unfair that such strikingly handsome girls should 'blush unseen' among just a handful of people here in this remote place where the rigours of life would wither their beauty all too soon.

The following day we gave our friends an extra piece of bear meat each for looking after us so well and left the bearskin to be retrieved on our return journey. Powlussie asked me if he could affix the inflated bear's bladder to our mast and as he had a length of sealskin line already prepared I happily agreed. We were in good spirits as we left the little harbour and cruised along quite comfortably for several miles with everything seemingly in our favour.

The coast line on this side of the bay softened as our journey progressed. The cliffs did not rear up to such a height, nor were they quite so harsh and unfriendly, and since traversing the bold promontory at the entrance to Ward Inlet we had passed some lower land with a surprising amount of vegetation.

We sailed along the coast of the big island of Kikitukjuak, but did not stop there, changing course instead to go eastward back towards the land as we had been edging out to the middle of the bay. In the fading light we could see that the coastline backed away quite sharply to the north to form the sound named after the Countess of Warwick by Martin Frobisher in 1576. Polly, as usual, appearing to know exactly where the camp would be, brought us through the dusk to a flattish point of land where a few dim lights were twinkling in welcome.

These people greeted us with as much excitement as if they had not seen us for years. Willing hands unloaded our gear in no time, then set about putting up the tent as this was to be our base for the duration of our stay in these parts. Polly, changing her role from that of navigator to housewife, began establishing a home for the four of us right away. Soon a lamp was giving out steady warmth with a pleasant light and a stream of visitors came to call. Some of them I knew, others by name only. Among the callers were Annawa and Savik, which made me wonder what, if any, solution they had found to their disagreement over the women.

My resolve to be flexible over the timing of the whale hunt was immediately put to the test when we discovered that Koojesse had gone down to Bear Sound to fetch some meat and 'might' be back after two nights. We agreed that rather than wasting time waiting for Koojesse, Nikoo would join the men from the camp on a walrus hunt. The practicalities were soon settled. I would not accompany them, never having had any great success in this form of hunting, but would supply boat and petrol in return for a fair share of any meat obtained.

Nikoo and Powlussie set off quite early with two other men the next morning. What had not really registered with me when we made the arrangements was that, with the men away, Polly and I would be left by ourselves in the home. I thought this rather alarming, but the situation seemed to amuse my friend, who sat smiling to herself as she made repairs to one of her garments. I sat deliberating how to raise the matter without embarrassment, until Polly revealed that she had arranged for her sister, Agiaktok, whose husband had gone off with Nikoo, to join us with her small son until the men came back.

Polly's sister arrived during the morning well loaded with all her paraphernalia, followed by her son clutching two large rolls of skins. Agiak had a large, round, plump-cheeked face which was always on the verge of a smile. She was the jolliest person I had seen for a long time and seemed ready to burst into uproarious laughter at the slightest provocation.

As they had not seen each other for some time, the two women settled down for a good gossip. I brought out my book but must have dozed off for a short while. When I next registered what they were saying it was concerned with the affairs of Annawa and Savik. I heard nothing very informative until Agiak suddenly said, 'Annawa became very angry about his dog.'

Polly did not answer this, but looked over at me as I sat up with the intention of joining in the talk. What they were saying was undoubtedly meant for my ears. I took up my cue by asking, 'What happened to the dog?'

This was not going to be a straightforward question-and-answer session, but Agiak beamed at me very kindly as she said, 'It was Annawa's best dog, he said, and had been working with him for five winters.'

Hoping to ascertain precisely what had happened to it, I asked, 'Will Annawa be able to use it this winter?'

'I don't know. Probably only having one ear will not stop it from working.'

'What happened to the other ear?'

'It's been cut off.'

'Are you telling me that someone cut the dog's ear off?'

'Yes. Savik did it with his snowknife.'

As one part of my mind was digesting this extraordinary piece of news, the other was reflecting upon the possible reasons for it. Surely no one would suppose that maiming a dog was likely to influence a man to give up his wife?

Once I had been told about the ear, other information started to flow more freely. Shortly after the party returned from the trading post, Savik, though apparently still disgruntled, had given up his tactic of harassment, so that though the two men were less than friendly, there were no open demonstrations of hostility, until Ali somehow returned from the east coast.

The woman stayed in the home of her brother and his wife, showing no intention of rejoining either of her husbands. This caused renewed dissension between the two hunters, because Savik claimed, with some justice, that their agreement should now be honoured by Peeta returning to him as promised.

For some reason or another, Annawa no longer wished for Ali to return to him, so made no attempt to complete the exchange, while the woman herself appeared to be totally indifferent to both hunters. Determined to demonstrate the depths of his displeasure, Savik then decided to remove the poor dog's ear.

When these facts had been related, Agiak moved back to tend her own lamp as though her account was finished, but Polly, who no doubt already knew the whole story, thought otherwise and prompted her sister, 'Tell Issumatak about the shooting.'

Agiak looked up from her lamp.

'One day when the men were down at the islands hunting walrus, a bullet went through the top of Savik's anorak and no one knew where it had come from.'

Oddly, Agiak did not seem to think this incident to have been of much importance, for in reply to my query as to how such a thing could have happened, she simply shrugged her shoulders as she replied, 'Perhaps the bullet had bounced off a rock.'

Polly must have thought that the shot had been fired on purpose, otherwise she would not have made Agiak tell me about it, but for once she had no comments to make when I tried to get her to tell me what the general feeling in the camp was.

This new development was too serious to be ignored. Normally, of course, the police would have investigated happenings of this kind, but as there was no possibility of getting into contact with the relevant authorities, all I could do was endeavour to restrain the quarrelling men from injuring each other.

In the years gone by, Innuit life was occasionally hampered by outbreaks of rather mindless feuding. Murder was not common, but the trouble was that when it did occur any murder had to be avenged. If a hunter felt himself to have been humiliated or grossly misused by another, he might resort to killing to re-establish his pride, but then his victim's family would feel obliged to satisfy their honour with retaliation. It would not matter whom they killed of the other family – it could be a young child or an old woman – but once started the likely result was the death of a number of perfectly innocent people.

It was unlikely that Annawa, if it was he who had aimed the shot, had any real intention of killing Savik, but the future possibilities were ominous unless the matter could be promptly settled.

As I went round to visit various homes that day, a little clique of about four or five young people attached themselves to me, all of Nyla's age or younger. They had never before come across a young European who could speak their language, or anybody other than the missionaries for that matter, and had an obvious and healthy curiosity about life in other places.

My little party accompanied me on a walk along the river

bank, where they showed me all the items of local interest, mainly connected with hunting and fishing. We sat on the grass for a while to talk. They were interested to hear about their counterparts in my country, but were mystified when they heard that many Europeans had never been hunting, as they obtained their food by growing things in the ground and keeping herds of animals to be killed off for food as necessary.

One bright spark suggested that the Eskimos should do the same thing with seals and deer, but his friends pointed out the difficulties which would arise, particularly with regard to the seals, so the scheme was abandoned, and anyway who would want to miss the fun of hunting?

The girls were mainly interested in the clothes they had seen pictured in a magazine one of the women had obtained some-where. They wanted to know all about the garments, how they were made, whether the girls made their own outfits and other details that I was quite unable to supply.

What struck me as the talk went on was the urge within the younger generation to be part of the wider world.

Back at the tent that evening, I got out a pack of cards and Polly's face lit up immediately. One of the most attractive things about my friend was that, although a highly competent person in many ways, she had a wonderfully childish enthusiasm for the simplest of pleasures.

After a while, the hearty laughter emanating from the sisters as they trounced me in the simple games we played attracted visitors from nearby homes wanting to see what all the fuss was about. We soon had a full house. The game became so altered by the introduction of various amendments as to be practically unintelligible to me, so I was quite relieved when they decided to have their tea.

I thought it would be hospitable to share the section of mother's birthday cake which I had brought with me, so I cut off a small piece each for everyone present. Polly watched me closely, then accepted her share, outwardly at least with pleasure, which quietened whatever suspicions the others may have had about this unusual food. Soon they were all munching away with expressions of approval. What a pity that I had no method available to record this rare scene: a cake from the kitchen of a remote sheep station in New Zealand being enjoyed by these hardy people of Warwick Sound, whose ancestors had confronted Frobisher and his party of would-be settlers more than two centuries before Captain Cook even sighted New Zealand.

My thoughts drifted off to my family down in the sunny South Pacific. Their spring would be just beginning as we were preparing for the winter. It would be hard for them even to imagine the rugged bleakness of this formidable island. Mother would be pleased that her cake had been much praised by my northern friends, as we ate our supper sitting round on the cosy deerskins while the flickering light of our oil lamps played with our shadows on the tent wall. Her interest might have turned to concern, had she known that her youngest son was to share the sleeping platform with two quite presentable Eskimo women and a small boy. She would never know that I was much more afraid of these women than they of me and that this fact was well known to them.

Our visitors departed with suitable expressions of thanks and praise for the cake, which they knew would please me. What they actually thought, of course, I do not know, but there was no doubt that they had enjoyed themselves as they straggled off into the night laughing and joking.

Left to ourselves, we made our preparations for the night. Polly had her bedding at one end of the platform, by her lamp, with Agiak in a similar position at the other end; the boy was between me and his mother.

My eyelids had already begun to flutter when it became

apparent once again that my friends were telling me something in a roundabout sort of way.

The subject of their discourse now was the woman Ali. From what I could make out, Ali was enjoying being the cause of dissension between the two men and since arriving back from the east coast had behaved provocatively enough to keep the fires burning. Such behaviour is unusual among the Eskimos, for few people, either men or women, have enough time on their hands to indulge in emotional drama, but here was an apparent exception to the rule.

My eyes had been closed as this information arrived in my ears and sleep now overcame me as the sound of their voices became a background drone, then faded out altogether.

I awoke once during the night with a feeling that something odd was happening. Agiak had somehow or another got herself slanted across the platform, so that although her head was over by her lamp, her feet had strayed across the bottom of the space and were poking into my deerskins to press up against my leg. As they were pleasantly warm, it seemed pointless to evict them, especially as this might only succeed in disturbing her peacefully sleeping son between us. But in turning my head into a new position, I observed that much the same thing had happened to Polly, except that in her case it was her head that had come over in my direction. She was smiling in her sleep and I reflected that between the head of one and the feet of the other of these two good sisters, I was unlikely to come to any harm, so drifted back to sleep again.

Waking early, before daybreak, there was time before stirring for the day for me to review the information which the women had given me. The sisters had once or twice introduced the name of a relative of Ali's who appeared to have considerable influence over her. Working on the assumption that the best way to cure a problem is to eradicate the cause, perhaps this older woman might be able to persuade our troublemaker to go back to the east coast, leaving Annawa and Savik to settle down again.

When we had finished breakfast, I announced my decision to visit Ali's relation and Polly said that she would come with me to show me the way.

The woman, Ikuma, greeted us with a pleasant welcome, but Ali, who was seated on the deerskins, gave Polly a rather venomous look as though she expected trouble. She did not wait to hear what we had come for, but departed forthwith, saying that she was going to visit her friends. One thing about all this puzzled me. If, as everybody thought, Ali was the *femme fatale* of the piece, it did not say much about the men, for she was about the plainest Innuit woman I had ever seen.

Ikuma responded unexpectedly well to my suggestion, though in loyalty to Ali as a member of her family, she did not admit to any wrongdoing on her part, ascribing the trouble to the men's bad behaviour.

My next port of call was Savik's home. The man was there eating a breakfast of seal meat. After some conventional greetings, I asked my key question: 'Why did you cut off the dog's ear?'

The man looked mystified, as though the reason for this violent act ought to be obvious to anybody. At first it seemed that he might not even reply, but then he scratched his head in puzzlement before saying uncertainly, 'Because it seemed the right thing to do.'

This explanation did not hold out any hope for a logical discussion, so with my next question I attempted to appeal to the man's better instincts by arousing sympathy for the injured dog. This failed abysmally, for in Savik's view owner and dog were inseparable to such a degree that the animal had to suffer for the shortcomings of its master. The man was quite clearly astonished at my even thinking that any separate consideration should be given to the animal.

My mild admonishments having thus fallen on deaf ears, a more severe line of reproof seemed necessary.

'The police do not allow people to attack animals without good reason. If they were to hear that you had cut off this dog's ear, they would be very angry.'

Savik did not like this and began muttering to himself, the gist of his complaint being that it was better to hurt the dog than to shoot at people. Of course, he did have a point there, so to prevent him from dodging all responsibility for his wrong-doing I responded quickly, 'But you hurt the dog before the bullet went through your anorak.'

The hunter simply continued with his mutterings, so I cut him short with a rather pompous pronouncement:

'You must not do such a thing again, for you are not allowed to harm other people's dogs just because you are angry with the owner.'

Without waiting for an answer, I moved on to Annawa's home. Here things were likely to be slightly more difficult, for whereas Savik, by freely admitting that it was he who had mistreated the dog, had laid himself open to reprimand, Annawa had never, as far as I knew, accepted any responsibility for the shot fired at Savik.

I tried to explain to Annawa, as tactfully as possible, how dangerous it was to fire a rifle in the direction of other hunters, and that if a man or woman was killed or hurt in this way, the police would not be easily persuaded that it had been an accident. Though many months might pass before anything happened, the officers would come in the end to take away anybody whom they felt had broken the law.

'Where would they take them to?' asked Annawa, a disconcertingly innocent expression on his face.

'Somewhere where the police could decide what their punishment should be. Perhaps they would be shut up in a little room for a long time.'

Then, suspecting that Annawa was diverting the conversation into a discussion of police procedures, I brought the talk to a close: 'That is why the people must not fire their rifles in any way that might be dangerous to others.'

Having delivered this final warning, I left the home with the feeling that nothing much had been accomplished and that my vague threats had done little to resolve the problem.

I awoke very early the following morning, to find pattering on to the canvas of our travelling home a gentle rain which was at first quite soothing but then developed into a steady downpour drumming above our heads. Around dawn, the wind got up, hurrying the rain before it in intermittent bursts, so that our tent pole creaked into a slow sway and little puffs of cool air seeped in through the lightly fastened flaps. These quiet disturbances penetrated the sleep of the others without actually waking them as they shuffled restlessly into new positions.

My mind ranged back over the past few years in Baffin Land. The events of the summer had drawn me into the Innuit community to a much greater degree than ever before. A year ago, I would never have thought it possible that I should find myself sharing even a temporary home with two young Eskimo women who would not find my company either strange or embarrassing, though Polly still did not understand why I had not made an 'arrangement' with any of the young women of Frobisher Bay.

A memory of my last year at school floated before me. I was in the housemaster's study where the poor man was struggling to explain the basic facts of life prior to my coming confirmation. A lifelong bachelor who had never been seen in the company of a lady, he probably had only the vaguest idea himself as to what it was all about, but he did his best to point us in the right direction. What would he have made of this scene: his erstwhile pupil on a sleeping platform sandwiched between two black-haired Eskimo females? Would he have credited that my companions and I had no intentions towards each other beyond a desire to share what warmth there was available?

Koojesse and Nikoo returned the next day and the following morning we were finally able to set off. Koojesse had brought with him all the meat he had cached down around Ishitukjuak, commonly known as Bear Sound, and Nikoo had secured five walrus, a sufficient haul under the circumstances, as we would hopefully have a heavy load to take back to Ward Inlet after the whale hunt.

The men got down to a very thorough checking over of the gear. They brought up an old man whom I had never seen before, Allukie. He had been a very noted whale hunter of his day, whose services had been much in demand when the British and American whaling ships still operated along the east coast of Baffin Island.

I reflected that he must be one of those hunters so adversely affected when the whaling industry dramatically collapsed in the early years of the century. The industry in those days was primarily concerned with obtaining great quantities of baleen, the flexible bone from the back of the whale's mouth, which had been ideal for the making of ladies' corsets, so greatly in demand in the latter half of the nineteenth century. The whaling masters established bases at various points along the coast, giving summer employment to a large number of Innuit. Although the wages were minimal, it was possible for the Eskimos to purchase rifles, which had superseded the primitive weapons upon which they had been dependent, and other important items in return for their work. They were also free to help themselves to much of the carcass of any animal killed to feed their families and provide warmth in their homes.

The baleen, in such great demand but very limited in supply, rose to astronomical heights in price with an obvious result. A cheap and effective substitute was developed so that the corset manufacturers withdrew their support from the whaling industry, and in the absence of any great demand for the other whale products, few, if any, ships undertook the long, expensive journeys up into the arctic waters. The Innuit of the Eastern Arctic, who had adapted their way of life to make use of more modern equipment, found themselves thrown back, almost overnight, on to their own resources until the first traders arrived.

Allukie gave us much useful advice as to the best method of hunting the Greenland whale. The men listened attentively to their elderly friend, although a few of them had themselves had experience with the whaling crews before the expeditions ceased.

All our equipment was checked into the boat: gun, bombs, rope, lances and harpoons, well covered to keep out the rain, so that everything was prepared for an early start. By sunrise, conditions seemed ideal for our departure. It was a strange daybreak, for an uncanny silence hung over everything. Where normally there was the stirring of the sea or the wind or even the seabirds at this time of day, this morning all was still, while along the seaward horizon the dawn was emerging with a rosy flush.

If the hunters thought these conditions to be somewhat ominous, they did not suggest that such a start might indicate less favourable weather later in the day. Perhaps my own insistence that we set out without delay stifled any comment.

The whole camp turned out to watch us pull out of the harbour. As so many hunters wished to take part in the expedition, Koojesse had decided to take his boat as well as mine so that the man on the gun should not be cramped for space when the time came for action.

Savik, one of the handful of hunters remaining behind, stood alone outside his home at the far end of the settlement. It struck me again that my handling of the trouble between him and Annawa had been too feeble to be effective. The sisters were standing outside our tent at the opposite end of the camp. They were to keep each other company until we returned from the hunt, when normal living arrangements could be resumed. This was just as well, for although Polly's behaviour had been perfectly modest and natural while we were living at such close quarters, over a period our association might have become embarrassing. Increasingly my suspicion was that she was slightly offended that I had not made wife-sharing arrangements with Nikoo.

We headed out of the harbour, westward at first to clear the cluster of islands, then altering course to cross the mouth of the sound in a south-easterly direction, with the aim of cruising on a line parallel with the coast between Warwick and Ishitukjuak Bays.

I did not want to go too far beyond Ishitukjuak. Nikoo had told me that the stretch of water was an awesome strait, a foaming cauldron swirling with the current and the tide among the rocks and little islands.

The first part of the morning was spent sealing, after which the men agreed that we should press on with our main object while the weather was still favourable. Already the signs were that the docile dawn had masked the approach of a less pleasant weather front, for the wind, though not yet stormy, had swung round to the north, from which direction came frequent gales and blizzards.

Now that we were in the area where we might expect to find our prey, we kept a sharp look-out on every quarter to ensure that we did not miss anything. One of the hunters, who had brought his telescope, concentrated on our starboard side, while Nikoo and I took turns with my binoculars on the port section.

The day slipped by as we moved down the bay, the shadows from the hills darkened and the wind gusted ever more strongly and coldly. We had almost reached our agreed distance when Nikoo suddenly picked up a tell-tale 'blow' of spray at some point right ahead of us.

We kept our course, directly astern of our sighting, where we could not cause any premature alarm. As we closed the gap between us and our prey we could see that there were actually two whales travelling in convoy about twenty yards apart. We prepared for action at once; the gunner, already in position, checked his weapon and Nikoo made sure that the coil of rope was free to run out easily. With everything ready, we braced ourselves for the onslaught.

The whales had been aiming north-eastward across the mouth of Frobisher Bay, so that if we were not careful we would be led into Bear Sound, which I for one wanted to avoid. Keen as we were to capture one of these great creatures, thus solving our winter supplies problem, my boat had already taken a great deal of punishment these past weeks and I did not want to expose it to the dangers of that awful place.

We decided to risk alerting our quarry and advertised our presence by swinging round to place ourselves between the whales and the shore. But with the wind no longer behind us and a cross-sea, our speed dropped so that we could not narrow the gap remaining. In our intense concentration on the hunt, we had ignored the fact that the steadily increasing wind, catching us unpleasantly amidships, spelt danger, as we headed out to the open sea to be subjected to an even heavier buffeting.

Koojesse had apparently digested these warnings, for he was already dropping behind, presumably with the intention of breaking off the hunt, when suddenly and quite inexplicably the whales made a turn which would take them in a line to come right across our bows. These great sea creatures did not as yet appear to be aware of our presence and Koojesse rejoined us to press home an attack.

There followed a few moments of manoeuvre to place ourselves astern of the nearest whale as it passed. With the wind now blowing across us, we had almost turned about as we closed in for the final stage of the hunt. Our position was ideal. We should have been able to kill the whale with one bomb, but something went wrong. The bomb only grazed the creature's back, causing it to swerve sharply in startled surprise and making a collision inevitable. We ran up on to the animal's huge frame and as the whale rolled, its fluke catching our bow and pushing us down into the water so quickly that we hardly had time to appreciate the gravity of our situation as the sea poured into the boat.

We owed our lives to Koojesse, who at the critical second lunged a spear into the great black body and caused the whale to swoop out of the water, releasing our bow as it streaked off ahead of us. We swung upright, slopping with water but otherwise not seriously damaged, and retrieved our rope, which was now dangling astern of us in the sea. We were still reeling from the narrowness of our escape when the storm, which had been threatening for several hours, burst upon us in full strength.

I had heard of the suddenness with which these violent storms are liable to gather in this infamous sea, but had never before experienced the astonishing speed with which a moderate wind can turn into a raging fury. The gale shrieked around us, sweeping the icy sleet and snow into our faces as Koojesse, approaching as close to us as he dared, shouted a warning of perils to come unless we made for shelter at once.

Koojesse steered into the dense blanket of sleet and snow,

edging his way through what seemed to be an impenetrable curtain. The coastline loomed through the murk, then was swiftly gone again, giving our guide just a fraction of time to correct our course so that we should neither miss the narrow entrance to our hoped-for shelter nor fall foul of the rocks and reefs ahead of us.

Closer to the land, ugly sharp rocks reared up on both sides, but with no other option than to trust in Koojesse's ability to bring us to safety, we followed him as nearly as we dared. Aware of the difficulties we might encounter in our larger boat, our friend kept an anxious eye on us in this perilous situation where a single mistake might have landed us in the sea; which was just as well, for we were suddenly caught by an enormous buffet. The bow swung round with enough force to ground us on a rock and once again we were seconds away from disaster, saved only by Koojesse's vigilance and prompt action. As the bow tilted on the obstruction, the stern sank far enough into the water to sink us. At great risk to his own safety, Koojesse came alongside to give us one huge shove, practically man-handling us back into the sea again and somehow or another we moved away from the reef towards the shelter we were seeking.

This was no peaceful spot. Being so close to the open sea, the violence of the water was not completely checked, but at least we were now spared the swift currents and pounding wind which had so nearly brought about our downfall. We stopped well beyond the reef and put out our heavy anchor and a grapnel, which held us reasonably securely for the time being.

We now had an opportunity to assess the damage we had suffered, which fortunately was confined to an area of wood-work above the waterline where a couple of timbers had split with the impact of the whale's weight. The whaling gear was intact, the petrol drum had been well enough secured to prevent any water seepage, while the provisions had been safely stowed amidships, well clear of both our incidents.

On a personal level, I had fared worse than the others. Apart from the water penetrating my protective clothing, the bag containing my dry clothes and sleeping bag, stored in one of the stern cupboards, had at some stage been completely submerged, reducing my outfit for both day and night to the sodden garments I was wearing. Despite this mishap, I was overwhelmed with thankfulness that my crew had had such an instant and competent reaction in such extreme danger.

Now they were laughing and joking as though they had been out for a summer's afternoon jaunt. The swinging and plunging of the boat made conditions too awkward for any cooking, but we got the Primuses going to make a hot drink. Koojesse managed to get across from his boat for a talk about the whales. He thought that they would still be somewhere in the area. There was a chance that the one wounded by the lance had been more seriously affected than we had imagined, in which case its companion would probably stay with it, for these creatures do support each other in an hour of need. Nothing was further from my mind at that moment than the thought of setting off after the whales again, but after all the trouble we had gone to we owed it to ourselves not to go home empty-handed if we could help it.

The bedding in the other boat had not suffered to the extent that mine had, so very kindly, seeing what a state my possessions were in, Koojesse produced a large deerskin for me to wrap around myself during the night.

We spent the night in the boat, which though uncomfortable and exposed meant we should be able to tell if anything untoward started to happen.

I dozed in short, nightmarish bursts. Later in the night the wind eased a little but shifted a few points so as to blow more directly into our harbour. As the violence moderated to a degree, the snow drove in more thickly, finding every possible opening in my deerskin cover.

I lay in a position of extreme discomfort across the boat in order to use any possible shelter provided by the engine housing, with my feet pointed upward on one side and my head similarly tilted on the other. My lower back and thighs reacted painfully to the strain of this unnatural posture, while the additional hardship caused by the penetrating snow drifting into my face or down my neck, according to how my head was turned, was almost more than flesh and blood could stand. Pressed up against the engine on one side, with Nikoo rambling into my ear on the other, there was no question of being able to turn in search of a relieving position.

In a desperate attempt to divert my mind from this bodily anguish, I began mentally to compose a letter to my family, setting out the details of my sufferings of the past few hours, and commenting extensively on the insouciance with which they had allowed me, the softest member of the family, to lay myself open to such a dreadful ordeal. Strangely enough, in a welter of self-pity, I fell into a sleep from which even Nikoo's cacophony could not arouse me.

Waking in the morning, my first sensation was one of intense surprise at the speed with which the awful night had turned into a blustery day, which was quickly followed by a growing suspicion that I should never be able to walk again.

Nikoo, though such a noisy man at night, had been very quiet and careful that morning. With typical Eskimo resource, he had made a little shelter in the side-locker to light the stove and prepare a hot breakfast. Under these circumstances the men would not normally have bothered to cook for themselves and this solicitude for my welfare gave me a real lift to start the day.

Nikoo actually had to pull me to my feet, then hold me steady until my limbs were ready to take the strain, but once the blood flowed back everywhere and my young muscles loosened up again, I was more than ready to eat breakfast.

We did not move that day, but by evening the weather had quietened to such a degree that the wind had become little more than a stiff breeze. We were able to set up a makeshift shelter with our sail, from the engine house to the stern, and with a little reorganization arrange our bedding along the boat instead of across it, all of which enabled us to get a reasonable night's sleep.

We left the harbour early the next morning, not sorry to see the last of it, on a dull featureless sort of day, taking a course south-westward as before, but moving away from the coast so as to avoid the rocky debris at the entrance to Bear Sound. After several hours of aimless cruising, I began to think that perhaps we should swing round and head for home. Koojesse was reluctant, not wishing to be proved wrong about the whales' likely movements, so we compromised by settling for a wide sweep off the mouth of the sound before heading back.

We had resigned ourselves to returning empty-handed when the two whales appeared again, emerging from the other side of a small island almost dead ahead of us to swim quietly across our bows at no great distance from the shore.

After our first failure we had come to the conclusion that the gun would be better situated in Koojesse's boat, which was more like a traditional whaler than our clumsy craft.

At first it looked as though we were going to misfire again, for our prey altered course rather abruptly to come round us in an awkward loop. I reversed our engine, backing away from the immediate vicinity to give the hunter complete freedom of movement. Koojesse followed the curve of the swimmers' course, until he reached a point where he could cut into position behind them. Having selected his victim, he followed quietly behind it to get within range, took careful aim and fired the bomb. There was a tremendous flurry in the water as the injured creature shot up, then plunged back into the sea. Koojesse had evidently taken careful note of all that Allukie had had to say about the firing of the gun, for after an initial struggle, all resistance died away as the whale rose to the surface to float quietly beside its pursuers.

The men were overjoyed at our sudden spectacular success, for even those hardy sailors from Scotland and America, with all their expertise, had not often achieved such a swift, clean result. This would be the occasion for considerable rejoicing at the camp, although the chief beneficiaries were to be people who had lost their hunters and had had no chance to reorganize themselves for the winter.

Our problems were not yet entirely solved. The prize would have to be brought as close as possible to the encampment for the people to get on with the cutting up without delay, without having to waste time travelling backwards and forwards by boat.

We progressed slowly, but with such a heavy tow, our petrol consumption increased alarmingly, bearing in mind that there was still the treasure hunt round Warwick Bay to be undertaken. At dusk, the wind fortunately increased in strength to fill the sails which we had hastily unfurled in both boats, and this, together with the benefit of a good flowing tide, gave us the momentum we needed.

Koojesse guided us past Sharko at a safe distance from the reef and rocks, then turned into the entrance to Warwick Bay, so that we could come round Niuntellik Island on the inside to aim for the point of land close by the settlement, within easy access of their homes.

We beached the huge whale without much difficulty, though

we could not get the carcass as high up the beach as we would have liked. The men got out their knives to slice off strips of the black skin, known as *muktuk*. This is about three quarters of an inch thick and quite a delicacy for the Innuit. Koojesse also cut off a layer of the whale fat and a long piece of the fresh meat, so that we should arrive home with visible evidence of our successful expedition, to an enthusiastic welcome from the ladies of the camp.

Polly and Agiak, much concerned when they saw the state of my clothes and sleeping bag, urged me to remove all my damp garments at once so that they could dry them off without delay. I had a few dry things in a bag which had been left behind, so in a act of contortion I managed to change clothes in public, but beneath the deerskins, much to the amusement of my friends. We ate the *muktuk* without any cooking. I had never before tried the skin of a big whale like this, but had always found that of the smaller white whale quite palatable.

Our warm, brightly lit home had an air of luxurious comfort after our two hard nights on the boat. But for the pangs of hunger which assailed me, I would have been quite happy to stretch out on the dry deerskins for a good sleep. The women had boiled up a pan of the fresh meat, so that followed the *muktuk* on the menu, and then Polly gave me a slice of her bannock.

Overcome by exhaustion after the meal, I retired to the deerskins, where, warm and comfortable for the first time since we left, my eyelids fluttered, then closed in sleep, while my companions discussed the details of our outing.

I awoke in the morning after a deep, sound sleep to find my clothes, all dry, in a neat pile beside my head and Polly sitting beside her lamp smiling at me. I thanked her for all she had done since our return and asked how she had managed to dry all the things so quickly. She said that her sister Agiak and her other friends had taken some of the clothes to dry them in their own homes. Mention of Agiak reminded me of her husband's quick action in spearing the whale to save us from being wrecked, so I described it all to Polly, who, though she must have been told the whole story the night before, behaved as though she knew nothing of our adventure. Not for the first time it struck me what good manners my friends had.

Polly had also bought news of a welcome surprise. During our absence from the camp, Ali had suddenly returned to Savik to become his wife again, thus bringing the affair to an end in such a simple manner as to be almost unbelievable.

This made me a trifle suspicious as to how it had all come about. At first Polly pretended not to know what had happened, but applying pressure, I extracted the truth from her. Ikuma, who had agreed to persuade Ali to go north again, had decided on a simpler approach, telling her relative that if she did not go back to Savik, Issumatak was going to send up one of his women for Savik, so that Ali might easily finish up with no husband at all.

The people began work on the whale that morning, while I checked over my boat in preparation for our search for the unlikely green rock. While walking home the old man, Allukie, came over to ask if he could come round the bay with us. He said that he knew the places where the Europeans had made their homes for a short while a very long time ago, including the small island which had been the main object of their interest and which had been named Kudlunarn, 'the place of the strangers'. Allukie told me that the island had been so named long, long before his grandfather's day, so it probably related to that short-lived sixteenth-century 'gold rush' sparked off by Martin Frobisher and his men.

Setting out from Twerpukjuak the next morning on our search for the green rock, I was glad to have Allukie as a new companion. He told me that his father, Ungarn, a great hunter with several wives, had accompanied an American man who, on a journey of exploration in this sound, took a particular interest in the islands Niuntellik and Kudlunarn. They had discovered things 'that had not grown there', such as a deposit of coal, some bricks, tiles and oddments that Europeans might leave behind them. This had been many years ago, when the hunter was quite a young man, but in later life Ungarn frequently told his son about the journey and the objects they had found on the islands.

We could easily have completed our examination of the various bays and inlets in time to have returned to Twerpukjuak at nightfall, but as the old man still had things to show me, we set up camp on Kudlunarn Island. It turned out to be a much smaller island than I had supposed, considering that this was the spot where Frobisher had intended to establish his settlement so long ago.

We had an interesting evening. First Allukie regaled us with the stories of the island which he had heard from his father, then, later on, Nikoo began asking me about my rifle, which he examined very carefully. I may have been wrong, but I had the strangest feeling that there was more to our talk than met the eye. Polly had an odd expression on her face and it seemed to me that we were actually discussing some sort of 'deal' involving the three of us and the rifle.

I answered all Nikoo's questions without allowing my suspicion to show or suggesting any inclination to make a deal, and hoped that Polly would not feel slighted by my failure to respond. Despite her enthusiasm for telling me all the bad news almost before it happened, I thought highly of my friend and respected her many talents.

But however I might have felt about Polly, there was Innuk to be considered. After the death of Akshut, who had been the official company employee for some time, Innuk had made every effort to be useful at the post. The usual procedure would have been to appoint a new assistant from among the hunters, but our hunting and trapping strength had been so reduced over the previous two years that we could not justify taking away another good hunter. In Nikoo's case, for he would be the obvious choice, we should also have lost Polly's trapping efforts, for I knew that they operated a joint trap line very successfully, being well ahead of anyone else in the number of furs traded.

That night, when everything was quiet, and even Nikoo, though asleep, was silent, it passed through my mind that we might be the first people actually to have slept on this minute island since that motley crowd of sixteenth-century adventurers abandoned their attempt to establish themselves here. This was not a spot which the hunters, with well-established camps in the vicinity, would have frequented, nor would the whaling people have had any reason for heading in this direction.

We returned to Twerpukjuak the next afternoon. I was sad to say goodbye to Allukie. Without him the second half of my expedition would have been tedious, but the old man with his fund of information and reminiscences diverted my interest to such an extent that the subject of the green rock almost dropped out of my mind.

We had intended to take a good portion of the whale meat and fat home in two journeys, but with Nikoo's large cache of walrus meat this was not possible, so Koojesse offered to fill his boat and accompany us home. We could then return with Nikoo's whaler and clear up everything in two trips.

We arrived back at Ward Inlet to a splendid welcome from everyone. They were suitably impressed with our huge and varied load; we seemed to have brought with us at least a sample of many of the known sea animals of the area as well as the remnants of the polar bear.

Koolee had sighted us while we were coming through the narrows, so Innuk had got the fire going and was already in the process of making a batch of bread. Koolee was so obviously pleased to see me that I got carried away and whirled the slight girl round in the air before giving her a big hug, all of which caused her to shriek with pleasure.

We had a real homecoming gathering in the kitchen. Everybody came to see us, including Nyla, who had made further progress. We told them all about our adventures before, with a busy day's unloading ahead of us and another long journey to bring home the rest of our supplies, it was time for bed.

I went outside for a few moments before retiring to enjoy a breath of air. The moonlight was streaming through gaps in the clouds, reaching out like a brilliant searchlight to cross the tops of the hills behind our home, already clean and dazzling with the first fresh snow of winter. I wondered what the next few months had in store for us at Ward Inlet, thankful that despite the last disastrous months we had been able to regroup and prepare for the coming winter.

XIII

BY THE END OF SEPTEMBER our load had been carefully stowed away in various parts of the encampment. The whale fat was piled up along the end wall inside the store and the meat was in three rock caches. There was little else we could do towards preparing for the winter, except continue catching seals in the nets until the ice began to form.

To warn us that time was slipping by, a ferocious north wind launched a powerful assault early one morning before daybreak, driving snow and sleet across from the river gulley with sufficient strength to force open the porch door. I shut it firmly but had quite a battle to push the door back into the frame, then scurried back to bed to escape the penetrating draughts which seemed to be billowing into the house from several directions.

The sickness was far behind us, though because of the deaths our weeks of trial were not easily forgotten. Nyla was still only a shadow of the former bonnie Eskimo girl she had been and an ever-present reminder of the great summer misfortune.

When I awoke again Koolee was standing beside the bed talking to me. After my previous efforts to deceive her by pretending to be asleep, she now appeared to believe that I was always at least partially awake. Her voice stirred me into wakefulness, as I heard her say, with some irritation over my delayed response, 'Tell me about the whale.'

I sat up, quite pleased to be jolted out of my overlong slumber.

'It was very large,' I said.

'How large?' queried the girl.

I used my hands to indicate a creature of substantial proportions, then went on, not entirely accurately, 'It was so big that it nearly pulled us down into the sea.'

The girl gazed at me solemnly for a few moments as though estimating the likelihood of this before accepting my statement.

'How did you kill it?'

I explained about the bomb, and was demonstrating how Koojesse had used the gun so successfully when Innuk appeared. She waited quietly for me to conclude my dramatic reconstruction of the whale's last moments before giving me her news. She said, 'Ookoodlea's aunt and cousin have come to stay for the winter.'

I knew that some extra people had travelled in Nikoo's boat and had not known who they were until Innuk enlightened me.

'The aunt's name is Koko and the other is Ooleepika and they have come because the family they lived with have moved to another camp.'

This meant that we should have another two mouths to feed, which did not please me very much, but as these people had already arrived there would have been little point in objecting.

The weather had moderated somewhat since daybreak, but Nikoo thought the boats ought to be moved to a more sheltered spot none the less. As the tide was well up, it seemed to me that our best course would be to bring them into the cove below the Innuit homes, where they could be beached fairly easily.

We beached Nikoo's boat without much trouble, perhaps because, doubtful of the weather conditions, he had anchored quite close to the reef line in the shelter of an inlet at the other end of the harbour from the river. The hunter's doubts about the weather were soon proved to be well founded, for as he and I made our way out in the dinghy to the post boat, a strong northerly wind whipped up the sea around us into foaming whitecaps. After a very long quarter of an hour or so, we were able, with some difficulty, to pull ourselves aboard.

Once or twice the storm almost threw us off course, but gradually we nudged our way towards the cove where Powlussie, along with some women from the camp, had set out some rollers to help us drag the vessel to dry land. Without the buoyancy of the water our little group of three men and several women did not find it easy to move the boat over the rollers, even though the tide was almost full, but in the end we got it far enough for apparent safety, with the bows securely propped on both sides.

My friends had all worked very hard in extremely unpleasant circumstances, so I invited everybody to come to my house for refreshment. This also gave me a chance to meet the newcomers and to find out how people were going to organize themselves for the winter without setting up any new homes to cause an extra drain on our resources.

Innuk, as usual, took charge of the proceedings, assisted by Koolee, so while the rest of them were waiting for their tea, I glanced round the group to check who were to be my companions for the winter. Nikoo and Polly would probably move off to their trapping grounds. The old couple living with Innuk, Sharni and Kokoshun, would be staying, as well as Nyla, who apart from still not being very well, now appeared to be bereft of close relatives, except for an orphan boy called Tuluka, who was in some way connected with her. Ookoodlea had an establishment of her own, which, as well as her own two children, Peela (boy) and Itualuk (girl), housed a blind man and another boy – Netchil and Tooshak respectively. Finally, there were the newcomers, Koko and Ooleepika, who for the moment also seemed to have come to rest in Ookoodlea's home. Koko was a voluble and apparently somewhat opinionated woman, which was unusual for an Eskimo, while her daughter was a tall, cross-eyed, rather sad-looking girl who kept well in the background.

The effect of the tea was much the same as the one a round of drinks might have had at a golf club. The chat became increasingly loud and mingled with hearty bursts of laughter as my friends reminisced about past storms and the mishaps that had occurred to the less fortunate hunters, while my house shuddered and creaked as the wind, now rising to a crescendo, tested our defences.

When my companions had gone I must have drifted off, because I awoke in the fading afternoon light to find Ooleepika trying to wake me. In my bemused state, what she said did not really register, but it suddenly came to me that her name, which had puzzled me, was the Innuit version of a biblical name and I said, 'Rebecca.'

The girl looked at me with some alarm. She said in a whisper, as though afraid to speak out loud in case it might anger me, 'I am Ooleepika.'

She looked so uncertain and frightened that, fearing her to be on the verge of tears, I reassured her by saying, 'Don't be frightened. That is your Eskimo name but it comes from the *kudloonas'* Bible and there it is Rebecca, which is not easy for you to say. Did you want to ask me something?'

The girl reached into the hood of her parka and without a word, brought out a pair of moccasins. Made from cured deer-skin, the slippers had been carefully stitched, with a very neat design on the top of each slipper.

The detail represented a group of hunters after a polar bear. On the left slipper, some stick men were emerging from their homes to sight a distant but clearly identifiable bear; on the right slipper the hunt had reached its climax with several of the men confronting their victim. In both cases, the detail was enclosed within a framework of beads. The appeal of the work lay in its neat simplicity, but it was most unusual to find an active design like this rather than a bead pattern. I asked Rebecca what had made her think of working a hunting scene on the moccasins because I had not seen it done before. She told me that an uncle of hers who did similar hunting scenes, inlaying soapstone on ivory, had shown her how to do the same thing with a needle and thread.

The girl was a much more articulate person than I had imagined. Her moccasins were a trifle on the small side as a trade item, though quite suitable in a woman's size, possibly with a new design. Doubtless she would be able to make larger slippers with the hunting pictures which would be acceptable for a male design. Whatever the design or size, original and attractive work of this kind had to be worth encouraging, though the powers that be did not show much enthusiasm for handling local craftsmanship.

Rebecca waited silently while I examined her handiwork, then explained rather anxiously that she had made another pair with a different picture, of a seal hunt on the ice, but her mother had said that the one with the bear hunt was better for the traders as most of the *kudloona* knew something about bear hunting. A look of real pleasure came over the girl's face when I told her that I would take both pairs, but she said she did not want to trade them. She and her mother, having come to live at the post for the winter, would be using our supplies, so she wanted to give something in return. Rebecca was very reluctant to accept any payment for her work, but eventually admitted that her mother, who had presumably experienced better times, would be pleased with a small gift of tobacco which she would come to fetch in the morning.

The weather had quietened since the middle of the day, but as darkness fell the storm built up again, so after the girl had gone, it seemed unlikely that there would be any more visitors that night. In fact, the door blew open once more for Innuk to make a rather more noisy entrance than usual. Obviously very angry, she rushed into the kitchen, and said, 'The woman Koko says that I should not be working here because there should be a man to work at the post with a wife who can help.'

This took me aback considerably, first because what happened at the post was no business of Koko's, and secondly because what she said did hold some truth.

'She has nothing to do with the company. Why does she say these things?'

'She says that Nikoo should be the company man in the normal way.'

Innuk looked so distressed that I calmed her at once by saying, 'Koko can say what she likes, but I shall decide who is to stay here at the post, and if she interferes in my business, she will be sent back to Twerpukjuak for the winter.'

Innuk was watching me very intently as though uncertain as to what my real intentions might be. I had never actually confirmed the situation which had arisen when Akshut died and she had continued her normal attendance at the house. Now that the winter organization was gradually falling into place, it did seem that a certain amount of jockeying for position was going on. Nikoo and Polly were clearly waiting in the wings with some justification, for they were the obvious choice under ordinary circumstances, but with their previous success as a trapping team, we could not afford to have them doing anything else that winter. In any case, I had grown used to Innuk and her sudden appearances had come to be part of my post life.

Having arrived at some conclusion from her study of my face, Innuk decided to broaden the discussion by asking, 'Is Nikoo to stay here for the winter?'

'No, Nikoo must have a trap line this winter,' I replied, with a fair degree of certainty that that was what Innuk had intended me to say. At all events, the angry expression left her face to be replaced with a smile and after announcing that she would send Koolee over with some of their seal stew when it was cooked, she opened the porch door and forced her way out into the boisterous night.

The truth of the matter was that I liked Innuk. Clearly the only way to restore complete peace to the camp was to enter into a closer relationship with her, thus halting all speculation concerning the post set-up for the winter. My friend had already succeeded, despite my complete ignorance of the ways of women, in unmistakably informing me that such a development would be quite acceptable to her – in fact the decision was really hers rather than mine.

Nikoo quite happily accepted my explanation as to why it was preferable for him and Polly to work on a trap line rather than stay as a post employee for the winter. We had never even discussed the possibility, but Koko had certainly put the idea into people's minds. Before they and Powlussie left for their trapping camp on the north shore, they helped get my boat into its winter quarters. Somehow or another the process turned into a hilarious affair. The children began it after we had spent quite a while examining the hull. Tired of standing around, they started a game, a sort of tag gradually involving the rest of us until everybody was running and jumping about as though we had just been let out of school. Rebecca proved to be quite an acrobat and Innuk turned out to be much more nimble than had seemed likely. Poor Ookoo went so red in the face that I feared she might upset herself, but she came to no harm as she retired from the fray to rest on a rock despite the pleas of her children. I was sorry to say goodbye to my hunting companions, among whom I of course included Polly. They had proved to be very real people with enough courage and endurance, combined with extraordinary practical resourcefulness, to leave most of us far behind.

*

My suggestion one late fall evening, that we should hold English classes for the boys and girls during the winter months, was so well received that everybody other than the two elderly folk and the blind man wished to attend. Even the voluble Koko appeared keen to learn. My prospective pupils apparently anticipated an immediate start to their lessons, for they began to gather in the kitchen straightaway, giving me no time to plan for their instruction, which it had not been my intention to commence until the winter evenings. Eventually it was agreed that school should begin on the day of the next full moon, though it was quite plain that no one could understand the need for such a delay when they were all so keen to get started.

With the start of the trapping season so close, it was essential that I formulate my own plan of action for the winter months. This was quite simply to set out a line of traps overland towards the head of the main bay and the great fish river. There was one important difficulty. All the travelling gear, the sledge, harnesses and equipment, not to mention the dogs themselves, had been Akshut's and now belonged to Innuk. I did not wish to assume control over her property without prior discussion, although there was little doubt that my friend would be agreeable.

The flatter land from the river delta, right across to the cliff base and the edge of the reef, was by now hidden beneath an unbroken cover of pure-white snow. It appeared to merge with the lower slopes, so that our toehold on the shore, usually dwarfed by the great hills behind us, seemed to have expanded into a wide-open space stretching all the way from the black rim of rock high up on the cliffside down to the thickening sludge of the dark grey, early winter sea.

It was not long before the inevitable wind sprang up, twisting the light snow into spirals, whirling first this way then that, until the first blizzard of the season was upon us and the timbers of my house were creaking and trembling once again with each blast of the gathering storm.

I was very surprised that evening when the door burst open with the force of the wind and Innuk and Koolee appeared, as if by magic, before me. They had come across, very bravely on such a wild night, for me to try on a deerskin outfit which Innuk had made from the skins obtained on our hunting expedition. The fitting took a little while, but when we had finished, with my trapping plans foremost in my mind, I took the plunge and said, 'I have been thinking about your dogs, Innuk.'

Mother and daughter looked at me quite blankly, mystified as to why anybody should be thinking about dogs on such a stormy night, so to cover my embarrassment I blundered on, 'I would like to use the team to set traps over near the fish river. Perhaps we can use the dogs together.'

Innuk's face at first clearly registered astonishment, but her expression changed quickly to suggest that what she had heard pleased her greatly. Then she said what sounded like, 'As one for the trapping at the river.'

It was my turn to look blank but the suspicion that our conversation did not refer solely to the setting of traps was heightened when Innuk, perhaps dismayed by my failure to respond to her last remark, asked a little sadly, 'Am I not a good person to go with then?'

This was the key question, the answer to which could commit me to a firm association with Innuk. The moral scruples implanted in my mind since childhood still fought against this association, but Innuk was a fine, decent person, who I thought must be fully aware that a manager of a small outpost like this could never be more than a temporary resident. She had already unmistakably indicated to me that that was no bar to an arrangement between us, so I said, 'You are a very good person, Innuk, and we shall remain together.'

I was not sure what I meant by this, but felt certain that the situation was somehow passing out of my control.

I was pleased to receive a visit from Ookoodlea and her small daughter, Itualuk, the next day. She seemed quite at ease in the house, as indeed they all did now. She had come up because the fact that she was drawing from our stock of meat and fat without doing anything in return had begun to trouble her. Perhaps our friend Koko had been making some more sharp remarks. At all events she felt the need to inquire if there was any work for her to do.

It is customary among the Innuit that as well as hunting, men and women should do whatever they are best at doing, whether it be carving, harness making, spear fashioning or anything else that might contribute to the well-being of the camp. I assured Ookoodlea that now the trapping season was at hand, there would soon be any number of pelts to be dried and cleaned, so there would be plenty for her to do.

Little Itualuk, a faithful miniature version of her mother complete with a round beaming face framed in a very straight fringe of jet-black hair, was tidily dressed in a tiny new sealskin outfit. She had been gazing solemnly from one to the other of us during our talk and now looked inquiringly up at her mother.

'Where is the *kudloona*, mother?'

'Here he is,' replied Ookoo, pointing to me.

'That's not him,' piped her daughter in a shrill, childish voice, 'that's only Issumatak.'

Poor Ookoo looked rather embarrassed at this, but it seemed a compliment to me, so I laughed and told the child that I was really both a *kudloona* and Issumatak. At this the child gazed at me more intently than ever but accepted the fact of my dual role without further discussion. Ookoo told me that her daughter, having heard from the other children that they were to be taught to speak 'like the *kudloonas*', had announced that she too intended to come to the class. Her mother said that she did not know whether Issumatak would allow this because she was so small, but as Ookoo herself was going to be a pupil, I said that she could bring Itualuk along to see how she got on.

Later on, Innuk came over with Koolee and Nyla, bringing the dog harnesses so that we could check them over in the kitchen. This was Nyla's first visit to the house since her illness. She was trying to take part in the life of the camp in any way she could, although most of what needed to be done was too strenuous for anyone in her condition. She was still very emaciated but was in good spirits and drank a glass of milk before bringing out her needle and sinew to help in any repair work that was necessary. We had quite a jolly afternoon. These people could make any working session enjoyable because of their readiness to laugh whenever possible. Young Koolee kept up a constant chattering as we sorted out the traces. Each dog had its own individual harness, so Innuk had marked them to make them easy to identify.

Once she had explained all the markings to me, she also gave me a brief outline of the various animals' virtues and faults.

We tried out our travelling arrangements the following morning with an outing across to the river, which was now well frozen, to fetch some ice for my water tank. Nikoo had already put new runners on the sledge as well as repairing the crossbar lashings where they had become worn at the end of last season, so we were really quite well organized for winter travel. We even had a spare sledge which Ookoo had brought with her. She also had some of her husband's dogs, but did not bring the whole team because we did not have a sufficient supply of meat.

Nearly all the able-bodied people in the camp turned out to see the fun as we gathered the dogs together for their first outing of the season. The animals joined in the light-hearted approach to the business by galloping off before we were quite ready, so there was a mad rush to avoid being left behind, with order only being restored when the sledge became lodged behind a big boulder. While this was going on, Rebecca, who had hitched up Ookoo's dogs to the other sledge, swept past us in a most professional manner, causing Koolee considerable annoyance, who was all for making a race of it until restrained by her mother.

After the ice blocks had been stowed away in my water tank, we fed the dogs their first proper meal of the winter. Rebecca came to help, as she had taken charge of Ookoo's team. I feared that we still had too many dogs in the camp for our limited food supply, but thought we could see how things went for the first month or so. Innuk came over to the house a little later to say that they were going out to see if they could find any hares near by and would I go with them because they only had one .22 rifle between them?

For once we set off quite quietly despite the fact that almost everyone in the camp had gathered for the outing. I later discovered that there was a very special organization about hare hunting which would be upset by too much laughing and shouting.

Innuk, Koolee, Ookoo, Tooluka (Nyla's relative), Koko, Peela, the boy Tooshak, Rebecca and myself made up the party as we headed across towards the river. Under Ookoo's guidance, we formed ourselves in a line to ascend the slope on the far side. Ookoo herself and Rebecca took the lead, followed at a short distance by the two armed members of the party, Innuk with her late husband's .22 and myself with my small rifle. The rest of the group, the boys Tooluka, Peela and Tooshak with Koolee, brought up the rear.

We trudged silently up the hillside, then each time we neared the top of a ridge, Ookoo waved us to a stop while she and Rebecca peered cautiously down the other side. Just as we were beginning to think that we had picked a bad afternoon for *okkalilks*, our leaders stopped us very firmly a short distance below the hill. They beckoned Innuk and me to take up position, then stood up and began singing a strange chant while moving away from each other on either side of a dip in the slope just ahead of us. In the middle of the dip sat two hares quite transfixed by the singing, presenting Innuk and me with a simple stationary target.

I had a most instructive afternoon. Innuk told me that the Eskimos had been hunting hares in this way for generations. Sometimes, with a particularly persuasive singer, it is possible to go right up to the animal while it remains motionless. This did not happen with us, but one more hare succumbed to the charm of our the women's voices, so we could all look forward to a meal of hare stew.

Intent on our hunting activities, we had hardly noted the passage of time, so that by the time we reached the river on our northward journey, darkness had fallen. It was a cold, crisp, starry night and a magnificent display of the northern lights began as we made our way along the river bank to our crossing-point just above the delta. A few thin clouds drifted across the moon from time to time and the aurora hung beneath them, shooting up and down in lines of brilliant golden light.

With the coming of darkness, our spirits flagged somewhat and the silence, no longer necessary, became oppressive, so I stopped the party and asked if we should sing our way back home. The suggestion being greeted with unanimous approval, I hummed a few bars of 'Onward Christian Soldiers', which seemed to be known, in some form or another, to everyone.

Off we marched to the tune of the hymn, faltering a bit at

first, then gathering confidence as everyone picked up the words of the first verse. We repeated it over and over, until we were able to send our chorus swinging upward as we tramped our way across the snow and rocks. After that I was able to get the tune of 'John Brown's Body' going so strongly to a variety of words that the sound seemed to leap up to the flashing lights, then echo faintly back to us from somewhere in the sky high above the hilltops.

By the time that we had crossed the river on to the flats, we had reached such a swinging momentum that we startled the people who had remained behind sufficiently for them to emerge from their homes to see what was going on. Then, with a last admiring look at the now fully developed aurora display, we retired to our homes, allowing peace to return to the empty land.

During the evening, Innuk came across to return a cooking pot. When she had washed it out and replaced it on the shelf, my friend made no move to go. I realized that this was not just an ordinary visit and hoping to clarify the situation between us, I said, 'How shall we arrange about the dogs, Innuk?'

She looked at me in some surprise, as though this was a question that had already been decided.

'The hunter uses the dogs as he wishes.'

'The hunter?'

'Are you not a hunter then?'

I had modest success on the deer hunt but hardly enough to classify myself as a hunter.

'Not like an Innuit hunter.'

'Did you not shoot more deer than the other men and have you not just hunted the whale with the new gun?'

Neither of these achievements really gave me the right to call myself a hunter in this land of hunters, but there was no reason for me to have a disagreement with Innuk about it. I told her that as the company man, it was necessary for me to put out a longer trap line than usual because we had lost so many hunters that unless we made a special effort we would not catch enough foxes and the managers might decide to close the post. Innuk's expression seemed to imply that the actual details of the line did not really concern her and that it was up to me to decide how it should be arranged.

My lamp, not having been properly attended for several days, then began to smoke rather badly, which diverted my friend's attention. She went off to fetch a candle from the other room, dismantled the lamp, cleaned it, trimmed the wick and in a very short space of time brightened the kitchen up considerably. Innuk, having several times caught me either sitting in the dark or huddling over a fluttering candle, undoubtedly believed my abilities in such matters to be childlike. Once things had been organized to her liking, she sat down more confidently opposite me where Koolee usually sat, seemingly ready to continue our discussion.

I felt myself to be at something of a disadvantage because of my uncertainty as to just what our agreement was. Innuk said, 'It was said that we would use the dogs and sledge together for setting out the trap line over at the river.'

It dawned on me what I had done. My clumsy attempt to ask Innuk the other night if I could use her dogs, had amounted to a proposal that we should work together on the trap line. In Innuk's mind the matter was settled. Any second thoughts would be an insult to her, which she now pointed out in a roundabout sort of way. Having received no response to her statement, she asked again, 'Am I not a good person for you to go with, then?'

I had had an easy relationship with Innuk ever since the night of our hopeless vigil over little Suzhie. My friend, who would not understand my reservations, had no doubts herself as to how things were. She had with her a bag containing some personal possessions, confirming that our arrangement had not solely been concerned with sledges and dogs. My inhibitions and nervous apprehensions had been delaying the inevitable, but there was no longer any way for me to evade the issue. Innuk's expression, which had become steadily more dismal as the silence continued, brightened immediately as I said, 'There is no one I would rather have with me than you, Innuk.'

We sat smiling at one another, and though my bridge had not been an easy one to cross, I knew that Innuk was a wonderful person without whom my winter prospects would be bleak. I hoped that she would derive at least an equal benefit from our alliance. Certainly the whole affair did not transgress any of the traditions or customs of her people. As we sat at either end of the kitchen table with the lamp glowing between us, I felt sure too that this unusual love scene did not disgrace the standards my housemaster had endeavoured to instil in me not so many years before.

The weather was clear for several days, then a night and morning of fine snow drifting on an easterly breeze covered the rocks and bare patches along the flats between us and the river. The sea had frozen out as far as the narrows and along the reef the force of the rising tide broke the ice blocks to become a floating link between the shore and the sea ice.

The people had not forgotten that they were to gather on the night of the full moon for school. Unfortunately I had, so that no preparations had been made for the first lesson when the door opened after supper and everybody filed into the kitchen. They were all spruced up for the occasion, owing, as I discovered later, to the fact that in the magazine she was so fond of studying, Koolee had come across a picture of a school class gathered for some special occasion in their best clothes.

Assuming that this was the normal wear for school attendance, she had warned the others as to how they should appear.

Innuk, Ookoo, Rebecca and Nyla had all put on dresses made from red, green and blue tartan plaid, which really brightened the place up. Rebecca looked particularly elegant as she was taller than the others and had a good figure. For once she did not give the impression of being poised for immediate departure, but rather of being quite at ease as she prepared to settle down for the evening. Nyla would have been the belle of the class had she been well, for she was normally a most striking-looking girl, but was still thin to the point of emaciation. But they had not come to be judged in a beauty contest. They were ready for their language lesson, and while covering my uncertainty as to how to proceed by carefully arranging my friends in a semicircle around me, it came to me that the most sensible way to start would be with a few simple phrases. So, when everyone had quietened down, I leaned against the table and said, 'Good evening,' in English, hastily explaining that this was a normal greeting for this time of day as I could see that hysterical laughter was about to break out.

This was the main difficulty at first, for the younger people seemed to think that everything I said was funny. Eventually, we got into the swing of it and by the end of the evening most of them were able to come up with a passable greeting for various times of the day with some idea as to what they were actually saying. It was clear that I would need to divide the class into two groups, because some of the children, although quite willing, had trouble keeping up with the others.

After everyone had gone, Innuk made some tea and we had a talk about the coming trapping season. She asked, 'Are we to set the traps along the fish river or round the bay up into Aggoun?'

When I told Innuk that I had not yet decided on the exact

area to be covered, she went on to tell me what she knew about Aggoun, Kumarkbik, Tunuchon and the other parts of the bay where we would be working. She had lived there a few years before and her knowledge of the district was to be most useful.

We had nearly completed the preparation of our travelling equipment and the dogs were being brought on to their winter routine of feeding and general care, so our next priority was to pinpoint the exact spots where we should concentrate our efforts. For a start, we decided to establish a base camp by the river on a central point of land known as Kumarkbik, then see how much territory we would be able to cover.

We set out one morning on a preliminary trip, heavily laden with meat, tent and traps, to set up a cache of dog food. Once safely arrived below Tunuchon we made our first camp and Innuk lost no time organizing food and warmth in our travelling home.

It was strange to think that the whole deep bay – it must have been about thirty-five miles out to the tip of Beecher Peninsula and at least twelve miles across – was entirely deserted of human life except for Innuk and myself. I was very glad of Innuk's company in this lonely spot and believe the reverse was true as well, for my friend had been rather nervy ever since we arrived there, starting at any unusual sound and clearly apprehensive for some reason or other. I plied her with simple questions about her previous visits, which gradually distracted her from her fears as she told me of her father's hunting feats when they had lived here in the days of her childhood.

We got off to a good start the next morning and made our way towards Kumarkbik. We found relics of past hunting parties when we reached the point and Innuk pointed out the site of an old meat cache. Quite a deep hole had been dug in the ground so we were able to put all the dog food there, then cover it with the rocks that were scattered about. The deer meat which we had stored under the rocks on the point of land just beyond Ujuk Island was still in quite good shape and certainly fit to be used in stews, meatballs and suchlike, so we picked that up on the way back home.

The weather remained reasonable for our journey back to Ward Inlet. Having unloaded all the dog food and the traps, we made good time, arriving home just as darkness was falling. As an experimental trip, it was very successful, and it overcame my doubts as to the wisdom of going about with Innuk like this. The speed with which she, and no doubt other Eskimo women, set up a home in the wilderness, utilizing every available resource to maximize the comfort, was really astonishing. I had to concede that the camping homes I'd experienced when travelling with a hunter companion had never come up to Innuk's professional standards.

Koolee and Rebecca came out to unload the sledge, then collected up the harnesses and fed the dogs. Rebecca had become most helpful and was almost as good as a young hunter in many ways. I worried, though, that she felt under some obligation because of her dependence on our supplies.

During the night, the heaviest snowfall of the winter began, so that by morning the whole area was completely white, with the snow continuing to come down so thickly that it seemed as if the sky was falling to earth. The silence was eerie. One might think that in a virtually uninhabited place like Baffin Island there would be very little noise at any time, when in fact all the small sounds of habitation seemed the louder by echoing over the empty spaces. Yet on that day the dogs were silent, the tent doors were not banging as usual and even the barrier ice had stopped creaking and cracking because of the low tides.

We could not do much in such weather, so we had a language class for a couple of hours during the afternoon, which finished with a spell of singing. I tried to teach them the words of 'Three

Blind Mice', but they went off into such paroxysms of laughter at my attempts to explain and mime all that happened to those unfortunate mice that we had to abandon the effort.

The snow did not let up for two days, by which time it was too deep and soft for any serious travel to be attempted.

Koko decided to put her oar in again while we were snowed in at the post. Innuk told me about it.

'The woman from Twerpukjuak says that Ooleepika should use Ookoo's dogs and sledge to set out a trap line, so that they can have trading money for the winter.'

Koko was clearly a troublemaker, but I couldn't deny that there was some substance to this suggestion. It did pose certain difficulties, however, which I pointed out to Innuk.

'That would mean feeding two teams of working dogs.'

'Koko says that they will have so little to trade.'

This was true enough. The girl could earn something by making moccasins and the like, but that would not amount to much. On the other hand, we simply did not have enough food to keep the extra dogs in working trim. I asked, 'Is there no one else who could give them some dog food?'

'The men will need all their meat for their own teams.'

Innuk looked at me very strangely, then astounded me by asking, 'Should Ooleepika come with us?'

At first, remembering how cross my friend had been about my joining up with Polly for the race, this suggestion bewildered me. Then it dawned on me. This was how the senior wives dealt with the problem when a home had more than enough work for one woman – by getting their husbands to take on an assistant of whom they approved. There was plenty of work for the three of us on a long trap line and I admired Ooleepika's ability, but I had no intention whatsoever of making any more arrangements. I protested, 'What will the missionary say when he hears that I go off trapping with two women?'

'He will say that you are a brave man.'

Innuk did not often attempt humour, but seeing the astonishment on my face, she continued in a jocular manner, 'Are you afraid to go off with two women? We heard that you were not afraid of Polly and her sister at Twerpukjuak.'

I had obviously underestimated Innuk's mental agility, with the result that the conversation drifted out of my control again. It was no longer a question of what the various authorities might say so much as what my personal reaction would be. Armed with the knowledge that I had quite happily shared a home with Polly and Agiak down at Warwick Bay, my friend was in a very strong position.

Why Innuk should have been so keen for Rebecca to accompany us on our travels still puzzled me, so I asked, 'Why do you want Ooleepika to come with us?'

'She is a very good sledge person and understands this part of the country better than some of the hunters.'

This was a very interesting comment. The Innuit had a great attachment to the land and to the animals that inhabited their area, a certain oneness with it all that made them a part of their surroundings and gave them a deeper understanding of the travelling problems which might arise. This would certainly be advantageous to us during the winter, but was not really the essential point for me. I said, more to myself than to my companion, 'What will everybody think when they hear that I went trapping with two women?'

Innuk very sensibly did not attempt to answer this. She was probably wondering why I was raising these objections. The idea of Rebecca joining us on the trap line would have struck her as being a useful, practical arrangement. The girl would be able to provide for her mother and herself. It would only be necessary for us to use one team, thus greatly reducing the strain on our supply of dog food and we would have an experienced traveller with us in case of difficulties. The realities of our position outweighed the other, more abstract considerations. There was no one here to answer the moral questions which arose in my mind.

Innuk was staring at me, waiting for a decision. Tiring of my silence, she asked, 'Shall I fetch Ooleepika?'

Without thinking, I nodded my head. My opposition had collapsed and yet the idea of this quiet cross-eyed girl coming with us pleased me. Innuk was most likely aware of this and also of the fact that what the missionary had to say in the distant future, if a report ever reached him, would be of little consequence. By then the likelihood was that we would all have dispersed to other places. I reassured myself that nothing untoward was likely to happen with Innuk in charge of the domestic arrangements, and in a few moments the two women came in to the kitchen. I said to Rebecca, 'Because we do not have enough meat to feed two teams, we shall have to send Ookoodlea's dogs down to Kikitukjuak.'

'Are my mother and I to go too?' asked the girl.

'Only if you want to go.'

'My mother wishes me to set our traps. Without the dogs I shall not be able to do this.'

'You will be able to set your traps over at Kumarkbik.' As I said this, I realized that Innuk had not spoken to Rebecca of this new possibility, for a look of bewilderment came over her face.

'Am I to go with you then?' she asked.

'This will be the best way,' I replied, 'because it will mean we shall only have to look after one team.'

At first our friend looked about as doubtful as I had been, but her hesitation was brief and she was soon discussing possible arrangements with Innuk.

As soon as she heard that her daughter was to join us over

in the bay, Koko was up to know if she could have one or two foxes in debt as she had not been able to do any trading for so long. This was strictly against the rules, but to stop her making a scene I gave her one fox on the strict understanding that the very first fur would have to be handed over.

Rebecca suggested that we take three of Ookoo's dogs with us to see if they would fit in with the rest of the team, then immediately set about making new harnesses and lines for them. Before we could put them to the test, we had a surprise visit from Nikoo and Polly. They had already set out their traps and caught some foxes, but the purpose of the visit was to bring us a couple of seals from their camp. Apparently the seal hunting had been good down there, so very generously the people thought of us all at Ward Inlet, knowing that their friends would be getting a little tired of whale meat and missing their favourite diet.

We decided to forgo our English lesson for a night and entertain our friends. After they had had their seal stew over at Innuk's, everyone, including the old people and poor blind Netchil, came across for an evening of fun. They brought all their bits and pieces for a real Eskimo 'do', Polly with her string to make her fancy animal shapes, Koolee with her ducks and carvings, while Netchil brought his drum. I was hoping to be able to avoid making a fool of myself, but after a while Polly began to agitate for the 'mirror story'. I decided to tell them about Aladdin and his lamp instead. They listened spellbound. Encouraged by their obvious appreciation of the story, I adapted the tale to fit in with their own lives, so that some of them appeared to think that the lamp might suddenly appear in the kitchen. Polly, although she was just as taken with the story of Aladdin as the others, was determined to have her choice as well and produced a hand mirror with a great flourish to round everything off.

XIV

WE LEFT WARD INLET for Kumarkbik in fine style two days later. Ookoo's three dogs seemed to fit in well with ours and Rebecca quickly proved her worth on the trail.

Mostly the going was good, with the snow well packed down, though every now and then we struck a patch where the sledge sank through with a sharp braking effect on the team.

Innuk and Rebecca complemented each other splendidly. Innuk could establish a warm and comfortable home out of a few square yards of wilderness, while Rebecca looked after the dogs, checked the harnesses, cleared the traces, and could ice the runners much more efficiently than I. All augured very well for our winter's activities.

We spent the first night, as before, at the camp below the big river. Having set a few traps on the way over, we then continued our line along the coast: into an inlet about four or five miles along from the mouth of the river, on several of the islands scattered about in the vicinity and on the point itself. I suggested that we pooled everything we caught and divided it equally. This was not the normal Eskimo routine, which was generally that whoever set the trap got the fox, but it appeared to please my companions greatly.

The next day we separated out. The women took me as far as the neck of the point of land on which we had our base camp (Kumarkbik), then they set off westward through a group of islands, making for the other river at the head of the bay.

My chief difficulty was to sort my load so as not to be too awkwardly laden for the long day's walk, as my essential gear consisted of the traps, snowknife, lumps of bait, my rifle and my lunch bag, which was made of deerskin to protect the contents from the cold.

The going was not easy at the start, for the snow on the grassy flatter land was still soft in patches and deep enough for me to sink almost up to my knees, but conditions improved along the river bank. After about an hour's walking, I came to a long flat plain where my thoughts, miles away with my family in New Zealand, swiftly returned to Frobisher Bay as I noted a herd of deer quietly nuzzling the grass through the snow not far ahead of me.

The caribou were surprisingly slow to move, so that I might have got off three shots in their direction, but with two of them in the bag it seemed pointless to fire again.

Fortunately, my two victims were both dead, saving me from having to indulge in any throat cutting. For me, the skinning was quite a slow process, so lunch was a welcome break. After cutting up the meat I covered it with skins and snow blocks until we could come and fetch it. It was well into the afternoon before I was able to continue with my trap laying.

The fading daylight reminded me that our camp was a long way off and that darkness would have fallen before I reached the mouth of the river. As I had feared, the light went very quickly, leaving me to flounder about in almost pitch darkness in the cloudy, moonless night, so that it was a great joy to hear the distant barking of the dogs. In a few moments they arrived to jump around me, followed by Rebecca, who clutched me quite fiercely by the arm, saying, 'We thought you might be lost in the darkness, so Innuk said I was to bring the team to look for you.'

The girl spoke rather apologetically, as though she feared that their lack of confidence in my ability to find the way home might upset me.

'Thank you for coming, because it would have been a long walk home. I have had to leave the meat under some snow a little way up the hill.'

'Meat?' queried my friend rather incredulously.

'Yes. I shot two deer this morning.'

Rebecca clasped her hands together and excitedly addressed the cold night air with a few complimentary remarks, such as, 'What a good thing our hunter was with us', inflating my self-esteem sufficiently for me to feel tempted to give her a big hug. Fearing that my behaviour might be misinterpreted, I restrained myself just in time. Rebecca was very keen that we should bring the meat down to our camp at once to ensure that none of it would be lost during the night, so we drove back, loaded the skins and the cut meat on to the sledge, allowed the dogs to gobble up the offal, then set off back to base.

Innuk's excitement matched that of her friend's. They fussed round me as though I had performed some phenomenal feat, until I retired to bed to watch the dancing shadows from the lamp flames flickering up and down the tent wall while my chattering friends continued on about their hunter.

I did not want to be too long away from the post as people from the other camps might be arriving with their first catches of the season, but after the distraction of deer my trap line was still not complete.

We stayed another day, completed our work and cut across from the river to the site of our first camp. There we spent the night before returning home the following day. Innuk thought it was possible to go back by way of the big river, cutting round to the hills above Ward Inlet somewhere up in the higher land, but as she was not certain of the route, we felt it better not to attempt this until we had had a chance to discuss the whole thing with one of the hunters. We took half the meat with us, caching the remainder under the rocks at Kumarkbik to await our next trip.

There were no visitors waiting for me at the post, but we had scarcely had time to put our gear away before they began to appear. These were people from the settlement where we had spent the night on our way down to the whale hunt. Their season had begun well, with the foxes which had last year been few and far between reasonably abundant, so they would be able to pay off a good part of their debt while still leaving money in hand for their present needs.

Innuk and Koolee came in to get tea and biscuits ready for the visitors, shortly to be joined by Rebecca. While the people were drinking their tea a bright idea occurred to me. Why should I not appoint Rebecca and Koolee as store assistants for days of heavy trading? Koolee was a little young but I was sure that under the guidance of the older girl she could certainly be of help. They were both very impressed with the idea of helping in the store, if a little apprehensive. These doubts were easily overcome when they heard that they would be paid a modest amount for their services.

As I'd hoped, my assistants helped greatly by saving me from a lot of running about fetching the various goods as required, which did cut down the time taken up by each hunter. When it came to money being spent by the women, however, the ladies, probably emboldened by being attended to by one of their own sex, tended to hold long-winded discussions concerning the minutest purchases, thus wasting the time gained with the men, so that finally I sent the girls back to the house and brought everything to a speedy conclusion myself.

We had hardly finished dealing with the first group of arrivals before our next lot of visitors appeared from further down the coast. They had also been reasonably successful to date and my assistants shaped up better on their second try, being now more familiar with the general layout of the stock and less inclined to chatter with the customers. Perhaps they were slightly ashamed of having to be sent home the previous afternoon.

Several of the men came in during the evening. They were very keen to hear about our line in Frobisher Bay, not appearing to be the slightest bit surprised that my team-mates were two women. One of them, Ushukaluk by name, had made his home in that area years ago, so was very informative. When he heard about our dilemma as to how best to head for base without retracing our steps, he drew an excellent map showing me how we could go round the whole line in an onward direction. He told me all the landmarks to look for as well as pinpointing many suitable spots for traps.

The post seemed quiet when everyone had left. I had enjoyed talking to the hunters; between them they had such vast experience, not to mention an encyclopedic knowledge of the countryside. Ookoodlea soon came up for one of her visits, however. She brought little Itualuk with her to ask whether she should continue attending the lessons, but it became apparent that her real concern was that her relations might be becoming a nuisance to me. She was especially anxious to know whether Rebecca was being really useful on the trap line. I swiftly reassured her on this point, but feeling that she wanted to explain further about her relations, I asked her to tell me what had happened to Koko's husband.

Some time back, Koko's husband, Itoodlu, had had a bad accident while travelling through a patch of very rough barrier ice, that left him with a severely crushed right foot which drastically limited his capability for hunting. Being of independent spirit, he would not allow his family to depend on scraps begged from others, so he taught the eldest of his two daughters,

Ooleepika, to hunt under his direction. In a year or two, she had become more like a hunter than a girl, and this, combined with her cross-eyes, had in Ookoo's opinion kept her from finding a hunter of her own. It was not that she was not a respectable girl.

I broke into Ookoo's story here to tell her that, from my point of view, Ooleepika was a highly commendable person. My friend looked rather surprised at this and I hoped that I had not inadvertently committed myself further than intended.

Though his eldest daughter had proved a great help to him, the hunter's physical disability did prevent him from achieving his usual level of success. Feeling out of place in a camp of generally above average hunters, Itoodlu decided to move away with his family to a place further down the coast. His friends tried to persuade him not to, but he insisted on going, so the family packed up all their belongings and set off. When they were about half-way to their destination, they were caught in a storm as they were passing a promontory. Koko and Ooleepika wanted to get on to the land before the wind became too strong, but Itoodlu would not agree to this, deciding instead to travel on until he came to a suitable patch of snow from which to erect a shelter. The sea ice round that point of land, never too secure because of the turbulent currents underneath, then broke off with the force of the wind. As their pan began to drift away from the main body, Ooleepika seized her mother and somehow dragged her across an ever-widening gap to safety, but Itoodlu could not move quickly enough to save himself and the younger girl. The pair on the solid ice could only watch as Itoodlu and his daughter drifted steadily away from them to be lost for ever. Ookoo paused in her narrative, looking at me to gauge my interest. To encourage her to continue, I asked how the mother and daughter had managed to get home from such a perilous situation.

Koko was so cast down with shock and despair that had it not been for Ooleepika's determination to bring her to safety, she would have remained with her husband. She also admitted afterwards that she would never have walked through the heavy storm, had not her daughter half-carried her for the greater part of the way. Eventually they arrived back at their former home on the verge of collapse, to be taken in and cared for by their friends.

I wondered vaguely whether Ookoo had come up especially to tell me this sad saga, and if so, for what purpose. Perhaps to explain how it had come about that her relatives were without a hunter to support them, or perhaps because Koko had suggested a visit for the extolling of Ooleepika's virtues. It was difficult for me to know quite what to say in response to Ookoo's story. My impulse was to say something complimentary which would please her, but I also needed to be very careful not to express an inappropriate interest in Ooleepika. I therefore confined my comments on the story to generalities, such as how fortunate for Koko that she had so capable a daughter, what a good thing for Innuk and myself that Rebecca had learnt so much from her hunter father and how I hoped that the pair would benefit from the winter on our trap line by trading her share of the furs.

Innuk came in just as Ookoo was finishing her story, so we all drank tea. Watching our visitor's beaming face as the two women talked, it struck me how over the past two or three months I had come to appreciate Ookoo. Behind what seemed almost a bland exterior there was concealed a strong character; her ability to help people through illness had been amply demonstrated, while her staunch loyalty to her family and to the traditions of her race became more evident every day.

That evening, my friends gathered for another lesson. My students had progressed quite well by learning phrases parrot fashion. To begin the class, each student stood up in turn, and the class called out, 'Who are you?'

The response came, 'I am so and so.'

Then the most popular of all, 'What are you?'

In answer to which everyone shouted, 'I AM AN ESKIMO.'

Then they all turned to me to shout, 'WHAT ARE YOU?' to which query would come my lone reply, 'I AM AN ENG-LISHMAN.'

After this noisy start to the proceedings, we would settle down to acquire one or two new phrases. I am sure this tuition would have been scorned by any academic institution, but we had a lot of fun, while most of them did learn a few expressions which might some day have been useful to them. We always concluded the session by singing. I tried to teach them the words to 'John Brown's Body', then later complicated matters by leaving one word out each time the chorus was repeated. We never reached a high degree of success, but always ended the evening on a note of great hilarity.

The first, and rather ferocious, storm of winter prompted Innuk to suggest her family move into a snowhouse before our next expedition to the trap line. We organized a snowhouse-making day, during which, in the absence of any proper hunters, but with much good advice from old Sharni, we teamed together to make two good-sized houses.

Innuk told me that both Rebecca and Nyla had some ability as builders if I could cut out the blocks. Sharni came with me to pick out a suitable area of snow, so we set about seeking out a large snowdrift of good consistency.

I was not altogether convinced that Nyla was in a fit condition to undertake this sort of work, yet but she seemed to have made up her mind that it was time for her to become an active member of the community again and she certainly seemed to have made a good recovery. The old man and I found a very suitable bank of snow quite close to the house for me to begin work straight away. My job was to cut the blocks for Sharni and the two girls to do the building. Everyone not otherwise engaged attended to the packing of the walls, filling any gaps at the edges with loose snow to form a secure joint. There was, as usual, quite a high degree of hilarity, particularly among the young people, but they did not allow this to impede the progress of the work. Innuk and Ookoo provided the midday refreshment, and before darkness fell the houses were in full occupation with the move completed.

The unexpected arrival of three hunters from Twerpukjuak delayed our second trip to Kumarkbik. Expecting to find her sister Polly here at the post, the jolly Agiak had made the journey in with her husband, but she made up for her disappointment by regaling me with the latest episode in the marital complications of Annawa and Savik.

The simplistic solution to the Annawa/Savik affair, which had apparently brought an end to the open hostility between them, had not proved enduring. Agiak gave me the facts as to the present situation in a sentence.

'Ali has left Savik again.'

Realizing the potential dangers which might arise from such a turn of events, I asked, 'What has Savik done about this?'

'He sits by Annawa and Peeta during the night as before.'

'Where is Ali now?'

'She is in the home of her aunt, Ikuma.'

It seemed to me that enough time had been wasted and emotions roused by these people's neurotic attitudes already without going into another phase of idiotic behaviour.

I asked Agiak, 'If I write to them will they understand?'

My friend obviously approved of this line of action. She beamed with satisfaction at the suggestion.

'Yes,' she said emphatically, 'they will understand a writing.'

I wrote three letters for Agiak to take home with her, one for each of the two men and one also to Ali's aunt, Ikuma. The message for the men was identical, expressing the hope that they would settle the matter by talking, without recourse to actions which might well get them into trouble with the police. The aunt was the more likely person to be able to control the situation, so to her the message repeated my prior suggestion that Ali be persuaded to return to the east coast, leaving the two hunters in peace. While this might not entirely heal the breach between the two men, I hoped that it would be sufficient to prevent any further outbreaks of violence between them.

Our trip around the recently laid trap line started off reasonably well. We had special success in the inlet near the big river and on the island lying across the entrance. Here it was clear that there were too many foxes for the available food supply. Probably the lemming population, stock diet for the predators, had been cleaned out earlier on, while the ptarmigan had moved to higher ground and the polar bears had not obliged by leaving the usual number of seal carcasses to satisfy the hunger of the scavengers.

We had equal success on the western arm of the river mouth as well as on the islands in the bay leading over to Kumarkbik, but the picture on the headland itself quelled our excitement. Around the cache where we had deposited the meat was a scene of carnage. We had set three traps there because of the known weakness of the foxes for burrowing their way into buried food. Each trap had evidently caught a fox, but they had all been devoured by a pack of ravenous wolves.

At first sight, it seemed they must have attacked shortly after we set the traps, but ominously, around what had been our tent site, there were fresh wolf tracks where the pack had been nosing about for any scraps of food. The loss of the three furs was annoying, but not nearly so serious as the continued

347

presence of these hungry animals in our vicinity. While my own experience of wolves was limited, it was fair to assume that they attacked human beings under certain circumstances which would almost certainly include ravenous hunger.

I was in some doubt as to how the women would react to the potential danger, so made no comment other than to bemoan the loss of the furs. Then, as we were finishing our snowhouse later that day, we distinctly heard the wolves howling at no great distance and I saw Rebecca shiver in alarm.

I could see they were at least apprehensive, if not frightened, and then Innuk asked, 'Will the wolves come to the house?'

I honestly thought this unlikely. So far as I knew these packs did not commonly launch direct attacks on snowhouses. I said, 'No, I do not think so. I think we should be careful tomorrow, though, because they will probably be somewhere not very far away.'

Despite my reassuring words, after we had eaten our supper I inspected my rifle carefully to make sure that it was fully operative.

The women watched me closely. Innuk asked, 'Will you be hunting the wolves tomorrow?'

'No. Unless they steal from our traps. If they follow us in the morning, we shall be ready for them.'

My friends appeared satisfied with this, but in the face of what might be danger, we made what preparations we could to repel any intrusion aimed at stealing our property, interfering with the dogs or an unlikely attack on ourselves. Innuk stoked up our travelling lamp so that we should have light in case of an emergency, while I kept most of my clothes on and my rifle close by me, ready for immediate use if necessary.

Rebecca must have remained reasonably alert, for I awoke in the night to find her calling my name and shaking me by the shoulder. There was no need for me to inquire what the matter was, as a sinister scuffling sound outside, accompanied by what sounded like groans and grunts, was clearly audible. The first thought that came into my mind was that the wolves were trying to dig their way up into the house. Then it occurred to me that the beasts had simply resumed their attempts to break into the meat cache alongside our igloo. The dogs, probably petrified with fear, were silent.

My immediate impulse was to retire under the deerskins in the hope that whatever it was would just go away, but somewhat braver thoughts gradually gained the upper hand. My plan was quite simple. The wolves were at work among the rocks of the cache, which was situated immediately beside our snowhouse, giving me the chance to launch a surprise attack through the wall of our igloo by quietly cutting out one of the blocks.

I got my rifle ready and signalled to my companions not to make any noise and to extinguish the lamp. I cut the hole fairly high up on the wall, to allow for the fact that our floor was below the outside level and to help me to assess the position of my targets as accurately as possible. Our visitors were busy on the far side of the cache and the only possible target within my range of vision was a small area of a wolf's behind over to the right of my view. The angle at which I had to position the rifle made it difficult to aim properly, but the bang of my shot was quickly followed by a screeching yelp as well as the scuffling sounds of hasty departure. The howling and yelping of the wolves faded off into the night, finally dying away altogether as the pack retired to a considerable distance from which they would be unlikely to return that night.

My friends must have been more upset by the proximity of the wolves than I had realized, for they were extremely relieved when they had departed, and once again rather overdid their praise for my achievement. Unfortunately, there was no reason to suppose that this had been in any way a definitive blow against the villains. Although my experience of wolf packs was confined to books about the north, I was far from convinced that we had eliminated their interest in our affairs.

Once we retired to continue our interrupted sleep, Rebecca moved closer to me and pushed her warm feet across into the bottom of my deerskin in case mine were cold. I knew that this was not intended as an advance of any kind, but simply as her contribution to the night's proceedings, in which spirit her gift was gladly accepted.

The next day we found two more ravaged foxes and two baitless traps. Then, happening to glance back toward's a low hill close to the river bank, I noticed a movement among the rocks. Three shapes separated themselves and trotted down the hill towards the plain across which we were travelling. Later, when we were attending to our line among the low hills above the bay, it became fairly clear that the wolves were following us closely.

My thoughts were not heroic by any means, but unless we took some fairly drastic action we were sooner or later going to have serious trouble with these animals. My inclination was to precipitate the confrontation without delay: much better for us to have a showdown in full daylight than to be at the mercy of these cunning creatures after dark.

We had brought one night's feed for the dogs with us on the sledge, which we could now use as bait for our followers. Rebecca and Innuk kept the dogs at bay while I unloaded it into a fairly prominent heap on the snow. We then drove off between two hillocks just ahead of us. I dismounted behind the nearest hill, telling the women to drive on for a few minutes to be quite out of sight and hearing, then climbed up the slope to station myself behind a boulder, from where I had a clear view of the dog food. Nothing happened for a few minutes, until two of the wolves came cautiously into view with a third creature dragging up the rear, slowed perhaps by a wounded bottom. The little pack moved forward quite cautiously, digressing from side to side in a thorough inspection of the area before continuing on, all the time following in our tracks.

It must have been at least ten minutes before our followers picked up the scent. They halted a few yards from the dog food to survey the area minutely, in apparent disbelief that such a prize should so easily be theirs, then hunger impelled them to make a final rush forward. The leader moved straight into the sights of my rifle, trained in the direction of the meat, and dropped with my first shot, the other two galloped off at once, but as they moved crossways instead of back in the direction from which they had come, gave me a chance for a second shot. Only the last member of the pack got clear away, at a speed that suggested little likelihood of return.

The second crack of the rifle was still echoing around the hills when my friends reappeared in the distance, running beside the sledge to encourage the dogs to speed over the snow so that they could find out what had happened. The second wolf was still desperately trying to drag itself away to safety, so I ran down the hill to put the struggling animal out of its misery.

My companions must also have believed that the third wolf would not bother us any more, for that night all traces of their apprehension had gone. I hoped that they would not have any future cause to regret their confidence, and sitting in our snowhouse miles up the river bank in this deserted corner of Frobisher Bay, the thought struck me that I had as great a need of them as they of me.

We followed Ushukaluk's route very successfully for the remainder of the trip, and once home and safe with our rewards it was clear that we had made a splendid start to the season.

The rest of the Twerpukjuak hunters were waiting for me

at the post. They had been there for a couple of days but had made good use of the time by hunting at the seal holes in and around the cove. They had secured four seals, to the great joy of the people, who had not enjoyed fresh seal meat, their favourite diet, for some time.

All the men had had quite a good start to the season. Many of the pelts were greasy, so there was plenty of work for Ookoo and Nyla, who had got on very well with the first lot brought in by the other men. Koojesse had been the most successful of the Warwick Bay hunters, with twenty-five pelts to trade, which was truly exceptional so early in the season. Evi, who had joined the travellers at Kikitukjuak for the journey in, greeted me like a long-lost friend, so our differences of the summer were evidently to be forgotten, which was a welcome development. Our new relationship began well with the hunter bringing in a dozen furs, all beautifully clean.

Mingumai, my visitor of the previous summer, came up later by himself. He shuffled about rather as though he had something on his mind, but naturally it took him some time to come out with it. He said, 'My wife told me to say that Savik is very angry again.'

The man spoke half apologetically, as though he did not like to bother me with such trivial matters. Regrettably, his wife had not accompanied him, so it was a hard battle getting the story out. I asked, 'Why does she think this?'

'Because at night time he does bad things.'

Thinking that this referred to a resumption of the night-time singing, the position did not seem to be much different from that reported by Agiak, but I asked, 'What bad things?'

Mingumai mumbled an answer, as though he had no desire to be put on record as having made some definite accusation, but he did say something about a gun, which immediately alarmed me. Mingumai was clearly unhappy answering these questions, but it was important for me to know exactly what was happening. I needed another source of information.

In the end it was Innuk who gave me an account of events at Twerpukjuak. She said, 'Savik began sitting by the sleeping platform again when the people were in their deerskins. After two days, Annawa told Savik that he was not to do this any more, but Savik replied that he would stay there until Peena returned with him to his own home. Then Annawa brought out his long knife and Savik went home. The next day your letters arrived, so nothing bad happened, but the night before the men left to come here, Savik went to the other home with his rifle. He stood outside shouting bad things about Annawa, then fired his rifle.

'Did he shoot into the house?' I asked.

'Not into the house but the bullet went through the skins in the porch and broke a piece of wood.'

'What happened then?'

'Annawa and his family remained inside the home, then Savik fired again, towards the sky this time.'

'He did not try to hurt anybody?'

'No, but he shouted that he was going to come back and it would be bad for them in that home if Peena did not return to him.'

Exasperated, I remarked in English, 'I am absolutely sick of these people.'

Innuk looked startled, as though she had understood my meaning if not the words, but she said nothing.

There did not seem to be any way for me to avoid making a journey down to Twerpukjuak.

Initially, I intended to accompany the hunters on their journey home, but there would not have been enough room at the stop-over camps to fit everybody in, so I decided to wait for a couple of days, then follow when the crowd had gone. Innuk surprised me by proposing that Ooleepika come with me on my journey. As Innuk clearly had no objection to me going on a journey with a lone female, and Rebecca would undoubtedly be a great help, I readily agreed to her suggestion and Rebecca and the two of us arrived at Twerpukjuak five days later.

Apparently, Savik had not attempted any more threatening demonstrations over the past day or two, and when I saw him in his home he looked as though nothing was further from his thoughts. But this time he was left in no doubt as to what would befall him if he went about shooting in the vicinity of other people's homes. If there was one more incident of this kind, he would be reported to the police and his credit facilities with the company would be stopped. He must settle his argument with Annawa by talking not by shooting. I suggested that if he needed a wife there were several excellent women living around the bay who had lost their husbands and would be only too pleased to find another hunter.

I told Annawa that he had not treated his friend well considering the agreement that they had had. Perhaps if they talked together, he could make a gift to Savik which might help to resolve the argument in a peaceful way.

In the face of my anger and the length of the journey I had taken to confront them, the men both gave me the impression that they would come to an agreement about the women. I remained unconvinced, but Mingumai's wife, Meelai, said that she would let me know if things did not improve between them.

We left Twerpukjuak by bright moonlight under a clear starlit sky with great hopes of a speedy journey. Within an hour, however, the clouds began to form, not angrily as in a pre-blizzard formation, but thickly and heavily as though by sheer weight they might shortly sink to the ground. The horizon disappeared behind a curtain of snow and fog, then the land vanished from sight, until we could barely keep the leading dogs in view. Occasionally, the snow lightened enough to allow us a glimpse of the coastline and Rebecca was able at once to confirm that we were still moving in the right direction.

The weather slowed our progress significantly, so it was another two days before we reached the last leg of our journey home. On our final evening, Rebecca was checking over the harnesses as usual, when I noticed an odd movement to her eye. I had noticed before that after a hard day on the trap line, Rebecca's eyes tended to wander rather badly.

Not wishing to upset the girl by asking questions which she might interpret as a criticism, I approached the subject in a roundabout way by commenting on the conditions we had encountered, and asking about the landmarks she had used to judge our position. Did she not find it difficult after a few hours of staring across the land to tell one cliff from another?

Rebecca thought about this for a moment, then she said, 'This is where we hunted when I travelled with my father. He had been here for many years and taught me how to recognize the hills which would be most help to us in finding our way to the camps during bad weather.'

'But do your eyes not get tired of trying to see through the snow all day?'

Once again my friend hesitated before replying, then she said, 'Sometimes my head becomes heavy and I do not see things clearly.'

'Where does it feel heavy?'

The girl passed her hand across her forehead, then indicated a blurring of her vision by moving the hand to and fro in front of her face.

'Is it like that now?'

'Yes, but by morning it will be well again.'

I rummaged in my box to find my dark glasses and gave them to her, telling her that she was to wear them whenever her eyes felt heavy because if she did not take care of her eyes, in years to come she would not see so well.

'Am I to put them on now?' asked Rebecca.

This was not strictly necessary in the comparative gloom of our tiny snowhouse, but I felt that it might be as well for her to get used to wearing the glasses, so I said, 'Yes. You must wear them whenever your head feels heavy.'

Rebecca put the glasses on. Actually they quite suited her, but our talk had made her conscious of her defect and she asked, 'Is it thought bad to have eyes like mine?'

'No. Many people are affected like this.'

'Do they wear the windows also?'

'Yes, nearly all of them have windows of different kinds.'

To take the girl's mind off her eyes we spent the rest of the evening practising the English she had learnt and playing cards.

Over the winter months, we were able to make another three rounds of the trap line, which yielded an ample supply of meat and furs. We brought back ten foxes between us on one trip alone, so that I was quite surprised by the efficient success of our little team. One morning, when the weather was too fierce for travel of any kind, my eyes opened to a scene of domestic hilarity. Innuk and Rebecca had heated up a quantity of snow and were washing themselves very energetically out of a bowl, all the time chattering away with much merriment as they mimicked the European people they had seen engaged in their ablutions. When I told them not to forget to wash behind their ears, they asked why that should be important, so I explained that that was what my mother had always said to me, at which they stopped laughing for a moment to cross-question me about my life as a child. They were much amused and clearly felt not a little superior on hearing some of the details of such a protected life.

Just two days before Christmas, Nikoo and Polly arrived,

looking a fine pair in their new deerskins. It was quite a sight watching them coming over the rough reef ice. Their dogs, keen to get up to the settlement where they knew there would be food, hurtled through the rough ice blocks, dragging the sledge recklessly behind them. Nikoo had to guide it through the gaps and out of danger by leaping from side to side with great agility while Polly braced herself at the back in an attempt to slow the mad rush. They had twelve dogs, all in fine fettle and splendid condition.

Our friends had set out a very long trap line in an area they knew well, so we definitely reaped the benefit of not having kept them more at the post. So far they had caught over forty foxes in two trips and Nikoo was building up to a new engine for his boat.

Nikoo was eager to hear about our brush with the wolves and was amazed at how bold the creatures had been in attacking the cache while we were in the snowhouse. Apparently, in days gone by, they were more aggressive, especially when the Innuit had been armed mainly with spears, but now that most travellers had rifles with them, the wolves were usually content to keep close enough at hand to take advantage of any scraps or leftovers.

The hunter and his wife spent several days with us, while Nikoo tried his luck at the seal holes. Innuk wanted me to go with him, convinced by now that it was only necessary for me to set off after an animal for it to fall into my hands. Hunting at seal holes, however, would be a different story altogether from anything I had previously attempted.

During the fall, when the sea starts to freeze, the seals begin at once to keep holes open where they can come out from under the ice for air during the winter. They do this by gnawing away the ice in several different places, thus keeping open an area under the snow sufficient for their needs. These holes require constant attention to keep the ice from thickening, an ever-present danger at these low temperatures. The seals are confined, during this period, to the area where they have made their holes, for should they wander off they would soon die of suffocation. A group of seals usually share their holes, thus forming the winter population of a given area.

The hunters used their dogs to scent out the places frequented by the seals. A man often had one special dog with a keener nose than the others, which he took out on a lead to find the exact spot. The hunter then probed through the snow with his spear until he found the open water, left a marker, then took the dog back to rejoin the rest of the pack.

In the deep winter, there was no special way of enticing a seal to come up at any one hole. It was just a case of waiting. At temperatures well below zero this was not an enviable task. The intended victim gave itself away when it blew on reaching the air. The watcher drove down his harpoon at once, so that the spearhead went into the seal, which dived, if it was able, back into the sea, paying out the line attached to the spearhead behind it. The loop at the end of the line was held by a spear driven into the snow, so that the seal could not escape, and all that remained for the hunter to do was clear away the snow, enlarge the hole by breaking the ice and drag his catch up on to the drift.

Although Innuk was most anxious for me to have a try, I persuaded her that it was better for me to stay at the post, so Rebecca went instead, teaming up with Polly to increase their chances of success. Our dogs most certainly benefited from a meal of fresh offal, for they had the hardest part of the winter still to come and not many chances of seal hunting under my care.

It was certainly fortuitous that I remained at the post, for the following days were spent in continuous trading. Heavy dark clouds obscured what little light there was, so our hissing lanterns illuminated the store. With Rebecca at the seal holes we were one assistant short and Nyla came to say that she wanted to help. This did not seem wise, for although much improved in health there was a fragile look about her still. The girl had quite made up her mind that she was to take Rebecca's place, so when I tried to tell her that she was not fit for standing about all day, her face crumpled as if she was going to burst into tears and my decision had to be hastily reversed. She came in to join Koolee, working most speedily and efficiently, but by the afternoon she looked worn out and was noticeably shivering. I suggested that it was time for her to go home and she agreed without protest.

The seal hunters came back with three seals between them, then another hunter arrived with two more, so there was plenty of fresh food for Christmas Day. My own feast consisted of a roast duck from my store. Innuk and Koolee between them made a very good meal, which included a Christmas pudding sent by my mother, like the cake, all the way from New Zealand. I was touched that Innuk, Rebecca and Koolee, knowing that Christmas was a special day for me, volunteered to stay for the meal. Feeling sure that they would all really prefer a seal feast, I sent them to join the others, but so that they should not think me unappreciative, asked them to come back to keep me company when they had finished.

Later on nearly everybody crowded into the house for an evening entertainment that began with some storytelling, followed by a performance from Netchil, who had brought his *keelown*. Holding the drum by the handle in his left hand, Netchil beat out a rhythm by striking the skin with a piece of bone in self-accompaniment to an extremely energetic dance. His friends sitting round the room greeted his act with bursts of song and laughter.

One or two others tried their hand with the drum, but it must have been a dying art for they could not achieve the same degree of control over the instrument as our blind friend, who was called back to accompany the ladies in a song. Afterwards, several of the younger women brought out their string to vie with each other in the rapid production of patterns resembling many of the animals of the area with great accuracy.

When the Eskimos felt that they had given me a sufficient demonstration of their entertainments, with typical good manners they invited me to take the stage. My first contribution was to suggest a game well known at Pond Inlet. The women and girls each remove one of their boots then turn their backs for a few moments, while one of the men jumbles the boots up in the middle of the room. Finally the competitors gather in a circle round the pile of boots to try and outdo each other in finding and replacing their footwear. They entered into the spirit of the game with real enthusiasm, laughing and tussling for the boots with so much energy that Innuk had to bring out the teapot and revive them all with a hot drink. I had hoped to escape a solo performance in front of this larger audience, but should have known better with Polly present, just itching to produce her mirror. My friends had taken the story over completely now, joining in the key parts in a chorus with such zeal that it must surely have become part of the folklore of Frobisher Bay. After that we took to singing, then eventually concluded the party with a reel, Sharni producing an old fiddle from somewhere to join with Netchil on the *keelown*.

In January, three hunters from Twerpukjuak arrived, and with two women in the party I was soon given a full report of the continuing affair between Savik and Annawa. I learned that while Savik had not altogether abandoned his protest, he had not indulged in any further shows of violence, confining himself to maintaining a kind of periodic silent vigil in

Annawa's home. Usually after the people had retired to bed, he would seat himself in front of the platform very close to the offending couple, at whom he directed a concentrated gaze, but after a spell of this silent contempt would depart home again. For me, this would be even more unnerving than an occasional outburst of violence, but from what our informants told us, Annawa, Peeta and their family appeared able to endure his surveillance without emotional distress. I decided it was time to disengage myself from the dispute.

The hunters finished their trading in a morning, then Ookoo came over with Nyla to sort the greasy pelts into the cleaning bag. Their excellent work must have added more value to the furs they restored than the small amount they were paid per skin, but owing to the large number requiring treatment that winter, they did earn a most satisfactory pile of dollars.

The same day Rebecca came over to say that she thought some of the dogs ought to be fitted out with tiny boots to protect their quite sensitive pads from injury on the rough ice. She and Innuk went through the team one by one to decide which of them were in need of this protection, concluding that Rebecca should make eight pairs of bootees.

As winter progressed the supply of heating and cooking oil became something of a worry. The pile of whale fat had diminished rapidly while replacement stocks of seal fat had not come in frequently enough to see us through the season. There were two possible solutions. The first was to adopt some form of rationing, which seemed unlikely to succeed amid the 'live for the day' culture of the Innuit. The second, more feasible possibility was to shut down one of the houses, thereby cutting consumption by a half at one stroke. This meant that a number of people would have to take up residence in my kitchen, an arrangement that would not receive the enthusiastic approval of the powers that be. Since several aspects of my behaviour could by now have cooled the official attitude towards me should they have been reported, one more downward step was not going to make much difference.

Innuk seemed surprised by my doubts about our supplies. She said, 'There is still some of the whale fat in the store.'

'But that will be finished before the winter is ended.'

'There are many seal holes not far away.'

This was all very well, but seal holes are not much use without any hunters. So far, Rebecca was the only person of our present community to have shown any aptitude for winter seal hunting. Innuk said, as I feared she might, 'Are you not able to hunt seals then?'

I was convinced that there would be little hope of my being able to spear seals successfully through holes in the ice, so to stop Innuk from driving the conversation down her chosen line, I said, 'It would be better if there were only one house to be heated.'

Innuk was not impressed by this suggestion.

'But we cannot all live in one house,' she said quickly and quite vehemently.

'No,' I replied, 'but some could come and live in this house.'

This novel suggestion silenced her. She stood staring at me, with her lips parted, then her expression formed into a smile. After her initial shock I was relieved to see that she did not find this new proposal displeasing. It certainly succeeded in deflecting her mind from the subject of seal hunting, for at last she said, 'Who would come to live in the house?'

Not wishing to accept responsibility for any future dissension which might arise, I answered, 'You must decide that for yourselves.'

'How many people could live in the kitchen?'

'Four or five, so that there will not be too many left for the other house.'

'Who should they be?'

'You must talk among yourselves to decide that.'

Innuk was now apparently quite converted to the idea of a few of the others taking up residence in the house, for she went out with a thoughtful look on her face, apparently already considering which of the others would be most suitable for such a move.

I was still congratulating myself on having evaded a discussion about seal hunting, when Innuk returned to say that everyone had agreed to the new arrangement. Koolee, Ooleepika, Nyla, Tooluka and Tooshak were to join her in the house, leaving Ookoodlea in charge of the other home. Koko could have come in to the house with Rebecca had she so wished, but she expressed a preference to remain in the snowhouse, which was perhaps just as well.

The reorganization was accomplished with great rapidity once the decisions had been made, my new housemates establishing themselves in the kitchen within the hour. Being used to fitting into restricted spaces with the minimum of fuss, they quickly set up a sleeping platform on one side of the room by spreading out a bed of twigs, covered first with a tarpaulin then deerskins on top of that. We moved the table into the other room and by the end of the afternoon one would have supposed my friends to have been resident for a considerable period.

XV

A RATHER HECTIC START to the season's trading tapered down to more occasional bursts of activity. Evi completed his rehabilitation in my eyes by being the most successful Christmas hunter on the post, but in general the trapping did not fulfil the promise of the early days. Our team of three maintained a steady success, however, and we were soon able to devote more time to the English lessons, which had been most encouraging. One or two of them were progressing quite rapidly and we had had some good fun with our singing too. Nyla was concerning me, though. She was active and cheerful in the mornings, but then lost all her sparkle by the afternoon, becoming quiet and withdrawn.

Meanwhile, both Innuk and Rebecca kept on at me about the seal hunting in a discreet sort of way. One afternoon, when the three of us were in the post house, Innuk said, 'Powlussie told us that there are several seal holes beyond the narrows, but he did not have time to wait there because he wishes to visit his traps again.'

When I did not reply, she commented, to no one in particular, 'He does not hear me.'

Rebecca looked up from her sewing.

'Our hunting person would soon find a seal near by.'

Feeling obliged to speak, if only to stop them from swirling their conversation around me, I said, 'Why not take the dogs and go down there tomorrow?'

'Because we are not proper hunting people.'

This gave me an opening: 'I too am not a proper seal-hunting person.'

A sudden shout from outside announcing the approach of a visitor saved me from further pressures. The new arrival, Koojesse from Warwick Sound, had brought a seal with him, so I was able to make my escape.

By March, the trapping season was coming to a close, but with the lengthening days ahead we decided to squeeze in one last round of Frobisher Bay.

The journey up into the hills from the head of the bay began with a morning of smooth travel which gave promise of a quick passage to our inland snowhouse, but shortly after lunch our adventures began when we came across fresh bear tracks. The dogs were immediately alerted and set off with a great burst of energy, jerking the sledge behind them in a frantic effort to catch up with the unsuspecting animal. Even the women behaved, in true Eskimo fashion, with no little excitement at the prospect of confronting 'Nanook'.

My reaction was somewhat more subdued, but I did recognize the importance of an opportunity to replenish fresh meat supplies at a bad time of year, quite apart from saving myself from a cold trip to the seal holes. A careful examination of the tracks revealed that there were actually two bears, a mother and an older cub by the looks of things. The pair must have made a very early end to their winter hibernation for these animals were not often seen until April at the earliest.

Shortly the two came into view, making their way down to the plainland on the eastern side of the river without any great haste, presumably unaware of our presence. We cut the traces of two dogs nominated by Innuk as being the best hunters, releasing them to make full speed after our prey in the hope of slowing them down sufficiently for the rest of us to catch up.

The speeding dogs caught up with the bears quite quickly, but did not cause them much delay until the larger one, becoming exasperated, stopped to deal with the annoyance by seizing one of its attackers and throwing it into the air to land some distance away. After one or two doses of this treatment, the hunters lost a certain amount of interest in the proceedings, so by the time the rest of us arrived a stalemate situation had been reached with the dogs running to and fro in front of the bears, yapping in frustration. We released the remainder of the team at once to join their fellows jumping up and down around their quarry.

The difficulty for me was to get in my shots without injuring the dogs, who were flashing about most dangerously in my line of vision. It was this thought that was exercising my mind as I checked my rifle and, seated on the box at the front of the sledge, took careful aim. My first shot was aimed straight at the larger bear's head, but to my amazement, apart from a slight shake of its body, the animal appeared to be totally unaffected. Almost at once another opportunity occurred, but this time, at the very moment I pulled the trigger, the cub lunged across and intercepted the bullet. Pandemonium broke out: both bears roared, the dogs barked furiously and the large creature broke off the engagement to dart off into the rocks while the other collapsed to lie motionless on the ground.

The growing darkness led us to break off the hunt at once, since in that sort of light we would be placed at a significant disadvantage. I did this with some trepidation.

On a night when we had been camped not so very far away, Beevee had told me of some of the dangers associated with the hunting of these great creatures. According to his rules, what I had just done was to commit one of the most serious blunders of all, for he had given a most solemn warning concerning the folly of injuring or killing a cub while its parent remained alive. The cub, although it had still been living with its mother, was already a good-sized animal if nowhere near as big as the parent. While the women completed the skinning and cutting-up process, I attempted to recall everything Beevee had said to me on that night. Gradually it all came back. In this kind of situation, the hunters must drive away from the scene at an angle to their proper course, in case the angry bear should try to pursue them. At a later stage, they should then take a sharp turn back in their true direction in order to confuse the infuriated bear, who, charging along with head on one side, would most probably miss the turn-off and career away on the wrong course.

My friends had clearly not heard of this piece of folklore, for they did not understand why I insisted on setting off in the wrong direction, but they accepted my decision without argument. We had travelled for about a mile on a course heading away from our true destination before I turned the team right round to head back over our own tracks before making a sharp turn towards our hill snowhouse. Whether this complicated manoeuvre would be successful in sending an irate bear astray remained to be seen. While not wishing for a night-time confrontation, there was good reason to hope for an encounter under more favourable conditions the following day.

Innuk and Rebecca showed no surprise in the morning at my announcement that we were going to travel back towards the spot where the confrontation between bears and dogs had taken place. We could not afford to waste this opportunity to add so significantly to our shrinking food supplies and it was not right to leave the area without making an effort to locate a bear which was almost certainly wounded.

Incredibly, crossing back over the first ridge, after less than a quarter of an hour's travel, we could see blood on the snow down below us. As we came to the bottom of the dip, we found the body of the bear behind a big boulder. It had not been dead very long, for although it was beginning to stiffen with the frost, we skinned and cut it up without too much trouble.

Innuk, who seemed suddenly to have found her voice again, proclaimed that it had been my remarkable achievement to have shot two bears with one bullet. I insisted, however, that this was highly improbable, as my first shot had definitely hit this bear but for some unknown reason had failed to cause immediate death. Innuk would not have it and became quite argumentative. There had been no bullet in the cub's head, she said, because it had gone straight through the softer skull to go on to kill the mother.

Despite these differences of opinion, we were a jovial group that night and with good reason. In this round alone we had added more than twenty pelts to our collection as well as securing this large stock of meat just at the vital period of the winter. The people of Ward Inlet would be very pleased to have a change of diet; indeed, it immediately had a very favourable effect on my friends, for that evening there was no restraining them. Rebecca even favoured us with a rendition of her 'hare stopping song', which I applauded quite freely, though admittedly more to show my approval of her character than in appreciation of the artistic content of her music.

Before returning to the post, we cached some of the bear meat carefully under the snow as there were no rocks available, then set several traps round about to discourage any foxes which might show an interest.

We returned to find that Nyla was not well. She had a low fever and aching limbs, so we had to put her to bed in a little side-room where she would be warm and undisturbed. I was cheered the next day when our faithful friends Nikoo and Polly came in to see how we were getting on. We were pleased to be able to reward them with a hunk of bear meat in return for the seal meat and fat they brought us. It had been my intention to go up to the meat cache with Rebecca to bring everything back to safety as it was fairly vulnerable just buried under the snow, but after they had done their trading, our visitors announced that they were going sealing, either at the holes or at the floe edge, according to how things turned out.

Happily for me, this presented Rebecca with an opportunity to go hunting for everyone's favourite food without me, for she could take half the dogs and Ookoo's sledge, returning to the post independently when the others went off. Meanwhile I could take the rest of the team and fetch the remainder of the bear meat from our snowhouse.

My first solo outing began well. The day was mild and sunny at the start so there was no reason to anticipate the near disaster which ensued. I got over to the camp without difficulty and found that nothing had been touched. There was one fox in a trap by the cache, but it had done no harm, and though there were fresh tracks about, they were heading down towards the long stretch of plain along the head of the bay.

With the drop in pulling power owing to the small number of dogs, the day was well on before I could have started back, so I spent the night in our little trapping home not wishing to overstretch my half team. The place was quite soulless without my friends. The snowhouse was cold with no lamps and I could see how hard it was going to be when and if it was necessary to resume solo or all-male travel arrangements. This line of thought lodged in my mind as I prepared to sleep, but with it, to shock me awake again, came the realization that my year at Frobisher was speeding towards its conclusion. Geordie's warnings about involvement, so easily pushed to back of my mind to be ignored as it suited me, sounded loud and clear. I knew it would not be easy to part with my friends when the time came. Although our worlds were miles apart, the ties that had formed between us, living together so interdependently, could not be broken without painful scars which would take time to heal.

The sun came up quite warmly as I started down towards Ward Inlet the next morning, and the warmth, combined with the after-effects of my wakeful night, must have lulled me off to sleep, in which state I fell off the sledge to roll down the bank and strike my head a severe blow on a sharp rock.

The blow knocked me out cold and the afternoon was well on by the time I came to. The sun had disappeared, but whether it had gone down or just slipped behind the clouds I could not tell as I had no idea how much time had elapsed since my accident. The dogs were nowhere to be seen, but a haze of snow hung in the air like a white blanket making accurate vision impossible beyond a yard or two.

My ability to cope with these difficult conditions was greatly impaired by my head injury, which, with the full return of consciousness, was causing me pain, nausea and dizziness. I felt as though I was operating in an unpleasant dream, my mind suspended half-way between snow-hazed reality and hallucination. Only the vaguest memories of my wanderings remained with me afterwards. I remember sheltering behind a rock with the strong impression that someone was talking to me, but so quietly that the sound of their voice drifted away on the air without ever forming into words or sentences. Then, moving on again for a while, I had an eerie feeling that something was crunching the snow beside or just behind me.

The muddle prevailing in my mind kept me from making any sensible effort to consider my position even half clearly, so instead of thinking about returning to our snowhouse, which could not have been far behind me, I was urged forward by all my remaining energy in the direction of the much more distant post. By the time night descended it no longer mattered; in a state of complete detachment, I had no idea as to where I was or in which direction my footsteps were taking me. Strangely enough, some part of me must still have been responding to the stirrings of instinct, for as it happened my route, haphazard though it was, did not become circular, as is often the case, but kept to a true enough course for home.

The night passed somehow, fortunately without the temperature dropping too low, but the wind increased with the day to whirl the snow about, blowing it uncomfortably into my face and down my neck. I remember an awful retching as nausea and sickness gripped me, then a sudden glimpse of the sun, which something inside tried to tell me was important, but my weakened mind could not grasp the significance before the light disappeared and dusk began to fall again. Whether my body could have withstood another night in this bleak wilderness is doubtful. More likely it would have followed my mind, which was already withdrawing to its last defences.

Rebecca found me. She asked me what had happened, but getting no reply, understood that my movements were purely mechanical. I might have lurched straight past her had she not taken hold of my arm to lead me to the sledge, and her questions, such as should we go home or back to our camp and other immediate queries, went unanswered. Rather frightened by my unstable appearance, Rebecca decided to take me home after first preparing a hot drink, which was mostly spilt on the snow owing to my lack of coordination. She then had a problem getting me anchored securely on the sledge because of my tendency to slip off on to the snow. Eventually she got me more or less wedged in, sitting in front of her, where she was less likely to lose me, and we journeyed home.

I remember nothing of this, but Rebecca gave me a full account of her stewardship afterwards, down to the last detail. She had returned from the ice almost at the same time as my dogs came down the hill with their traces trailing behind them.

The seal hunters had had a successful first day but the weather worsened during the afternoon, much as it had with me, so the next morning Nikoo had suggested that Rebecca should take two of the three seals they had secured and go home.

At first people thought that the dogs had just broken away, abandoning me somewhere up the hill, but when they found the sledge jammed between two rocks on the crest of the slopes they realized that the team had probably been wandering driverless all night. There was no sign of what had happened to me. Innuk and Rebecca had toiled up the hill together with all the dogs, but on reaching the other sledge split them up again so that Innuk could bring the meat back with a few of her team while Rebecca went on to search for me.

Innuk apparently took charge of me when we got home. She washed my head, then tied it up with a strip of material because she knew that this is how the *kudloona* treat wounds of any kind, before putting me to bed. Some time during the night I began to recover, coming back at first to a semi-conscious state, feeling very warm, which was hardly surprising as I was sandwiched between two human bodies. Gradually I registered that my friends had decided to restore me with the warmth of their own bodies. I did not stay awake long at that stage, but before dropping off again saw that Ookoo was sitting on the side right at the end of the bed and wondered if she had been singing or talking to me with that melodious voice of hers. Innuk and Rebecca were both sound asleep, but Ookoo was wakeful, and when she saw that my eyes had opened, she got quietly off the bed and went out of the room.

When I awoke next morning, Innuk and Rebecca were up and dressed, sitting on either side of the bed and watching me intently. Seeing me smile, they realized their attempts to restore me to health had been successful and started talking together rapidly, expressing their pleasure at my having been returned to them. Then Koolee came in with a friend and soon the room seemed full of people, all expressing their relief, which, being pleasant listening if a little embarrassing, soon lulled me off to sleep again as their murmuring voices dwindled gradually into silence.

The time passed in a haze of confusion and a headache which in the absence of painkillers of any kind simply had to be endured. Fortunately sleep intervened for reasonably long periods with beneficial effect. During this time, my friends were constantly attentive, determined not to allow me to slip from their grasp and completely undismayed at having to assist me in various basic ways. In one quite lucid spell, I woke to find Ookoo sitting by the bed talking to me, but with her words not seeming to make much sense, I asked her, 'What are you saying to me, Oookoodlea? I do not understand your words.'

She did not explain but replied, 'When you were a long way off, you asked me to talk to you because you said it was good for your ears. This is why I am speaking to you in this way.'

I accepted this without any comment, presuming that the sound of her voice had drifted into my mind to soothe my jangled nerves. I was grateful and later said so.

The fog in my head dulled my mind for about three days, then, one morning, it had gone, leaving only a slight ache behind the eyes and some heaviness.

One very ominous sound that had punctuated through the haze of my lost days was the sound of Nyla coughing. It was not a very noisy or vigorous cough, but dry, continual and to my fully conscious mind, alarming enough to send me searching for the thermometer and the cough mixture as soon as I had recovered sufficiently. The cough mixture, quite rightly seen as useless to combat the summer plague, now redeemed itself somewhat by having a moderating effect on Nyla's spasms, though it did not subdue them altogether.

373

With my returning health there came an opportunity, when all Innuk's and Rebecca's friends had gone across to the snow-house one evening, to thank the two of them properly for their care and attention. They looked a bit taken aback at receiving my special thanks. Although human contact in the Innuit world lacked the romantic element present in my own, and even the bonds of affection seemed much weaker, there was a very real and deep-seated commitment in the family group to the support of one another without reservation or limitation. The precise boundaries of this commitment were not easy to define, but in my time of need I could feel their constant determination to maintain a link through to my mind and keep me from slipping away from them.

By mid April we had a steady stream of hunters coming in, all of them rounding off the season with a few furs to trade, but the excellent promise of the early weeks had not been fulfilled, reflecting the shortage of trappers. My decision not to hold Nikoo and Polly at the post, combined with the efforts of my little Frobisher Bay party, underlined the wisdom of the autumn planning, for jointly we contributed a very reasonable proportion of the post total. When the time came for Innuk, Rebecca and me to share out our booty for the season, we had caught seventy-five foxes between us. At $10 a pelt, this meant a credit of $250 each.

Innuk was to have the wolfskins, and Rebecca the cub bear-skin, while the larger bear came to me. My partners were almost overcome by the size of their share, but I overruled their suggestions that more should come to me by assuring them that their efforts had greatly increased our total bag.

Meanwhile, the spring hunting had begun with Nikoo bring-ing us the first whitecoat of the year. The growing warmth of the sun brings a change in the hunting procedures. When the seals have their young, they make themselves a little house under the snow, by enlarging one of the breathing holes and clearing a space above, so that they can lie on top of the ice. Within her refuge, the mother gives birth to her young, a small replica of herself, but covered in a sort of white-green baby fur called a whitecoat. The seals are very vulnerable to their chief enemies at this time of year: the polar bears and the hunters' dogs. The polar bears are well equipped to locate the seal shelters by their sense of smell, which leads them unerringly to the spot, where they proceed to jump on the roof and crash into the shelter. The mother is frequently able to make good an escape but rarely manages to rescue her baby from the bear's clutches. The bear will then often use the baby as bait by seizing its rear flipper, pushing it back down into the water and swinging it backwards and forwards, coaxing the mother to come close enough to be grabbed with the bear's free paw.

The Eskimo hunters, always ready to pick up pointers from the highly respected polar bears, adopt a similar ploy for this early spring seal hunting, but because they do not have a bear's sense of smell, they use their best dog to track down the homes. The men break into the shelter by jumping in the same way as the bear and use the same tactics for capturing the mother, except that they can lower the whitecoat much further by securing the hind flipper to a good length of sealskin line.

Nikoo also brought the good news that he and Polly and Powlussie and his wife would be returning to our settlement, believing that the hunting should be good there as so few men had been operating. It was a relief to have real Eskimo hunters back in the fold who could superintend some proper sealing outings and therefore keep the homes supplied with meat and oil.

Nikoo and Powlussie rebuilt the snowhouses so that some of my winter lodgers could move back into more familiar surroundings. There was some doubt in my mind as to whether it was wise to let Nyla go back to the snowhouse, but it would have done no good to isolate her from her friends. Besides, she had responded fairly well to the cough mixture, which also helped her to sleep. I watched her sleep for a few minutes one day before she left the house. Her face was relaxed like a child's, with her lips slightly parted in a half-smile. She looked young and innocent but the flesh that had fallen away from her cheeks in the last year's awful onslaught had not come back. There was a look about her of a battle fought and lost.

With our new organization and the adequate supply of food available, it had been reasonable to suppose that my hunting services, such as they were, would no longer be in demand. Innuk had even stopped talking about seals, but then Rebecca came in one afternoon to fetch something for her mother and said as she was leaving, 'The people are going sealing on the ice tomorrow. Should the dogs go out to be fed?'

I walked straight into the trap that was concealed within this apparently innocent question.

'Yes, it will be good for them to be out hunting with the other teams.'

'The hunters will be leaving early in the morning. Shall we go with them or wait and follow afterwards?'

This question puzzled me. Rebecca was perfectly capable of deciding what time to leave for a hunting expedition, but I played along, saying, 'It will be best to go with the others.'

My assumption that Rebecca had used the plural 'we' in the sense of being inclusive of herself and the dogs was now shown to have been foolishly optimistic, if not downright stupid.

'I will fetch you when the dogs have been harnessed then.'

So that was that.

A fine day turned the routine hunt for food and oil into a camp outing because, in the morning, it seemed that nearly everybody wanted to come. Our three sledges were loaded with people, but we made a sort of race of it out as far as the narrows. Innuk and Rebecca, running up behind our team to urge them on, kept us in the lead until we were well through the narrows, but I suspected the other hunters were just being polite. After that, we spread away from each other to cover different territories.

We aimed towards a point of land about seven miles or so out from the post which the women thought would be the most likely spot for our hunt. Nikoo travelled on towards the gap between our big island and the smaller ones to the south, while Powlussie stationed himself between the two of us.

My friends each detached a dog from the sledge with its line then went off in different directions to see what they could find while Koolee and I remained to look after the team. Innuk's dog galloped off at full speed, dragging her behind him, and in a matter of minutes was scratching away at the snow not far away. Koolee ran over to fetch the dog, then came back to tell me that her mother wanted me to go over to break into the den because she was not heavy enough.

The whitecoat was inside and for a moment I feared that Innuk was going to ask me to fish for the mother, but thankfully Rebecca had seen what had happened and ran over to do the fishing. We were well rewarded when our hunter hooked a big seal on to the ice. This was our main success of the day, for though Innuk managed to locate another whitecoat with her best sealing dog, we could not tempt its mother to come to the rescue.

Powlussie and Nikoo had three seals between them, as well as the whitecoats, giving us a satisfactory bag for the day to replenish our stocks. It had been a beautiful spring day and I was already in high spirits that evening when Rebecca brought me a really lovely pair of moccasins. The design on the left slipper depicted me waiting for the wolves that day up in the hills, while on the right one was an illustration of the three of us standing beside our slain foes. To make the triumph complete, she had depicted all three wolves as having been killed.

She would take nothing for her work, this time refusing completely, saying that it had been good of us to have allowed her to come along and earn all the money. I tried to tell her that she had earned all the money herself by hard work and that without her we would not have done so well, but she just looked at me. Not knowing what else to do to show how much her gift was appreciated, I went over, took her by the hand and kissed her on the cheek.

I continued to visit Nyla every day through the late spring to check her stock of cough medicine, take her temperature and keep her believing that she would be back to her old self again by the summer. Secretly I feared she would be gone long before the geese flew south again.

The melting of the snow and lengthening of the days made me realize how soon my time at Ward Inlet would be over. I had been so immersed in the day-to-day problems confronting us since those dreadful weeks of sickness and their after-effects that there had been little time for me to worry about my coming departure. As the weeks had gone by, I had become increasingly attached to my friends of the winter, which made the thought of my leaving less and less welcome. With Nyla slipping away from us, it seemed that the long shadow of that ill-fated summer would now stretch out to cover my whole year in a final backlash of the battle we thought we had won.

Innuk especially had been my constant companion. The mission would probably have said that I ought to have married her, but it would have been impossible for me to live for ever as an Eskimo hunter, just as it would have been impossible for her to live happily in any other environment. Our union seemed somehow to become inevitable, necessary and entirely suitable yet without any permanence. Now the penalty of a painful parting had to be suffered.

I had not had this kind of involvement with Rebecca, yet her constant faith had created a need in me to try and live up to her expectations.

Innuk had clearly been considering her own position, for one morning, while we were talking in the kitchen, she suddenly inquired, 'Shall we be going to Kumarkbik for the trapping again?'

This unexpected question floored me for a moment. It had never occurred to me that my friend had been thinking of the present situation as anything but temporary. The Innuit knew that traders seldom stayed long at one post, especially at the more remote places like Frobisher Bay, but her interest was quite justified and deserved a serious answer. Knowing this, it was wrong of me to temporize when my reply could have been definite. I said, 'When the ice has gone they will probably send the *Ungava* to take me away to Lake Harbour.'

'Do you not wish to stay here?'

'Yes. I would like to stay but will have to go if they tell me to.'

Innuk saw my probable departure as a reflection on her own merits. She said, 'I cannot have children any more. Suzhie was not born easily and there cannot be another.'

I began to realize how little I really knew about my friend. It seemed incredible that she might think that her inability to have any further children could in any way lower her in my estimation or bring about my departure. My confusion must have shown in my face, but misinterpreting the cause she said, 'Ooleepika is a younger person.'

My astonishment that Innuk should apparently be openly recommending Rebecca's qualities as a wife gave way gradually to an entirely new line of thought. Looking back over our winter travels, it dawned on me that Innuk had been deliberately encouraging the development of a relationship between the three of us because of her own fancied shortcomings. Quite possibly the people of Frobisher Bay already thought of Rebecca as a junior to Innuk. There could be no point in dwelling on these thoughts now that the year was nearly up. I said, in an attempt to extricate myself from this extraordinary conversation in a diplomatic way, 'Ooleepika must marry a hunter. She is a good Eskimo girl.'

Whether Innuk would have accepted this as a terminating point for our discussion is in some doubt, for though she was not an aggressive person, she was quite capable of pursuing her objectives with determination. However, at that moment the door burst open to reveal an agitated boy who had been sent across by Ookoo to tell us that Nyla was bleeding badly in a coughing fit.

We rushed over to the tent (in the warmer weather the snow-houses had become too dilapidated to be used). Nyla's paroxysm had quietened down, but the evidence of her haemorrhage was all around her on the deerskins. Deep down, I had suspected for some time what the trouble was, but in the absence of any definite proof had persuaded myself that her symptoms could indicate some less mortal illness. Now that last faint hope had gone and it was not within my power to deaden the symptoms or in any way lessen the suffering. Ookoo was talking quietly to the girl as she cleaned up the blood and washed her face, so there was not much for me to do except pour out a larger dose of the cough mixture. Nyla was breathing very rapidly and in obvious distress, so when Ookoo finished cleaning up, I tried artificial respiration for a while to try and restore her breathing pattern. She relaxed gradually and some colour came back into her cheeks as she drifted into sleep.

The swift progress of the deadly disease was fearful to watch.

To see a young person disintegrating with no possibility of being able to help, except in very minor ways, was like a form of torture. What a cruel fate that after her long, practically unaided battle to live, so malignant an enemy should rise up to destroy her.

*

It was not long before another perfect spring day encouraged the hunters to try their luck at the floe edge. It occurred to me to return Rebecca's kindness in making the moccasins by asking her to come out hunting with me, instead of the reverse which was usually the case. Innuk went over to the house to ask her and the girl appeared like a shot out of a gun. She burst into the kitchen and asked, 'Am I to come hunting with you, Issumatak?'

I hastened to reassure her, 'Yes. The sun will bring the seals out down by the islands.'

My decision to go out was not made entirely from gratitude. Looking out over the bay through my binoculars, I had noted several seals basking in the sunshine. This meant that the time had come for a new and for me vastly preferable form of hunting. Instead of jumping about on the little snow shelters and using the baby to ensnare the mother, now it was a straight-out stalk. The idea was to use a pair of binoculars to select a suitable victim, then, with the aid of a portable screen, approach to a range where the seal could be killed with one shot.

The screen consisted simply of a piece of white material fixed on to a frame and pushed in front of oneself as cover to prevent the seal taking fright. A hole in the middle of the material allowed the rifle to be pushed through with sufficient space to line up the sights. The first shot had to be effective, because if the prey were merely wounded it would slip easily back into the water over the frozen blood never to be seen again.

In days gone by, the Eskimo hunters, not having any white material, had done the stalking without a screen. Instead they pretended to be another seal worming its way across the ice by raising and lowering their heads at about the same frequency as the intended victim. Sometimes, as they got closer, they used a chant to persuade the seal to remain stationary long enough for them to be able to use their rifle or spear. As might be imagined, this method was rather long-winded and not always successful despite a long and patient shuffle across the watery ice.

Beevee once told me a tragic story in connection with this technique about a sealer in Pond Inlet who had brought his son with him to look after his rather restless team of dogs. During the afternoon, the boy wandered away from the sledge to play. Pretending to be a seal enjoying the spring sunshine, he lay down on the ice and began raising and lowering his head. Suddenly, with incredible speed, the dogs were up and off, growling and straining as though they had gone mad. Their wild excitement affected two other teams waiting unattended near by who bolted after them. By the time the boy saw what was happening, there were nearly thirty dogs pounding savagely towards him. The child screamed. Everyone dropped their harpoons and ran, desperately striving to head the team off. His father fired his rifle, shouting as though he had just killed a seal in the hope of distracting the snarling hunters. The boy got up, still yelling and shouting, but too late to save himself. The huskies tore into him, so that he went down again, disappearing beneath the swarm of ferocious, drooling dogs.

The hunters arrived quickly on the scene, but it was several moments before they could drive off the hunt-maddened teams. The pitiful remains of the partially devoured child were lifted off the bloodstained snow, then laid carefully on to Beevee's sledge and covered with a deerskin.

Rebecca had not made herself a screen yet so I said that we would share mine and take turns with the stalking. By a stroke of luck, my first stalk was successful. Although my approach had been very cautious, the seal altered position at the last moment, then obligingly turned its head round to look in my direction just as I pulled the trigger to bring about its own destruction, clean and immediate.

Rebecca, who was quite the best possible hunting companion, behaved as though no one had ever shot a seal before when, arriving with the dogs a minute or two later, she jumped off the sledge to rush over and express her admiration. Her genuine delight over this seal was so infectious that it overwhelmed all my reservations and cautions, so I took her by the hands and hugged her as we jumped up and down on the ice.

In a few moments, we came back to earth again to get on with our business of skinning the seal and decided to feed the dogs right away.

Rebecca wanted me to do the stalking again, but I insisted that she take her turn as arranged. There were two seals apparently sleeping close to the western shore of our inlet, so we moved off in that direction and my companion set off to creep towards them.

Rebecca made a good approach towards her prey, except that she was awkwardly placed with regard to the seal's head at which she had to aim. Manoeuvring without alerting the prey to its danger at close range was not easy, but the girl crawled patiently round to correct her angle, took careful aim and fired. The seal rolled towards the water, but Rebecca, dropping everything else, rushed at it with her hook just in time to haul it back on to the ice. I hurried the team over to the scene, where we celebrated the second kill of the morning, though with slightly more restraint this time.

We had had a good day, and yet throughout it my talk with

Innuk had been weighing on my mind. My answer the other day had not been entirely honest, for it was no use maintaining the pretence that my coming departure was a matter of chance. The arrangements were definite and final as made last year when the powers that be had decided that my appointment at Frobisher was to be for one year, followed by removal to Southampton Island in the north-west corner of Hudson's Bay. Perhaps it was my subconscious wish to remain here with these good friends who had supported me so well, certainly it would never have occurred to me at the same time the previous year that leaving was going to be so difficult. Now the time was near, it was hard to know what to say in a way that would not hurt their feelings or let them think that it did not matter to me. When we had finished our tea on our return, I tried to explain to them both by saying, 'The big company boss told me last year in his letter that they would be taking me away this summer, so when the *Ungava* arrives I shall have to return to Lake Harbour with them.'

'Can you not tell them that you wish to stay with us here? Then they will send you back again.'

'They would just get angry if I said that, but they would still make me go.'

Innuk did not reply to this, but Rebecca put her word in.

'Now that so many of our hunters are dead, would they not allow you to stay and help us?'

'They would not think that I am a proper hunting person.'

The women fell silent, probably accepting the fact of my departure. I did not feel that my friends could realize from this brief conversation how much I had appreciated their company and support, but we had to move on to practical details.

'You both have many foxes of credit in my book. Do you want to spend that now or wait until the new stock arrives?'

Rebecca had already made up her mind. She said at once,

'My father's rifle is very old and does not shoot well. Is there enough for me to buy a new one?'

I was pleased to be able to help by buying the rifle at cost price through my own account, which would mean that she would only have to pay about half the price. The company would not approve of such a move, but Rebecca had been a great help to us and deserved some extra recognition. She accepted happily and Innuk came down to the store with us to watch her make her choice. She deliberated quite expertly over the two rifles that were available, then made her selection on strictly practical grounds, though it somehow seemed wrong that a fine girl like this, probably only about my own age, should have to be buying a rifle in order to keep a home going instead of having a hunter of her own. Rebecca bought a few other items, mainly for her mother, then went off home with her new weapon, cartridges and the rest, still leaving a substantial credit for future use. Innuk made no purchases so would be quite a wealthy lady, at least for the coming year.

*

We lost Nyla at the end of June. Late one evening, Ookoo came over because her patient had had another terrible paroxysm of coughing. That Ookoo had come to the end of her resources was in itself an indication that we were losing control of the situation and one glance at the sleeping platform where Nyla lay was confirmation enough. The skins were in disarray where the girl had pushed them aside in her battle for air and, as she coughed, blood spattered in all directions.

Fully aware of the futility of trying to fight death with cough medicine, I nevertheless got the girl to swallow a dose, then tried to counter the laboured breathing with a period of artificial respiration. Shortly the awful gasping relaxed a little and Nyla lay propped up on my knees in a kind of exhausted peace, but when I tried to substitute a folded deerskin for my knees, the tears began to run down her cheeks in silent despair. Perhaps she was weeping for all the years she would never see or for the children she would never have. Perhaps the tears mourned the mother who could not be there to comfort her daughter in those last hours, for a hand reached slowly out from under the skins to grope for mine, and this so distressed me that the kindly Ookoo reached across and gripped my arm.

In a little while, the crying stopped, and suddenly Nyla spoke in a hoarse whisper, 'When am I going to die Issuma?'

I could only answer truthfully, 'I don't know, Nyla, I don't know.'

'You will live to be an old man. Why do I have to die so soon?'

There was no answer to this, and as if to fill the heavy silence, Ookoo began speaking and her deep soothing voice seemed to give the sick girl some sort of calming reassurance for her eyes closed and her breathing became more even.

I looked down at the deep-sunk eyes, the skeletal cheeks, the bloodstained lips and my mind went back to the night of the storm and the bonnie Eskimo girl who had helped us so efficiently. What a long battle she had had to endure, only to have to die by inches in the end.

There was silence in the home except for Ookoo's voice. The lamp began to flutter and outside a dog barked, then at last Nyla fell asleep for a time, and though I knew that my help was only minimal, there was some satisfaction in feeling her hand slipping out of mine and watching her face relax in peace.

I hardly knew what to expect the next morning, for it had seemed unlikely that Nyla would last more than a few hours, so it was no surprise to find her already detached from the world in a restless coma, though still battling for air with laboured and rattling gasps, a sure sign that her ordeal was coming to its end. She did not react at all when Ookoo wiped her face with a flannel, but her breathing became more and more difficult, so that her back arched with each desperate effort to draw in air, until her strength gave out and with one long, rough sigh of despair, she was gone.

We buried Nyla up on the river bank beside Suzhie that afternoon, but this time I did not read the poem for it was clear that she had not had that sort of attitude to dying. Instead we gathered round the bend in the river, then, with the damp mist hovering about us, sang the hymn which had almost become a theme song for our little group since that night we had marched home from the hare hunt beneath the northern lights. We sang as loudly as we could, because, regardless of whether Nyla could rightly be classed as a 'Christian Soldier' or not, if one had to die so young, it was better to march away with your head in the air than to crawl into eternity on your knees.

The sea ice soon swept out of the harbour. The winter covering had hung on so long that it was pitted all over with black pools of water, but showed no sign of movement until one morning our old adversary the north wind took a hand in the matter, rushing down the gulley and out into the cove, smashing the ice on either side of the narrows before sweeping it away into Frobisher Bay.

Nikoo and Powlussie had been hard at work on my boat for most of the previous week, repairing the damaged timbers, caulking, puttying and painting to restore it completely after the damage sustained during our expeditions the previous fall. We were tempted to push it straight down into the water when everything was dried and set, but decided to wait until the weather moderated for our first outing.

We had a surprise a day or two later when a boat arrived from Twerpukjuak, but they told us that the strong wind had cleared the ice right over to the far side of the west coast, leaving them an open passage all the way down. They brought us a box of eggs of various kinds to provide us with a welcome change of diet.

A shock, but a welcome one, was to see that both Annawa and Savik were members of the party. It turned out that Ali had after all gone up the coast. She must have had some quality that was not apparent to the eye, for her hunter friend up there had so pined for her company that he made a special trip down by sledge at the end of the winter to lure her back, which so astonished Savik and the others that she was gone before they had had time to react.

The biggest and best surprise of all was that Savik had come to ask Ookoo to be his wife and to take her family back to Warwick Sound with him.

She accepted gladly, thus settling the long-running dispute and ensuring that she would now have a hunter and a home of her own, all of which was excellent news.

We got our boat safely into the water, and then of course we had to have an outing to celebrate the launch. The whole gang wanted to come with us, so we packed in as many as we could but had to take the Twerpukjuak craft as well to accommodate the overflow.

This was to be an entirely carefree day out; we would, as always, seize any opportunity which might arise to stock up the larder or the fuel supply, but it was clear from the level of noise as we set out that everyone intended to enjoy themselves to the full.

Our first stop was made at the island to allow the young people to hunt for eggs.

Nikoo and one or two of the others went off again to see if they could find any seals, while Innuk, Rebecca, Ookoodlea, Polly and Koolee sat on the rocks with me. They were talking about some of the events of the past winter, but in such a way as to suggest that they had not yet fully realized our days together were coming to an end, or that my departure would mean a change in conditions for most of them.

Our extraordinary year together, brought about by the disasters which had almost overwhelmed us, would never be repeated in any of our lives, but thankfully my friends had the ability to accept whatever circumstances life imposed upon them. Our experiences had had a greater effect upon me than upon my companions, for I had never before lived as part of such a close and interdependent group for whom, for a time, simply staying alive had been the only real objective.

As they talked, my mind went back to my first days at Ward Inlet. At that time these women would have seemed all much the same to me, now I knew and respected each of them. Innuk, with quiet patience pursuing her objectives to a successful conclusion. Rebecca, the willing worker, whose long slender fingers indicated artistic talents which were never likely to be properly developed. Polly, who would have been an outstanding person in any community. Koolee, the bright, inquisitive child. Ookoodlea, whose ability to help the sick was highly respected, yet who never pretended to be anything more than an Eskimo housewife.

I lay back on the rock pondering such thoughts while Rebecca fanned the flies away from my face. My faithful Eskimo friend. I suppose it was because she flattered me so and said such nice things about me, but I was going to miss her as much as Innuk who had been my closest companion.

Sleep must have overcome me, for suddenly Rebecca was shaking me, 'Issuma, Issuma.'

My mind flashed back momentarily to our snow homes at the head of the bay in a confusion of bears and wolves, but it was only to tell me that the hunters were down on the beach with their seals and should we boil the kettle?

Later on, we went across to the mouth of the river to hook fish out of the pools with Powlussie's home-made gaffe. It was great fun and when we returned home Innuk cooked a lovely fish supper to round off the day.

I am glad that we had that last happy outing together, all of us, in the sunshine of a summer's day, for just a little more than twenty-four hours later I would pass that same river mouth again, but this time in the *Ungava* on the first leg of my passage to Hudson's Bay.

After the excitements of the day, we had a quiet evening, although nearly everybody came up to the house to talk about one matter or another. Polly, who was sitting at the table and surprisingly had not yet produced her bit of mirror, suddenly looked up and motioned the rest of us to silence. In the quiet we could hear the distant, but unmistakable bark of the *Ungava*'s engine as the vessel approached our harbour.

My thoughts had been much occupied over these last days with the problem of what to give my special friends as a parting gift. They both had a reasonable nest-egg of money from the winter furs and to increase this sum seemed too impersonal. I wanted the present to be something special to show them how much I had appreciated their company and support during the winter. The only things in my possession that would tell them this in a way they would understand were my two rifles, so when they came into the kitchen to tidy things up, I told them that this was what I wanted to do, giving Innuk the big rifle and Rebecca the .22

My belief that such presents would impress my friends was correct. They looked utterly astonished, but in a few moments their expressions relaxed and I could see that they had understood what I was trying to tell them. Innuk handed the big gun back to me, saying very quietly, 'A woman should not take the rifle of a hunter.'

I managed to persuade Rebecca to take the smaller weapon, but Innuk, quite adamant about the other, asked if she could have the playing cards and the draughts game instead.

Everybody gathered outside the house to say goodbye when the time came. After shaking hands with them all, I gave my two trapping companions a big hug each before turning quickly to go down towards the shore where Nikoo was waiting with the dinghy.

The *Ungava*'s engines were already running and we were on our way before Nikoo had even reached the shore.

I stood staring at the little group of people who were waving and shouting to me and sent a last, silent message over the water.

'Goodbye, Innuk. Goodbye, Rebecca. I know that I shall never see you again but you will not be forgotten. Thank you for being such lovely people and may the good spirits watch over you all the rest of your days.'

Fittingly for such a sad departure, the sun had hidden somewhere behind a drizzling mist that now closed around us, like a curtain falling on a year of my life, as we headed through the narrows towards Frobisher Bay and Hudson Straits.

EPILOGUE

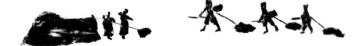

A FINAL, FAINT ECHO from my Frobisher days was to reach me a few years later on the northern grapevine.

The report said that Innuk had married a good man and that she and Koolee went off somewhere up the east coast with him when he took a job at an early-warning station.

Nikoo and Polly, the reckless pair, had gone from the bay. Rumour had it that they had taken one risk too many. Caught by a sudden winter storm at the floe edge, the story was that they had been blown out to sea, and like Itoodlu, never seen again, but no one knew for certain whether this account was true or not.

Of Rebecca and the others there was no news.

Nyla was right in predicting that, for me, life would go on into old age and my promise has been kept too, for every now and then over the years, the ghosts have slipped out from the past and I have kept brief company with my friends of long ago.

This Agreement, made this   Seventh   day of

April   . A.D. 18 30 .

Between   Edward Beauclerk Maurice .

of   Pulteney House, Pulteney Road, Bath

in the County of   Somerset   , hereinafter called "the party of the first part," of the first part

and   George Birney, acting on behalf of

the Governor and Company of Adventurers of England Trading into Hudson's Bay, commonly called
The Hudson's Bay Company, hereinafter called "the Company," of the second part

1.   The party of the first part, for the consideration hereinafter mentioned, agrees to enter into the
service of the Company and to serve the Company at such place or places in North America as the
Company or its officers shall direct, in the capacity of Apprentice and in such other capacity as the
Company or its officers shall from time to time appoint, for the full term of five years, to be computed
from the date of embarkation to Canada A.D. 1830 and for such further terms as is hereinafter provided ;
and that he will, during the whole of such time, diligently, honestly and faithfully serve the Company and
perform all such work and services for the Company as he shall be required and directed to perform by
the officers thereof, and abide by all rules and regulations now or hereafter made by the Company and
applicable to his employment.

2.   That he will not (during the period of his engagement hereunder) engage nor be concerned
either directly or indirectly in any trade or employment whatsoever except for the benefit of the Company
and according to its orders, and that all goods obtained by barter will the Indians or otherwise which
shall come to his hands or into his possession or within or under his control or direction shall be held or
controlled by him for the Company only and shall duly be delivered up to the Company, its officers or
agents.

3.   The party of the first part further agrees with the Company that in case he shall not give at
least twelve months previous notice in writing of his intention to quit the service of the Company at the
end of the said term of five years (which notice shall be given to the officer in charge of the post where he
then is, or in the event of his being himself in charge of a post, then to the officer in charge of the district
where his post is) he shall remain and continue in the service of the Company for the further period or
term of twelve months after the expiration of the term above agreed upon, on the terms and conditions
herein contained.

4.   The Company hereby agrees with the party of the first part that in consideration of the services